Cat & Fern's Excellent God Adventure

Daily Inspirations for 365 Days of Heaven on Earth

CATHERINE HICKLAND

and

FERN UNDERWOOD

with Lindsay Harrison

INTRODUCTION

Life is a funny adventure. It comes complete with High Risks, High Highs and Low Lows. We meet people through strange and unexpected situations that we sometimes call "coincidences." I am not of the mindset of "coincidences." I believe everything and everyone that come into our lives have a purpose, even if the purpose is to be a change-agent for us, whether it's in a good way or a painful one. It helps me to forgive and move on, knowing that someone who may have hurt me came into my life to teach me something valuable. I can bless them and send them on their way without harming myself with negative feelings, thoughts of revenge, and resentment. It only makes sweeter the great people who come into our lives to shine their light on us, and to show us that we, too, have a light to shine on the world.

I met writer Lindsay Harrison on a trip to Los Angeles. (I was living in New York and working on the television soap opera *One Life to Live* at the time.) I made that trip without booking a hotel in advance because I'm the ultimate adventure monster. Unfortunately, the Grammy Awards were being held the same weekend, and when I arrived I discovered there wasn't a hotel room to be had in the entire city of L.A. I literally thought I was going to have to sleep in my rental car! I texted a friend back in New York to tell her of my adventure-gone-wrong, and she told me she had a friend she could call and ask if I could stay at her house. I felt weird about it—what an imposition! But the call was made, and the answer was yes. Enter Lindsay Harrison into my life. She opened her home to me, and we felt as if we had known each other forever. Talk about a change agent! Unbeknownst to me, I was about to go through some very challenging personal life changes, and this new friendship would transform my life in a huge way.

I knew I had many life lessons ahead of me at the time, which might explain my longing to seek a deeper connection to God, and Lindsay turned out to play an important role in my search. We became great friends, and every time I went to Los Angeles, I would stay with her and her fur (not a typo) children. A year later, my personal life began to fall apart. I was struggling with my emotions, pains, fears, and my self. Lindsay shared with me that her mother,

Fern Underwood, at the time ninety-two years young, had been given the gift of "automatic writing." Every day at 5:00 a.m., Fern wrote directives and conversations from the Creator and e-mailed them to her daughter. Fascinated, I asked if I could see them, and Lindsay checked with Fern. Another "yes."

So each day, back in New York City, my e-mail inbox would include Fern's daily dose of Jesus, forwarded from Lindsay. Those e-mails brought God back into my life in a deep and profound way. I eagerly awaited those daily conversations with God, as they were easy to read and understand, and they addressed many things I happened to be going through at the time. It was to be the first of several supernatural happenings that would finally bring me back to the *self* God created me to be.

Eventually I would begin to write as well. I started with daily inspirations and moved on to a healing book called *The 30-Day Heartbreak Cure* (Simon & Schuster), which Lindsay and I co-wrote.

I have always believed that Fern's writing should be introduced to as many people as possible, but it would take more than a decade for Divine Inspiration to intervene once again and this book was born—a combination of my personal inspirations and Fern's conversations with God. She's an inspiring and most humble woman who has never invited the glare of a spotlight, but thankfully she agreed to let Lindsay and me share her words with you.

She'll turn one hundred years old on February 7, 2015. In addition to being a homemaker and mother, and taking over her husband's auto parts business after his sudden death in 1973, she's traveled around the globe as a member of the World Methodist Council. She's won awards ranging from the local Chamber of Commerce for community service, to the Iowa State "Friend of Education" Award for her work with school children in her area, to the Iowa Governor Volunteer Award, to the Bishop James S. Thomas Leadership Award. And, at the age of 85, she founded what she called "Fun Church" at a rural trailer park near her small town in Iowa, at which, seated on a blanket, surrounded by the children who lived there, she introduced them to Jesus and His teachings and the sacred dignity and grace of their souls. (She wrote about Fun Church in a pamphlet she titled *To Come Alive at 85*. How inspiring is that?!)

Fern first experienced her gift of "automatic writing" at a spiritual retreat in 1973, when, in her words, "I had barely seated myself when I felt urged to take out my notebook. For one solid hour I wrote as fast as I could, the words seeming to come like dictation." She's so reluctant to take credit for these writings that when I asked if I could use them for this collaborative book, she replied, "I'd be honored, but you know, they're not really *mine*."

Please note: The italicized passages you'll read are many of Fern's inspirations which came, as she would say, "through" her, not "from" her, with Someone Else guiding her hand, and we're sharing them in these pages exactly as she received them.

And so, from Fern and me, thank you for letting us walk through the next year of your life with you. Enjoy each day, and know that you are *Blessed!*

Catherine (Cat) Hickland

JANUARY

JANUARY 1

"Faith is the assurance of things hoped for,
and the proving of things not seen."
– Hebrews 11:1

From Cat:

I'm so excited for you.

Simply opening this book means that no matter how your life is going—whether you're on a roll right now or things are looking pretty bleak—you're ready to do what it takes to make it better, to make you better. And you have the faith to know it's possible, the faith to know there's nothing good and worthwhile that you and God can't accomplish together, one step, one day at a time. No need to worry about tomorrow. God's already there, and you can't live it until you're in it. Today, the first day of the best year of your life, is your gift from your Father, your opportunity to lay the groundwork for every "today" ahead, so let's make the most of it and get started.

It's inventory day. Time to take quiet, honest stock of who and what you've chosen (and I do mean chosen) to include in your world. How much of it is serving you well, and how much of it is nothing but clutter that's taking up physical, mental, emotional, and spiritual space you could be putting to much better use?

I have a friend who cured her tendency to impulse-shop by training herself to ask herself, every time she found herself tempted to buy something, "Is this '*stuff*'?" If the answer is yes, she puts it back and moves on—and considers it a victory, by the way, when she comes home from shopping without having bought a single thing.

So I'm talking about taking an inventory of the *stuff* in your life—the useless things, the people who make you feel badly about yourself or use you or refuse to cheer you on, the negative thoughts and conversations, the worries, the self-doubt, the guilt, the anger, the grudges, all of it—and making a promise to yourself that every single day of this year, starting today, you're going to start weeding it out and getting rid of it. (You didn't accumulate it in a day, after all, so don't set yourself up for failure by expecting to eliminate it in a day.)

I call it "emptying the cup," making room for the new and better and more fulfilling that you deserve, and then having the faith to know with absolute certainty that if you do the work, you'll find it was out there all along, just waiting for you to unclutter the path.

I always say that God drags us kicking and screaming into a better life than we could ever imagine for ourselves. It's certainly been true for me, or I wouldn't feel qualified to write about it. There have been times when I actually found myself clinging to things and people and circumstances simply because they were familiar. Like most people, I found change uncomfortable, and thought I was perfectly comfortable with the way things were. I would fight change with all my might and all the anxiety that fighting change creates, usually to discover that the change I'd been fighting so hard to prevent was actually a breathtaking improvement over the "familiar" I'd been settling for.

That's how I (eventually!) learned to empty the cup and give up my shortsighted belief that I knew what I wanted and how to get there. In fact, I've related so well to my life coaching clients who can give me a long list of what they don't want but are a little hazy on the subject of what they *do* want. How are any of us going to successfully hit a target when we're not even sure what it looks like, let alone what it is?

And how are we going to find that target if we've buried it under piles and piles of stuff, instead of letting faith fill all that precious space and lead us there without a fight?

> Dear God, please guide my hands,
> my mind and my spirit today
> and every day ahead
> as I begin emptying my cup to make room
> for the wise, glorious plan
> You've created just for me. Amen.

3

JANUARY 2

"God is love."
— 1 John 4:8b

From Fern:

How interesting that little incidents throughout life stay firmly in memory. In the vast accumulation of experiences, certain ones that may not seem unusual at the time, in retrospect are recognized as life-influencing. There were nine children in my mother's family, but the youngest was my ideal. She was a teacher and seemed to me very beautiful. Her opinion of me was very important. One day when the family had gathered around Grandmother's table, my mother noted my lack of manners and whispered, "Don't take such big bites or Aunt Dorothy won't like you."

Aha! Love is earned. Love results from approved behavior. This simple statement along with other subtleties colored all my relationships, but particularly my concept of God. It remained until I heard a young lady testify, "I gave my life to Christ when I realized that no matter what I ever did, He would never love me any more; and no matter what I ever did, He would never love me less." Isn't that glorious? God's love is not a beacon in which light we stand if we live in a certain way. God's love *is*. Put another way, "God does not love us because of who we are but because of who He is." The truth is too wonderful to grasp! I stand in awe!

JANUARY 3

"Whatever you do in word or deed,
do everything in the name of the Lord Jesus..."
– Colossians 3:17

From Fern:

Dear _____ (your name), *the day is full of promise. Look forward. Greet it with enthusiasm and whatever your hand finds to do, do it with all your might. Give to it* my *touch, for I shall be with you and in you. To every person you meet, express my love. To every project, give full attention. This is the difference between living and existing. There is so much beauty to see when your eyes are open, so many lessons to learn when your mind is alert, so many wonderful people to love when your heart reaches out. My child, how desperately love is needed! To what gross and unsatisfying ways do hungry people turn when they long to have the evidence of love—to be touched, to be held. I appoint you to do that. It takes no extra time. Do it in the course of your day.*

Reach out. Stroke the hungry persons. Express my love. Tell them by word and by touch that I love them. And the most unlovable of all, by other standards, be sure *to tell them! There is so much said about world hunger, but there is no hunger as deep and as prevalent as that love that will not fail in any circumstance. Show and tell.*

JANUARY 4

"Be still and know that I am God."
— Psalms 46:12

From Fern:

Dear Lord, today my thoughts are like wild horses ready to bound into the day. I can hardly control them, to direct them where I would have them go.

Help me tame them. I want to be quiet in your presence, to concentrate totally on our time together. I need the strengthening of this period to approach the day's activities. I come with empty hands. I have nothing to give but everything to receive.

The day calls for wisdom, a new beginning, all past forgiven. I need energizing, refreshing, and the Spirit's filling in order to be ready.

Quietly, Lord, I wait before you. Calmly I dedicate this time to you. I breathe in, accepting you into my heart and mind. I breathe out all that has gone before. I breathe in peace, I breathe out pressure. I breathe in love, I breathe out ugliness. I breathe in Spirit, I breathe out self. I sit, now, quietly in your presence.

This is my preparation for the day. With this preparation I can meet all that comes, one detail at a time. Thank you, Lord!

JANUARY 5

"Is not my word like fire, says the Lord..."
– Jeremiah 23:29

From Fern:

O, Holy Spirit, set me afire! Take out of me any inclination to view my life as dull, routine, uninteresting. Scrub out of my thoughts any vestige of the opinion that the Christian life is one of obligation and restriction.

Jesus, your Spirit recreates me and leads me to the paths you chose. Your Spirit leads me to the Jordan, to baptism, which washes away all that was, and I emerge clean.

Your Spirit burns away, by holy fire, all the trash in my life and changes what was to what can be.

Set me afire, Lord, I repeat. Heighten in me a blazing desire to do your will, to be about your business. Excite me with opportunities you have for me. Give me the Pauline zeal to serve, to tell others of your activity in my life.

Dear God, burn away fear of being thought strange. Clarify the one path you have designated as mine. Set my foot upon it, with my face toward Jerusalem, and give me eagerness for the journey.

JANUARY 6

"Judge not, that you not be judged...
the measure you give will be the measure you get."
– Matthew 7:1-2

From Fern:

Dear Jesus, as I read your words about return, I think of circles upon circles. Days flow into nights and back to day. Weeks, months, seasons are in cycles. Growth proceeds from seed to plant, then back to seed.

Lord, help me to apply this to relationships; for I believe that what I send out in thought, or attitude, or opinion, does not proceed in a line, out into infinity. Nor does it go forth and fade into nothing. It is an energy form and has existence. It is circular, I hear you saying, and instead of harming someone else although it may, I can expect it to boomerang, coming back to me.

You, who desired for us abundant life, told us to love, for then we shall be surrounded by love. As we are generous, life will be generous to us. Whatever we sow, we shall also reap.

How important for wholeness, Lord, is this teaching. Cleanse me from unkind thoughts or feelings. I not only want to be rid of them because they are unlike my Teacher but because they are hazardous to my health.

JANUARY 7

"I have found that if you love life, life will love you back."
– Arthur Rubinstein

From Cat:

I had dinner the other night with one of my amazing girlfriends. She looked especially happy and beautiful, and I asked what was going on with her.

She smiled and announced, "I'm just not coasting through my life any more."

I almost fell over. The word "coasting" had been brought up to me several times in the previous weeks, and it's a word I rarely hear or use. Since I personally don't believe in coincidences (I'm a miracle and blessing girl myself!), I decided it must be a word worth paying attention to and examining more closely.

We all need to coast every once in awhile—take a break, stop pedaling, and let gravity briefly do the work while we catch our breath.

But as a way of life? Not a chance. That's not what we're here for, and we're short-changing ourselves if we put up with it for any length of time.

Coasting is letting life happen to us. It's doing the easiest possible thing, without challenging ourselves, or learning, or even trying. When we coast, we lose momentum. We don't think much, and we don't feel much, we basically just eat, breathe, and go through the motions, out of either laziness or fear. We feel continually anxious without knowing why. But the "why" is simple: there's no inner peace to be found by expecting too little of ourselves, by setting the bar so low for ourselves that we barely need to lift our feet to step over it.

If you're reading this right now and realizing that yes, you have been coasting through your life for awhile, because of family, work, obligations, routine, whatever...the great news is, no one but you

9

made the choice to coast, which means that you have all the power to put a stop to it.

There's a line from one of my favorite movies, *The Shawshank Redemption*, that I've never forgotten. Tim Robbins says, "You'd better get busy living, or get busy dying." Morgan Freeman replies, "Damn straight." I think of that line every time I'm tempted to tune out and just ride along on this journey. It acts for me as a simple, powerful reminder that life owes me nothing. Fulfillment, and joy, and dreams, and heartfelt peace aren't going to come knocking on my door and asking me to come out and play. It's my job to open throw that door, run out and join in. I'm entitled to nothing more and nothing less in this life I've been given than what I'm willing to provide, and coasting, providing nothing, demanding the least of myself, is just plain not good enough.

My beautiful, cherished friend, demand the most, the best, everything of yourself, starting today! Keep raising the bar higher and higher as you keep growing. God didn't breathe life into any of us so that we could just wake up every morning and go through the motions until bedtime. We owe Him all we've got. We owe ourselves all we've got, from this day forward. We owe it to ourselves, right now, to get busy living!

Damn straight.

Heavenly Father, I embrace this Call To Arms
that You've sent my way exactly when I needed it.
I'm ready to live this life You've given me
and settle for nothing less.
No more sleepwalking through it, no more coasting.
I'm wide awake again, an activist on my own behalf
and on Yours, in humble gratitude. Amen.

JANUARY 8

"Be not forgetful to entertain strangers,
for thereby some have entertained angels unawares."
– Hebrews 13:2

From Cat:

I was in the middle of a ten-day stage hypnosis engagement at the Central Florida State Fair. My crew and I arrived to set up for the first show on the main stage and were greeted by a classic Florida rainstorm so heavy and relentless that it looked as if the show would have to be cancelled. Oh, well. It happens. No big deal, I thought.

Apparently, though, it was a very big deal to a little girl who was standing with her mother under the technical tent, crying her eyes out. I resisted the momentary temptation to declare it none of my business and went over to ask what was wrong.

The girl was crying, her mother told me, because the Fair had promised she could sing a song or two on the main stage before my show started. But with my show being rained out, and nothing in the audience but row after row of wet, empty chairs, it obviously wasn't going to happen, and the girl was heartbroken.

The mother went on to explain that her daughter was autistic, and that singing was her whole life. She didn't care that it was raining, or that there was no audience. All she wanted was to sing for the sheer joy of it.

The easy thing to do: tell them how sorry I was, go find someplace dry and have some lunch. But "something told me" (always read "God") I could do better than that. I asked the mother if her daughter would mind performing just for my crew and me, because we'd love to hear her sing.

The girl was ecstatic. She hadn't spoken a word to me, or even made eye contact, so I admit we had limited expectations as we politely gathered to watch her.

And she blew us away.

I still get goose bumps on top of goose bumps remembering how fantastic she was, belting out Broadway show tunes and current

11

hits with the voice and skill and passion of a seasoned professional. It was nothing short of a privilege to witness.

Then, when she was finished—because she was, after all, a young girl at the Fair—she couldn't wait to race off to the midway and ride the rides.

Through her mother I asked if she'd honor me, my crew, and my audience by being the opening act at my Thursday night show. She accepted the invitation, and the audience loved her as much as we did.

God bless you, Bethany Burnette, you little inspirer. I'll never forget you.

I can't speak to the impact it had on that girl's life, but I can tell you that that one incident, that one simple gesture that cost me nothing, continues to enrich mine to this day. Listening to that "something told me" rather than ignoring it and moving right along with my own busy-ness allowed me to hear an angel sing. It taught me to slow down, pay attention, and look for opportunities to extend a kindness, no matter how small or how it's received, for the sheer joy of how it makes my soul and its Creator smile.

Watch for those same opportunities today. Make an adventure out of it. Open a door for someone. Let someone go ahead of you in line at the grocery store, or take that parking space you had your eye on. Pay a compliment to someone who looks as if they're having a bad day. Whether or not they turn out to be angels is beside the point. Your soul and its Creator will smile either way.

Just one quick warning, though: The joy you'll get back may be addictive.

Dear God, please keep me vigilant today
in my search for the anonymous angels You send my way,
and then help me remember to treat them accordingly.
Amen.

JANUARY 9

"Therefore, choose life..."
– Deuteronomy 30:19

From Fern:

My child, today you are concerned about the world, the chaos in the lives of many people, their lack of vision, the earthy level of their thinking.

Don't you know that this is not new? It has ever been. A difference is in the openness, communication, willingness to tell what is happening.

Do you not see that this is good? The Lord's truth is being proven again and again, in your time, before your very eyes. The commandments stand! Obedience leads to a blessed life; disobedience to devastation. God has put before each of the created a choice of life or death. Life has the aura of goodness. Spiritual death is a consequence of evil. It is plainly said that obedience to the commandments results in life and God pleads, "Therefore, choose life!"

You have seen how God, through the Holy Spirit, has touched this person and that one. God knows each one individually. God watches over all. God knows the precise moment when, and the best way—the how—to reach the beloved.

Trust God. Work with God. Pray and witness. That is your part.

JANUARY 10

"...Unless your righteousness exceeds..."
– Matthew 5:20

From Fern:

Holy God, Your word often speaks of the inward versus the outward. You look not as men look, who judge by outward appearances, while You look on the heart. Jesus talked about those who went about struggling with their religiosity when inwardly their lives were unclean and full of death and decay.

Paul warned against being men-pleasers, but how often I find myself attempting to satisfy the expectations of persons. I care too much about what others think. Their praise is too important to me.

Help me, Divine Master, to hold my ambitions up to the light of Your approval. Help me to test all that I do by the truth of Your word. You want only the best for me. You and I agree that we want this life to be productive, lived not for momentary purposes and pleasures, but that it will have a lasting effect. I do not ask to be great in any way, but to be a quiet, steady influence for good on those whose lives touch mine. Help my inward motivation to be a hungering and thirsting for righteousness, and regardless of acceptance or rejection by fellow travelers, keep my aim steady.

JANUARY 11

"Be merciful, even as your Father is merciful."
– Luke 6:36

From Fern:

Divine Parent, much is said in the Bible about our need to love. There are many reminders of Your love for us, which depends not upon what we are but who You are. It is Your divine nature to love, which entails giving, being merciful and forgiving. In my life there has been nothing equal to motherhood by which to feel this kind of love. Thank You for children!

What a privilege to do for them freely those services I could not be hired to do for wages. What a joy to give them that which causes their eyes to shine with pleasure.

Through them, God, You have given me a range of emotions: pleasure and disappointment, happiness and pain, patience mixed with impatience. But You have also given me understanding of Jesus' words of forgiveness, "They know not what they do." I see reproduced in my children my own weaknesses. I know the origin of many of their frailties and have loved them in their most extreme expressions of immaturity.

Lord, I need to see others with this same kind of insight. Broaden my sense of family that I may be more merciful than I have before.

JANUARY 12

"How can we who died to sin still live in it?"
— Romans 6:2

From Fern:

Dear God, our world is full of violence and hatred, of catering to the baser instincts and passions. Help me to have the proper response. Deliver me from seeing all of this as "them" but to know that I am a part of them and they a part of me.

With age my temper has been modified, my zeal lessened; but I confess that when I hear what seems unjust, I inwardly desire to retaliate, often against someone. Situations arouse my anger, at times toward a person or a group.

Help me realize, Lord, that it is those very feelings, exaggerated, that lead to violence. It is those very feelings that reveal to me that I have overcome sin. It lives within me.

Empower me, Holy Spirit, to grow stronger than these weaknesses. Live within me with Your loving presence in order that love will encompass my life and emanate to all I meet in person or in thought. Help me not to judge or to condemn but to empathize, knowing the feelings that prompt regrettable action.

JANUARY 13

"His name will be called 'Wonderful Counselor,'
'Mighty God,' 'Everlasting Father,' 'Prince of Peace.'"
– Isaiah 9:6

From Fern:

Just as the prophets were inspired to know the details of Jesus' life—
Micah His birthplace, Isaiah His role and mission, the psalmist
describes His death—so Joel and Zephaniah foretell a day of the
Lord.

And just as the disciples were unable to comprehend what Jesus told
them as He spoke about His death, no one can precisely anticipate
the end times. Of that day or that hour no one knows, not the angels
in heaven nor the Son, but only the Father.

But just as Jesus defeated the last enemy to be destroyed—death—so
there will be a final victory over the forces of evil. When the beasts
and the kings of the earth with their armies gather to make war
against him, the devil will be defeated.

For the Lord shall reign! The government shall be upon His shoulder,
and His name will be called "Wonderful Counselor, Mighty God,
Everlasting Father, Prince of Peace." Of the increase of His
government and of peace there will be no end, upon the throne of
David, and over His kingdom, to establish it, and to uphold it with
justice and with righteousness from this time forth and forevermore.
At the name of Jesus every knee shall bow, in heaven and on earth
and under the earth, and every tongue confess that Jesus Christ is
Lord, to the glory of God the Father!

JANUARY 14

"He remembers that we are dust."
— Psalms 103:14b

From Fern:

Dear God, thank you for remembering that we are dust, that we have an affinity for the world around us. It is so near, so loud; its ways are so present, and adopting its values seems to make us compatible with our neighbors.

But while You remember that we are dust, weak and prone to falling into temptation, help me remember that I am spirit. You are spirit and You made me in Your Image.

You have given me this duality and challenge me to find the balance. My duties, responsibilities, opportunities, are here in the earthly "dusty" realm. My strength, my source of wisdom and caring come from the spiritual realm. I invest myself physically and spiritually. I reap rewards physically and spiritually.

Dear Lord, help me to keep this clearly in mind and heart. Physical and spiritual health result. I *am* physical. I live *here*; but I am also a citizen of heaven, and in due time I will come to live with You in that other realm.

JANUARY 15

"I bless the Lord who gives me counsel;
in the night also my heart instructs me."
– Psalms 16:7

From Cat:

I recently had one of those sleepless nights when my mind
wouldn't stop chattering and the tapes in my head wouldn't stop
playing and let me sleep. I'm sure you know those nights and have
learned, as I have, that they're usually a symptom of unfinished
emotional business.

Finally, exhausted, I quietly asked God to help me get to the
bottom of what was holding me back from the sleep and the peace of
mind I desperately needed. Of course, there's no real point in praying
if we're not willing to follow it up by listening. So I listened, and what
came was a feeling, an intuition. (The way you can tell the difference,
by the way, between intuition and imagination is that imagination can
whirl you around all over the place and often leave you more
confused than you were before, while intuition always feels right,
makes sense, and immediately triggers a call to action.)

My unfinished business that night was all about anger—one of
the most damaging, peace-robbing emotions we can ever feel. In this
case, it was anger toward a specific person, someone who'd betrayed
my trust in an utterly mean-spirited, self-justifying way and, because
she's one of those people who takes no responsibility for her actions,
I knew there would never be a sincere apology headed my way.

It took me awhile, but I finally got in touch with a truth my
anger occasionally clouds: The only way to regain my peace of mind,
and a good night's sleep, was and is to forgive her. Really forgive.
And not just forgive, but bless her and wish her well so that I could
put the hurt and disappointment behind me and move on.

I put that forgiveness in the form of a prayer and gave it to God,
with every ounce of sincerity I possess. I said it out loud, identifying
her and every other person and situation and hurt and unkept
promise still rattling around making my soul hurt, forgiving them all
one by one and then blessing each one of them as He would do.

While I was at it, I asked God to help me forgive myself as well, for any and all pain I've inflicted in my life out of carelessness, thoughtlessness, self-centeredness, and/or ignorance.

As that long, heartfelt prayer reached its "Amen," I literally felt a weight lift from deep inside me, a light come on where I'd "gone dark," and an emotional exhale only God's cleansing can provide.

Anger makes us forget sometimes that forgiveness is not weakness. It's not permission to hurt us again. The Lord's Prayer says, "Forgive us our trespasses as we forgive those who trespass against us." It does not say "...as we continue to tolerate bad behavior from those who trespass against us," or "...as we cozy back up to every toxic person who's trespassed against us." Forgiveness is for our benefit, not theirs. It's grace in action. When it's sincere and given the added propulsion of a blessing, it's downright liberating. And make no mistake about it, withholding forgiveness binds you to the person you're refusing to forgive as surely as if you were to move in with them.

I forgave her, I blessed her and sent her on her way, I had a busy, productive day the next day that didn't include a single thought of her, and the next night, I promise you, I slept like a baby.

Forgive and bless someone, and yourself, today, out loud, in a prayer to God for His help with making sure you mean it.

It can be our secret, and His, that you're really doing it for you.

Dear God, I thank You
for cleansing me of my anger today
and for helping me be strong enough, and love You enough,
to follow Your Divine Example and forgive. Amen.

JANUARY 16

"We are being changed...
from one degree of glory to another..."
– 2 Corinthians 3:16

From Fern:

_____ (your name), *do you realize that every moment you are the product of all that you have received from your ancestors, as well as all that you are learning and experiencing every day? Do you know that you are constantly changing because of this? More than that, do you know this is true of all souls? Relate to others with this in mind. Do not be critical or intolerant of others, for you have not walked where they have walked, or seen what they have seen. You have not always heard what they were saying either in words or subtle innuendoes underlying their words. Allow persons to be themselves, to be different from you. Learn to appreciate the difference. Do not judge. Realize that all, like yourself, are in the process of becoming.*

Envy, suspicion, jealousy, resentment, fear—any and all of these can become a mindset; but all of them are opposed to love. They are, Paul said, the products of a life in the flesh. They are not characteristics of life in the Spirit. Recall that I asked the Father's forgiveness for those who had put me on the cross, for the reason that they knew not what they were doing. Relate to others in this way. Allow them space and time to grow.

JANUARY 17

The aim of prayer:
"If the soul is much with Him...its whole thought
will be concentrated upon ways to please Him
and upon showing Him how much it loves Him."
– St. Teresa of Avila

From Fern:

Dear God, whom I know as Divine Parent because of Jesus, whom I know as loving because of Jesus, whom I know as forgiving because of Jesus: Thank you for Jesus! Thank you for "caring enough to send the very best."

Thank You for so desiring us to know You that You came to earth in Jesus! What life was before Jesus, I cannot imagine—living, to please You, by an imposed law made far too complex for the average person to understand. God interpreted by words, by priests, God known only through ritual, sacrifice, and holy days!

And then You broke through, O God! And light fell upon the words which became the Word, and You made each of us a priest, and taught that love supersedes sacrifice and ritual.

You gave us a Person! And victory! A Spirit walking beside us in the happiest and darkest of times.

Praise you, Lord, for Jesus!

JANUARY 18

"Prayer is conversing with God."
– Anonymous

From Fern:

O my Savior, forgive this flesh its weakness; forgive the thoughts that wander in my prayers, my mind anticipating the day's activities instead of reaching upward to you. I would not have it so. Would that I spend my time in prayer, in prayer, absorbing that which would strengthen me for the day.

My child, I made your flesh. I set you in the world. I gave you responsibilities. Do not shut me out of them, or them out of your prayers. Allow me to be involved in them, and assist you with them.

When you bring them to your prayer time I am able to inject wisdom. I am able to remind you of facets to attend to. Bring to me all your life—don't compartmentalize it and give me only what you consider the "heavenly" part.

I invited, "Come to me, all who labor." Bring me your labors, your trials, your concerns and I will give you rest.

Peace be in your heart today, the "peace that passes all understanding." Go about the work assigned to you and I will be with you.

Go in peace.

JANUARY 19

"And He awoke and rebuked the wind,
and said to the seas, 'Peace! Be still!'
And the wind ceased, and there was a great calm."
— Mark 4:39

From Fern:

May the Lord bless us and keep us. May He make His face to shine upon us and give us peace.

PEACE

How sweet the word, how warm the feeling of that deep serenity that pervades in spite of storms without! As Jesus stilled the storms on Galilee, just so He stills the storms of the soul!

What causes our lack of peace? Taking our eyes off the Master, forgetting that God is Ruler yet over all life, forgetting that there is a purpose and a plan, a *use* for the trials of life.

For even in sorrow and tragedy, although the outcome cannot be anticipated, there can be a sense of God in it, walking with us through it, giving strength, comfort, and stability.

And in the end, at the conclusion of each event or life, God stands alongside, helping to evaluate and interpret—revealing that new strength of character attained because of the experience!

JANUARY 20

"Prayer is not to inform God of what God does not know.
It is an eye through which to see God."
– Sir Wilfred Grenfell

From Fern:

Dear Jesus, I bow before You this day with nothing to request except the infilling of Your Holy Spirit. I have no needs that cannot be met by the Spirit's fruits of love, joy, peace, patience, kindness, goodness, faithfulness, gentleness, and self-control.

All of these are intangibles, but I have come to know that therein lie the *real* possessions. Therein is the security for which I long, and nothing tangible has meaning if my life is not built on the basis of these fruits.

Jesus, as You demonstrated that abilities are to be used to bless those who come our way, and to the glory of God, let me be involved in that. Help me to see that the gifts are not possessions to be held but are for others, as life itself shall be.

For that I need You ever near. For that I need the daily infilling to replenish what I pass along. And so, each morning as I start the day, I come, open and receptive. Fill my cup, Lord.

JANUARY 21

"...His compassions never fail. They are new every morning."
– Lamentations 3:22-23

From Fern:

My child, reach tall this day.

Live it on tiptoe, for no day is without its joys, no day is devoid of some delights. Look around you at the colors and know that I have planned it all for your eyes to behold.

Look around you at persons, for they, too, are part of the plan. See the beauty of them, within and without. Look at their intentions more than at their actions.

Be sensitive to what their souls are saying, more than what their words are telling you. Appreciate them as unique creations designed by God to fulfill a particular purpose. Love them because they first were loved by the God Spirit within you.

Be alert, for no day is insignificant and no event within the day is meaningless. Be keen and sharp to look for it. Register it all in your mind for future use.

I will go with you through the day. I will nudge you from time to time to alert you.

I love to walk with my chosen.

JANUARY 22

"Coincidence is God's way of remaining anonymous."
– Albert Einstein

From Cat:

I was raised for a few years by my grandmother. (Another story for another day.) We called her Gram. She was my constant, my walking security blanket, my fiercest ally, and my biggest fan. She was a tough, no-nonsense farm woman who rarely, if ever, said, "I love you." She didn't need to. I knew it to my core.

My dad passed away almost thirty years ago, and in such an awful way that a year later Gram, his mother, passed away too. Amidst all the chaos in my childhood, for the last year of her life I didn't even know where my beloved Gram was.

After she passed away I thought so often of her. She would have been so proud of some of the things I've managed to accomplish, and I wished I'd had a chance to look one more time into those deep-set, soulful eyes and thank her and tell her how much of it I owed to her.

I was booked to play eighteen performances at the Delaware State Fair for the first time a few years go, a state I hadn't been anywhere near since I was a little girl.

As the date of the Fair got closer, I found myself thinking more and more about Gram. I vaguely recalled that she had relatives somewhere in Delaware, and I wished with all my heart that I'd known them. Gram would have been 110 by then, and her nine brothers and sisters were all very close in age, so I was sure they would all be long gone.

Two days before the end of my run in Delaware, I was alone in my hotel room when my cell phone rang. The angel on the other end was a woman named Bev, who'd tracked me down through the Fair and introduced herself as a friend of Gram's sister, Christine. I remembered meeting Christine a handful of times when I was a child, and liking her, but I hadn't seen her or heard a word about her since 1982.

27

I thanked Bev for going to the trouble of finding me and gently asked how long ago Christine had passed away.

"Passed away?!" she said with a chuckle. "She hasn't passed away. She's still here, and she's ninety-eight years old!"

Not only was my Great Aunt Christine still here, it turned out, but she was living a mere ten-minute drive from my hotel. I still get chills talking about this...I asked Bev if we could meet at Christine's the following day and surprise her. Bev was into it!

I was so excited when Bev led me into Christine's house the next day, fully prepared to explain to this 98-year-old woman who I was. Instead, it took her four whole seconds to recognize me. I knelt down and took her hand, and when I looked into her eyes, I saw my Gram shining out at me. Christine even sounded exactly like her!

I didn't let go of that precious hand for over an hour, with joyful tears streaming down my face as this sharp, wonderful woman and I, each other's family, reconnected. She'd lived in the same house since 1943, a house I'd driven past a hundred times in the last couple of weeks, and she was able to fill in all the blanks for me about my dear Gram's last year on earth. The honor and the miracle of just being with her took my breath away, and still does.

I know with absolute certainty why Gram had been so strongly on my mind before that trip and why Bev's efforts to find me, the timing, and the proximity between my hotel and Christine's house had fallen so perfectly into place: God and Gram orchestrated it as a sign that they were watching over me as always, and that we should probably eliminate the word "coincidence" from our vocabulary.

(And for those of you who are thinking, "Duh, of course your grandmother was on your mind when you were going to Delaware, you knew she had relatives there," I'll point out that I'd never been booked to perform in Delaware before. Who knows when the orchestrating began?)

What if coincidences are nothing more and nothing less than proof that there really is a divine Plan for each of us, more magical than anything we could devise on our own, if we'll just open our eyes and appreciate those signals when they come our way?

What if coincidences, and déjà vu, and those moments when we "just happen" to find ourselves in exactly the right place at exactly the right time, and a phone call from a friend we've just been thinking about for no apparent reason are actually hugs from God and those loved ones we mourn and think are gone, with the simple, amazing message, "I'm right here!"

To everyone who says, "How do we know that's what those things are?" I say right back, "How do we know they're not?"

Dear God, please help me today
to get past my mundane, earthbound thoughts
and help me recognize the everyday magic and the miracles
You quietly create for me. Amen.

JANUARY 23

"His disciples did not understand..."
– John 12:16

From Fern:

_____ (your name), *there are events reported in the gospels in which the attitude, not the incident, should have gained attention. John told of the time I washed the disciples' feet. Simon Peter could not bear to have me do this. He who had flashes of insight concerning my identity—the time in the early days when he fell before me, the day he perceived that I had come as Christ—but now as I knelt before him, he did not comprehend what I was doing. Nor could he have understood if I told him that in my heart, I washed them daily. I washed their minds from old ways of looking at life, to new.*

Neither Peter nor the other disciples had learned the difference between greatness in this world and in the kingdom. They argued about greatness, and the sons of Zebedee asked for special recognition. They had yet to learn that greatness in the kingdom is evidenced by servanthood.

Do you see what this requires? 1) Total loss of self-aggrandizement, a willingness to take the lowest place; and 2) fulfillment of the only command I gave, that you love one another as I have loved you. When my followers have my Spirit, they are able; without it they cannot.

JANUARY 24

"If you have bitter jealousy and selfish ambition in your hearts...
(this) is earthly, unspiritual, devilish."
– James 3:14-15

From Fern:

Lord God, I would love to think that I take no direction from the devil. "What have you heard from Satan this morning?" "Nothing! I have nothing to do with him," I would like to think.

But the Bible is my mirror and when I look into these verses, I cannot pretend that these ugly feelings are unfamiliar to me. Somewhere in my nature is a spirit of competition, of perfection. I not only want to be my best, I want to be *the* best. That is selfish ambition!

Jealousy is involved as someone else is recognized for being in the place that I want to be. Thank you, God, that through Your servant James You have made clear the origin of my feelings. Even as they come to me, I know that they are opposed to love, and I dislike admitting them.

Forgive me, I pray. You know that I long to conquer them. The way to do that is to be filled afresh every day with Your Spirit, who is love; to rely more and more on Your leading and guidance so that there is no room for the devilish urges.

JANUARY 25

"To the only God...be glory, majesty, dominion and authority..."
– Jude 25

From Fern:

Dear God, this verse goes through my mind, reminding me of Your divine Otherness.

One with Your created, as near as breath, still You retain the majesty that sets You apart.

You are Creator! You are King! You are God of justice as well as of love. Help me to remember that as I approach Your throne.

Keep my prayers from becoming folksy. Help me retain a sense of awe of Your omniscience, a reverence for Your divine power. The image of the God of wrath is not obsolete. You do not wink at wrong. Your divine goodness is offended by unrighteousness and injustice.

Our words are so inadequate to describe the divine. Our minds, created by You, cannot grasp the Maker any more than a clay pot can comprehend the Potter.

Help me to know this, Lord. Keep me from becoming comfortable in my concepts. Every day burst the old shells that I may gain new recognition of Your goodness, your holiness, your majesty.

JANUARY 26

"...He was bruised for our iniquities..."
— Isaiah 53:5

From Fern:

Dear Jesus, You allowed yourself to be put to death for (as a consequence of) our sins. You had the power to call upon the angels to rescue You. You could have walked away, as You had done before. But You put us ahead of Yourself. You made fulfilling a prophecy a priority in order that we could identify You. You made the ultimate sacrifice in order that there would be no veil to separate us from God.

O Savior, You died for (as a consequence of) our iniquities and You died for (as reparation for) them.

You cared so much that Your own life become unimportant to You, Your image inconsequential. Help me to care that much about others! Help me to be so concerned for the salvation of souls that I lose sight of what happens to me, if by my words or example they may know You.

John told us that You are the expiation for our sins. We are unfamiliar with the word and the concept boggles the mind; but You reach beyond our intellectualizing into our hearts and we *know* what You did, and why, and we love You for it.

JANUARY 27

"...Where I am there shall my servant be also..."
— John 12:26

From Fern:

Dear Master, where You are Your servant shall be, meaning that
where Your servant is, You are present; meaning that when I am
serving You, You are with me. How well I know this!

How often You have shown me that it is impossible for me to
perform a kind act, to do a good deed, to give, without it coming
back as a treasure to me. You bless it, increase it, and return it.

O, my Lord, thank You for so constructing the world, for building
into it these spiritual laws, then awakening Your children to them in
order that we can incorporate them into our lives, using and
benefitting from them every day.

Thank You for your nearness, which becomes more evident the
greater our need. Help me to live in that awareness. Move me
continually from my sense of self-sufficiency into reliance upon You
for decisions, for executing the plans we make, and especially in
giving the glory to whom it is due.

All of this I ask in the name and spirit of Your servant, my example
and my Lord, Jesus.

JANUARY 28

"They knew it was the Lord."
— John 21:12b

From Fern:

Dear God, how many times a day do I miss seeing You, when You are plainly before me? In persons, in situations, in ways in which events develop, You are here! And I know it not.

Omniscient God, open my spiritual eyes that I may see that You *are* everywhere. You have promised to be with us, and Your promises are true.

The failure is not with You, but with me. The busyness of my life distracts me. I take my mind off You, and I lose You in the crowd. My heart becomes impure and I fail to see.

Jesus, thank You for becoming physically visible, in order that Your disciples could write as eyewitnesses to Your actions and hearers of Your words. What they heard You say has come down to us, and we who know You now as Spirit experience Your presence among us, still speaking the same words to us. It is for You that I seek to live, and therefore I need to know You as You are, not as I imagine You to be. Help me to watch and listen for You every day.

JANUARY 29

"I am the Lord your God, who teaches you what is best for you,
who directs you in the way you should go."
– Isaiah 48:17

From Cat:

If you'd asked me several years ago to list a few "absolute facts"
about myself, the words "card-carrying Big City Girl" would have
made it into the top five.

Yes, sir. Big City Girl. I knew that about myself as surely as I
knew I require oxygen to survive. In different incarnations of my life
I'd lived in New York, Rome, and Los Angeles, because that's me,
and I've gotta be *me*. (I also have a passion for animals and have
always made sure I'm surrounded by them, against the will of a few
co-op boards who would have kicked me out on my butt if they'd
known.)

When my years on *One Life to Live* came to an end and it was
time to move on from New York, another fact I knew about myself
came into play: I had to live by the ocean. Let's see. City, by the
ocean. Santa Monica, California, here I come! I found an apartment
on Craigslist that sounded perfect, arrived at the door with my
luggage, and stepped inside to find a mess of a place with a floor still
waiting to be unpacked from its huge pile of boxes and installed.

Okay, I don't have to be hit over the head with a brick; maybe I
could postpone the ocean thing temporarily.

So this Big City Girl moved right on along to Las Vegas...

...reconnected with an old acquaintance, to whom I'm now
ecstatically married (more about him on another day, I promise)...

...and spend the vast majority of my time off happier than I've
ever been in my life, on his ranch in central California and/or in our
RV traveling around the country.

Got it? Just when we think we're the world's greatest expert
about ourselves and proceed accordingly, we find out that Someone
knows us even better than we do and will move heaven and earth,
even keep a laminate floor in boxes if He has to, to guide us to where
we really belong. And it's our end of the bargain to get over ourselves,

stop believing we know Absolutely Everything, and bow to His Expertise.

For the sake of accuracy, I should add that I'm still not much of a hike-all-day-and-then-sleep-on-the-ground-under-a-tent enthusiast, and my bathing-in-a-lake days ended one afternoon when I found myself nose-to-nose with a water snake. But Big City Girl loves walking barefoot in literal fields of clover; I got to feed a grizzly bear a Snickers bar with my teeth; I can be as mesmerized by a sunset as I used to be by TV; we have, adore, and personally tend to a wide variety of animals, including my husband's dog, Yipi, and my rooster, Nugget, who travels with me; and I thank God every single day for not giving me everything I thought I wanted, knowing it would have paled in comparison to where He was leading me instead.

And to think, if I'd seen this life on paper ten years ago, I might have said, "No, thanks, not for me."

Dear God, please help me keep my mind open today,
especially when hope runs low,
to remember that Your dreams for me,
so much greater than mine,
are on their way. Amen.

JANUARY 30

"The earth is the Lord's and the fullness thereof..."
— Psalms 24:1

From Fern:

Jesus, in many ways you likened the needs of the soul to the needs of the body. Will you speak about this?

_____ (your name), *when you are mature enough in the faith, you will become more and more aware that this is true. The body needs food. My food is to do the will of Him who sent me. The body needs water. I offer living water, a spring welling up to eternal life. The body needs light, and I am the light of the world.*

The Psalmist invited you to taste and see that the Lord is good. You have done this and you come each day to be fed. Now go and bring others to the table. Participate in the good life and bear fruit on which others may feed as well. Be a tree of life with fruit for the twelve months of the year, and leaves for healing. Sink your roots deep into the soil of the Spirit so that your nourishment will be pure, for this is reflected in the flavor and quality of the fruit.

Spread your branches like wings. Offer fruit to all, for the provision will never cease. Abundance is assured.

JANUARY 31

"Practice and observe what they tell you, but not what they do."
— Matthew 23:3

From Fern:

Dear Lord, give me, this day, enthusiasm for Your work, a zeal to seek and do Your will. Forgive me the times I have regarded it as duty or routine. Perhaps even worse are times when I have followed certain patterns in order to appear "good."

Jesus, those are times when I have forgotten You. I have let go of Your hand and am drifting on alone. My attention has snapped back to me and to this earthy life. But when You are at the center, and doing Your will is my highest goal, life takes on an aura that is totally different! I sense Your nearness. I receive Your direction. I am relieved of my anxieties and come to rest on my trust in You.

It is then, O Lord, that life becomes exciting and I expectant. There is a glow like that of first love that surrounds each moment. Will I see my Beloved today? Will I find Him in the situations that arise, the coincidences? Will I see Him within the persons whose lives touch mine? In some I must look more deeply than in others, but in the most unlikely places, I shall seek and I shall find You this very day, Jesus.

FEBRUARY

FEBRUARY 1

"Lift up your eyes...and see."
— Isaiah 40:26

From Fern:

O my Lord, I praise You for Your wondrous love! You who created heavens and earth, the seas, and all that dwell within them—who established a natural and a spiritual law and revealed both to humankind as rapidly as we have been able to comprehend and to use them.

O Master, You deigned to come to earth to walk among us, and to stay on earth in Your Holy Spirit!

Jesus, You are all the world to me! Beyond love of family, friends, certainly above *things*, Your loving nature keeps me steady. You are my gyroscope. As long as my eyes are fixed on You, my life remains on an even keel.

You do not divert my love from others to You. You enhance my love for all. Each of my family and friends becomes more precious, their good becomes more important to me, because of my centering in You and You in me. And for those whom I considered unlovable, I can now care deeply because they are cared for by You.

O, what marvelous change You bring to life when we lift our eyes and see!

FEBRUARY 2

"He who has ears to hear, let him hear."
– Matthew 11:15

From Fern:

Dear Lord God, I long to hear what You have to tell me. I desire to come to You each day, completely undistracted by what has been or what will be—just totally absorbed in this time, with intercommunication.

This I want: to talk to You about my loved ones, those for whom I am concerned, then to confidently leave them in Your care...to speak to You about the complexities of my life, to seek Your wisdom and find answers. This is my need.

Holy God, I was a long time learning to hear, to realize that You speak through thoughts rather than words, through feelings and urges, through the word written by those inspired by You, and through the life of Jesus.

Thank You for each one, dear Lord. Thank You for being near, for knowing and caring. Thank You for Jesus by whose life we may find our way. Though circumstances differ, the principles by which He lived, the priorities He chose, provide the guidance I need this very day. Let me hear in a new way all that You would have me know!

FEBRUARY 3

"Put on the whole armor of God..."
– Ephesians 6:11

From Fern:

Dear God, You have divided life into segments and we continually enter a new one. We leave the old behind, finished and sealed. However much we would like to, we cannot change it.

Lord, help me accept the past and leave it there. Help its joys, rather than its sorrows, errors, or embarrassments, dominate my memories.

Gird me for the new day, donning the armor that You provide: salvation, truth, righteousness, peace, faith, and the very Spirit of Your divine Self.

These equip me for confrontation with human contenders, with situations or with the "hosts of wickedness" which are present in sly and subtle ways. I do not know what this new time frame holds. I do not know how to prepare myself for it; but my heavenly Parent knows, and cares!

Lord, I place my hand in Yours and go confidently into the day. Thank You for the armor, but even more that You do not send me out alone. I love You and I love Your going with me, for fear can have no power or place when we meet life together.

FEBRUARY 4

"...Your youth is renewed like the eagle's."
— Psalms 103:5b

From Fern:

Dear Lord, thank You for this promise. I do not want to return to youth as mine was. I do not want to relearn those hard lessons; but I treasure the vitality, the exuberance, the expectancy of youth.

In the letter to Ephesus as John told in Revelations, the church was accused of having lost its early love. O my God, do not let that happen to me! Isaiah wrote about the eagle and the concept that as the bird flew near the sun, it gained strength. Just so, as I come to the Son each morning for our time together, renew me, recreate me, wash away the effects of the yesterdays so that I may go clean and fresh into today.

Precious Savior, thank You for renewal! Hold me steadily in the light of Your love. Help me to share my love for You with others, but most of all, help me retain zeal for You and Your kingdom.

Maintain my enthusiasm. You have created me for a purpose. Reveal it to me and help me see everything that leads to its fulfillment as opportunity. Keep me faithful, I pray.

FEBRUARY 5

"It's not time that heals all wounds,
it's what you do with that time."
– Anonymous

From Cat:

I've experienced a lot of loss in my life. I don't know anyone
who hasn't. Whether it's the loss of a loved one, a pet, a significant
relationship, a job you depended on, a home, or even a treasured
dream, it leaves you reeling, in the deepest pain, unsure what to do or
where to turn, if you can even summon up what it takes to do
anything at all.

One of the losses I was grieving when I left New York was the
end of my seventeen-year marriage to a wonderful man I'll always
love and consider one of my closest friends. (I don't care what
anyone says, love is not enough.) Among my many realizations in the
aftermath of the divorce was that I had absolutely no interest in
dating. None. Zero. Thank you, no. In addition to my whole "been
there, done that" feeling about it, I was sure I wasn't emotionally
equipped to make wise choices in the dating arena, and I've learned
(finally!) to believe in an old Spanish proverb that translates to,
"Better alone than poorly accompanied."

So alone it was when I ended up moving to Las Vegas,
determined to take a one-year sabbatical from dating, show business,
and the same-old-same-old in general. I was only looking for three
things: peace, a non-chaotic life, and me.

I couldn't afford not to work, and I'm not happy when I'm not
productive, so I revamped my cosmetics company (Cat Cosmetics), I
started producing my stage hypnosis show, I wrote a book based on
personal experience (*The 30-Day Heartbreak Cure*) and I began
developing a life coaching and hypnotherapy clientele.

But mostly, with the occasional exception of a few close friends,
I spent a whole lot of time alone, hard at work on self-examination. I
took long, tough, often painful stock of who I was, who I wasn't but
wanted to be, what my priorities were and whether or not they were
as worthwhile as I'd been giving them credit for. And I especially

focused on how I'd managed to come up with some of the choices I've made throughout my adulthood that, in retrospect, were completely inconsistent with my dreams and my most heartfelt beliefs.

It was eye-opening and soul-opening. There was no quick, easy way through it, but even at those times when I was tempted to give it up because it was too hard, I managed to keep going with the help of prayer and an old friend and pastor from a long-ago incarnation in Florida.

Finally, a year later, I woke up one morning and realized I was whole again—still a work in progress, as we all are and will be until we leave this earth, but whole, blissfully peaceful, on my own and fully intending to stay that way. I'd learned, among countless other lessons, that it was no one else's job but mine to make me happy.

And then, through a series of "coincidences" (turn to the day that talks about coincidences and you'll understand the quotation marks) I could never have orchestrated myself, I was re-introduced to an acquaintance I hadn't seen in about twenty-five years.

His name is Todd Fisher. He's the best, most extraordinary man I've ever met, and I've now been proudly and happily married to him for a year and a half.

Looking back, I know with absolute certainty that if I had spent that year staring blankly at my TV and eating ice cream instead of working very, very hard on myself, I would never have been healthy enough to be attracted to such a wonderful man, or to attract him, for that matter. It seems that while I was still in New York, my marriage crumbling, Todd was losing Cristi, his beautiful wife of more than twenty years, to cancer. He'd been alone getting healthy, too, not looking for someone any more than I was, and we found our way to each other not because we were lonely and needy and unhappy, but precisely because we weren't.

Whatever's going on with you right now—whether it's loss or depression or just a general sense of emptiness and futility—I promise you, it won't get better if you sit there waiting for the clock to tick it away. DO THE WORK! Get so busy making yourself better, for you, that you won't give a second thought to the wonderful surprise that's headed your way, and you'll love not having to show up to the party empty-handed. You'll be a better partner, a better parent, a better friend, and most of all, a much stronger, healthier, happier, more fulfilled example of God's Spirit shining through you.

Dear God, please take my hand today and
help me take just one step forward, just one step
toward the happiness that's waiting for me—
not "after enough time has passed," not "out there,"
but now, "in here," where You reside. Amen.

FEBRUARY 6

"All souls are mine..."
– Ezekiel 18:4

From Fern:

_____ (your name), *Ezekiel spoke for the Lord saying, "All souls are mine." Your soul is mine and has always been mine, although you rebelled and for years tried to claim it for yourself. You came and gave it to me, as though it had not always been mine. That constituted your commitment but did not change the ownership.*

Souls of all on your prayer list are mine. You are relieved of responsibility for them, even though your prayers are heard and are important. Your particular assignment is to deepen awareness of those with whom you associate, those who come under your teaching in one way or another. Keep seeking, yourself, to grow in order to share with them.

Your soul is mine, but you are responsible for its growth. The souls of all are mine but interaction gives you opportunity to help others grow. There are many who do not know about this growth, others who seem not to care; but it is because they have not been awakened.

Continue to nudge them until they stir and then be ready to lead them on. But you do not save them. That has already been done.

FEBRUARY 7

"Surrender to what is. Say 'yes' to life—and see how life suddenly
starts working for you rather than against you."
– Eckhart Tolle

From Cat:

I recently had to learn this lesson myself, so I'm especially eager
to share it with you today.

I've always associated the word "surrender" with the whole
concept of giving up, a concept that goes against my grain. By nature,
I'm not a quitter, so *seriously?!* Give up?! Fat chance!

In truth, though, "surrender" can also mean to stop fighting a
battle we can't win, a situation we're in that we can't do a thing about.
Surrender in much of everyday life is simply moving into acceptance
of what is. It takes strength rather than weakness to know when to
put down our swords, stop wasting our energy waving our fists in the
air, stop risking an ulcer or an anxiety attack, and stop filling valuable
head space with how some circumstance we're in "should" be.

Acceptance is only a negative approach when you could make a
difference but choose not to bother. When we know we can't make a
difference, no matter how hard we try and how fiercely we fight?
Acceptance becomes a useful tool for clearing our heads and making
our transition to something better a peaceful, healthy, smart one,
rather than some rage-filled knee-jerk impulse that's almost
guaranteed to land us in a worse place than we were before.

Scan your life today and look for opportunities to transform a
personal war into a healthy surrender to "what is." Take it from
someone who's just been there, it's one of the nicest gifts you can
give yourself.

Then say out loud, as often as necessary to make it a daily habit,
one of the most beautiful, useful prayers I know:

"God, grant me the serenity
to accept the things I cannot change,
the courage to change the things I can,
and the wisdom to know the difference."
– Reinhold Niebuhr

FEBRUARY 8

"God had foreseen something better for us..."
— Hebrews 11:40

From Fern:

Dear Father, this verse of scripture takes me back many years to a little girl who prayed for a pony and believed every morning when she came downstairs there would be this wonderful surprise awaiting her. She prayed, she believed, the perfect formula. But the pony never came.

God, the Hebrews author lists persons of faith and obedience, who had received divine approval. But the report concludes that they did not receive what was promised. They were obedient, faithful to their call, made known their desires, and did not receive, as the little girl did not receive the pony.

Father, the reason is the same. The heavenly Parent, as the earthly parents, foresaw something better. Earthly parents who care of the wholeness of the child realize that it does not come from gratifying every wish. The heavenly Parent we *know* cares for our wholeness and the same rule applies.

Forgive me, Father, for asking the wrong questions when my formula does not produce the desired results. Help me to trust!

FEBRUARY 9

"These men...have turned the world upside down."
– Acts 17:6

From Fern:

Jesus, how true it is that when You come to live in our hearts, You do, indeed, reverse everything. All that formerly seemed of utmost importance is now insignificant. Instead of receiving, I want to give. Instead of controlling, I want to yield. Instead of attracting attention to me, I desire to step aside and call persons to You.

And the miraculous part, dear Lord, is that the harder I sought for happiness and fulfillment in the old way, the more it eluded me. Now happiness has come as a gift, a by-product of this world You have reversed.

Thank you, Jesus, for showing us the way. You also reversed the order that we are accustomed to in the world. You, a King, came not to be served, but to serve. You, omnipotent, refused to use Your power to save Your life and thus claimed Your eternal life and power.

Everything that this world regards as important, You rejected, thereby leaving an example by which those who follow can find the true riches, the true power, the true life.

FEBRUARY 10

"Put out into the deep...and you will be catching men."
– Luke 5:4, 10

From Fern:

Jesus, Your servant Matthew told us that Your very last words were that we should go and make disciples. The first command You gave to Peter was to put out into the deep. It was day and fishing was done at night. It had not been a successful night, but You said, "Try it with my guidance."

Lord Jesus, I want to do what You told us to do. I want to bring others and I have specific others in mind. I have not been successful, but as I look at this account You give me clues. To put out into the deep is to risk being unsuccessful again. It makes me vulnerable. I have not been willing to risk very much. I hide behind not wanting to come on too strong, not wanting to turn people off.

But You sent Peter. He did not go of his own volition, but at Your command. You upset the normal expectations and the result was so great that all who saw it were astonished.

My Lord and my God, thank You for never telling us what to do without equipping us to do it. You never send us out alone, unaccompanied by Your Spirit. Help me to have Peter's obedience and faith to do as You bid me to do.

FEBRUARY 11

"You are the Son of God."
– John 1:49

From Fern:

Jesus, I praise You! May all that I do honor You. "You *are* the Son of God!" Write those words upon my heart, Lord Jesus, that they may be the motivating force in my life. Write them across my forehead so that in whosever company I am, my allegiance will be obvious.

Precious Lord, Whose spirit fills me, Whose directions bid me where to go and to whom, go with me every step of the way. In the daytime fill me with Your inspiration; and, while I rest at night, open my mind to receive, in order that You can equip me for the day ahead. The life that You give is pure and holy. It continually recreates. Your work, therefore, is never boring. I never tire of learning more about You.

Holy Father, Holy Son, Holy Spirit, help me to tell others of Your place in my life. Give me the boldness to declare all the wonderful deeds of You who brought me out of darkness into Your marvelous light. Excite me always, every day, with the wonderful truth of Your presence.

FEBRUARY 12

"...Shake the dust from your feet [and walk away]."
– Matthew 10:14

From Cat:

How's that inventory coming along that you started on your first day?

It's my educated guess that you might be struggling, at least a little, with weeding out some of the toxic people in your life. If so, there's a perfectly logical reason it's not easy for you: it's because, as a caring, loving person with a conscience, you don't want to hurt them, and you believe that somehow, if you hang in there long enough, you can somehow inspire them by your example to be better, happier, more reliable, more responsible, more...whatever. They are, after all, God's children, just like we are, right?

Besides, when we first met them, they were so charming, so much fun, so attentive, with so many interests in common with us, and maybe, if we refuse to give up on them, we can unearth that same wonderful person we're just sure is still buried in there somewhere.

Seriously, what did we think, they were going to walk up to us and say, "Hi! I'm toxic!"?

And yes, of course they're God's children. But no matter how often they attend church or how many scriptures they can quote off the top of their heads, they demonstrate by their behavior toward us and the rest of the world that they don't give God a second thought.

Toxic people should be easier to spot than they really are. They lie, they cheat, they steal, they manipulate, they have no conscience or sense of responsibility, and they take all the credit and none of the blame for everything that happens around them. If they hurt you, and they will, it's because you made them do it, and if you criticize them in any way, it's because you're too stupid, too shallow, or too jealous to appreciate them. Their world is all about them, their problems, their feelings, and their perpetual sense of being victimized and martyred. They play passive-aggressive games to keep you off balance, never addressing a disagreement head-on but instead turning morose, sullen, bored, grumpy, hateful, and/or indignant, without owning any of it, until you're sure it must be your fault and start scrambling to make peace. Even a lightweight co-dependent is bound to be kicked into high rescue gear, and before you know it you're mentally, spiritually, physically, and yes, sometimes even financially exhausted.

Any of that sound like someone you know?

Well, as Maya Angelou put it so beautifully, "When people show you who they are, believe them."

And while it might feel unkind at first to walk away, please give some thought to the fact that every minute you spend "helping them" with your patience, compassion and loyalty tells them that their toxic behavior is acceptable. How kind is that, really?

When you finally do walk away, keep it brief, clear and non-combative, and no matter how much drama they throw at you, or how hard they might try to reel you back in, here's your new motto:

DO NOT ENGAGE.

Remember, by refusing to abandon toxic people we've learned are draining us dry with no end in sight, we're abandoning ourselves, compromising our own beliefs, standards, health and well-being for someone who wouldn't dream of doing the same for us. As a therapist once pointed out to me when I was struggling with a toxic person in my life, "Nowhere on earth or in heaven do they hand out medals for masochism."

Of course, if that person happens to be someone you can't walk away from—a family member, an in-law, a co-worker, etc.—you can skip the official good-bye while still applying that same handy, foolproof motto:

DO NOT ENGAGE!

You'll thank yourself a million times over, and so will the truly good people around you who probably got tired of hearing about this person a long time ago. Aspire to take it as great news instead of a horrible thought that if you want to know where your life will be in five years, look at the people you've chosen to be in your life right now.

❤ ❤ ❤

Dear God, please help me find
the strength, the clarity, the courage, and the integrity
to surround myself only with those who live by and cherish
Your divine example,
and to leave those who don't to You. Amen.

FEBRUARY 13

"Be faithful unto death, and I will give you the crown of life."
– Revelations 2:10

In his latter days, Paul said, "If only I may accomplish
my course the ministry which I received from the Lord Jesus!"

From Fern:

_____ (your name), *take your eyes off the distant goal and focus on today. Do not try to do all, or even something significant, immediately. Just be faithful. Think of my life and three years of daily ministry. What was significant about opening the eyes of a blind man, healing even ten lepers, preaching to multitudes, most of whom did not comprehend what I was saying?*

Think of Paul's life. He did not think of 7000 miles of travel as he and Barnabas set out for Cyprus. In each case they were simply faithful to the day, responsive to the Spirit's leading. This is all that is required to accomplish the course and ministry you have received. Much of what you are called to do seems menial. With some activities you are impatient. Not every evening can you look back and see the results of your work. But I see.

Be steady, be faithful and you, too, one day can say as I said, "I have accomplished the work which thou gavest me to do."

FEBRUARY 14

"You are to them like one
who sings love songs with a beautiful voice..."
– Ezekiel 33:32

From Fern:

Jesus, help me to see the whole of Your message and not sift out only those parts that are beautiful to hear. It is wonderful to read of Your love and forgiveness, the abundant life You came to give, the offer to "come and I will give you rest."

It is comforting to know that You desire for us prosperity and good health, to have the peace You leave with us and to anticipate that You will come again and take us to Yourself.

But, Lord, that is not the whole story. There was also suffering and nowhere to lay Your head. There was servanthood and no greater love than to lay down Your life for Your friends. There is the promise that we are Your children, heirs with You, provided we suffer with You that we may be glorified with You.

Father, it is time for me to grow up and read the hard words along with the easy ones. The Dick-and-Jane approach gives me but half a life. It does not give me strength for the storms. It does not send me forth to win others to You. It centers on *me* when my desire is to center in You. Help me, Jesus, to view life by Your example.

FEBRUARY 15

"It is no longer because of your words that we believe,
for we have heard for ourselves and we know..."
– John 4:42

From Fern:

Lord Jesus, how significant are these words! We can hear someone's testimony and judge whether or not it is valid. We can read the Bible and interpret it as we will.

But true belief comes from knowing You personally, from knowing *You*, not knowing *about* You.

Knowing You begins with awareness that You had been reaching out to me, choosing me as surely as you chose Your disciples, loving me before I loved You. Knowing You proceeds with trusting You enough to accept You as Savior and Lord, and sensing that You are with me every step of the way.

Savior, I see the many ways that my response has opened doors for my growth. As with other acquaintances, I did not come to know You fully in our early meetings. You continue to reveal greater depths of Your divine Self, the more we walk together. Thank You for taking me beyond knowing You through the experiences of others, to the place where I know You personally, myself, and for the promise that I will come to know You better still.

FEBRUARY 16

"Do you want to be healed?"
– John 5:6

From Fern:

Jesus, sometimes I get very comfortable with what is. I do not know what may be, and I really am not sure I want to be healed. I don't know what responsibilities may be given me if I am whole. It is safer here, because at least I know *this*. I am handling *this*, although it is not the best.

But You, Lord, are not satisfied with our having to accommodate to a life that is less than You envision for us. You always say, "Go. Take up your bed and walk...Unless you love (something else) less than me, you are not worthy of me."

You call us forth to adventure, to risk, to explore the larger world, and to a life so exuberant that it breaks all the molds.

Jesus, help me to throw off fear, timidity, and put on boldness to follow You wherever You may lead. Out in the world are new friends to gain, new areas to explore physically, mentally, and spiritually.

Take my hand that I may not wander apart from You. Go with me and ahead of me, leading the way.

FEBRUARY 17

"He who is of God hears the words of God..."
– John 8:47

From Fern:

Dear Lord, among the choices You have given is the choice to hear whom and what we will hear. You have given each of us the prerogative to interpret all that happens.

Father God, when I am fully Yours, when I have the mind of Christ, I will hear *You*. I will interpret everything in the light of Your qualities of love, truth and forgiveness. I will trust the persons I hear, and put the best interpretations on what they say. I will interact with them in love, concerned for what is in their best interest. I will seek truth, not rumor; whole truth, not partial. Each encounter will be a new experience, uncolored by any resentment held over from the past.

O Lord, help me so to live this day. It shall not be difficult when I go empowered by Your Spirit.

Now I am Yours and I pray for the ability to resemble You, my true Father.

FEBRUARY 18

"What does God require...but to do justice,
to love kindness, and to walk humbly with your God?"
– Micah 6:8

From Fern:

Father, I am remembering the time I was stopped by a patrolman and accused of something of which I was not guilty. There was no way to prove it and I paid the fine.

I admit, Lord, that I still resent it. It was unjust. I was facing an authority who had the upper hand. I was a powerless victim. But as I think of that, I realize how many people in the world face this situation throughout their lives. There are whole bodies of people who are powerless, subject to authority that cares for them not at all. They are non-persons. And it is not only bodies of people. There are individuals who have never had a chance, and I pray for them this day.

You are a just God. You ask that I be just in my dealing with others; that is, justice for *all*, oppressed and oppressor. It is a difficult position, for I tend to side with one against another.

You have shown us, O Lord, what is good. You have told us what you require us to do—demand justice, love kindness, walk humbly. Be with me this day and empower me to do it. Help me seek justice for any who are oppressed, obviously or subtly, as diligently as I seek it for myself.

FEBRUARY 19

"If I had no sense of humor,
I would long ago have committed suicide."
– Mahatma Gandhi

From Cat:

I know, right? Mahatma Gandhi didn't just have a sense of humor, he could imagine killing himself without it?! Who knew?!

Which leads me to today's assignment: Laugh!

May none of us ever become so wrapped up in our problems, our circumstances, our careers, our responsibilities, our personal and spiritual growth, or just the unavoidable busyness of everyday life that we forget to laugh. There are few greater purges than laughter and few quicker ways to relieve a whole lot of stress and regain a glimpse of perspective. We're all on a tough journey on this earth, but that doesn't mean we have to be so grim about it!

It doesn't matter where you find laughter today—as long as it's not at someone else's expense, because you definitely don't want that karma. Call a friend who invariably makes you laugh. Watch an old sitcom or movie you've never made it through with a straight face. Find some hilarious video on YouTube. Make time to focus on your children and/or your pets playing and plug into that silly, un-self-conscious joy. If you don't especially need it for yourself today, share a good laugh with someone who does and help lighten *their* load.

And if you happen to be one of those people to whom laughter doesn't come easily, what better day than to get over yourself and *learn*?

Dear God, I know You've given me many gifts,
including the gift of laughter,
and a world full of humor just waiting for me to find it.
Please help me today to put those gifts
to their best possible use,
to contribute more light than darkness
to this life You created. Amen.

FEBRUARY 20

"Create in me a clean heart, O God,
and put a new and right spirit within me."
— Psalms 51:10

From Fern:

_____ (your name), *prepare your heart to receive my word. Send from your mind all impure thoughts, criticism of others, or any attitude that prevents my entry. Hate what is evil. Hold fast to what is good. In other words, clean the house that is your mind. Prepare your life, which is my temple. Make ready to receive me, for I choose to come to sup with you.*

What shall be our conversation, our table talk? I, the Lover, choose that we speak of love. I, the Master whom you desire to serve, choose to encourage you in order that you will know that whatever I assign you to do, you will be able. I, the Friend, desire to hear, also, of you—the joys and sorrows you experience; and, as we talk together, answers to decisions you must make will become clear. Joys will become more joyous. Your sorrows will be comforted.

For my love for you is unbounded. It is understanding love, for I walked where you are walking. I felt what you are feeling. This is not only past tense, for in Spirit I know all that is happening in your life. Lo, I am with you always, to the close of the age.

FEBRUARY 21

"The dead were judged by what...they had done."
– Revelations 20:12

From Fern:

Blessed Lord, Father of our Savior Jesus, Distributor of the Holy Spirit, may I enter Your presence? May I call upon You, worship You, adore You?

For You are holy beyond any holiness to which I can attain. Before Your goodness, graciousness, and power, I stand in awe. Yet You bid me come. You give me audience.

Precious Lord, hear my prayer. Feed me with the spiritual food that my soul craves. Refresh my life with the living water to wash away the dust into which, as Creator, You breathed the breath of life. Restore the image in which I was made that I may proceed into this day to fulfill its purpose for my life.

Do not send me forth alone. Accompany me, direct me, sustain me. Make each day, Lord God, a preparation for that coming Day when I shall be called to give a final accounting.

Or is there a sense in which each day is judgment? May I conclude this and every one with a report of which I am not ashamed.

FEBRUARY 22

"He who is faithful in very little is faithful also in much."
– Luke 16:10

From Fern:

Dear God, characteristics of a Christian life are love, peace, patience, forgiveness, integrity, and others. These are not flashed on and off according to present company. They are the deep-seated, natural response to persons and situations.

Lord, You know how far short I fall. Can I be like Paul who was not already perfect but pressed on because Christ Jesus had made him His own?

This is the key, isn't it? I do not gain Christ-likeness by my own endeavor. The harder I try the more it eludes me. But I know that what or whomever I worship, I resemble.

I have chosen to worship You, and You have made me Yours. Your Spirit transforms me and I gain Your attributes. Many decisions, therefore, are already made! I do not judge a person to know if I will love. I simply love. I do not decide if I will be honest in a certain situation. I am honest, and patient, and forgiving.

I am at peace! Thank You for this slow but steady transformation.

FEBRUARY 23

"The spirit indeed is willing but the flesh is weak."
— Mark 14:38b

From Fern:

Dear Jesus, I, too, am one of Your sleeping disciples. Even as I read a brief section of Your word, my mind slips off the subject and goes flying in a dozen directions. I hear You saying to me, "Could you not watch one hour?"

Busyness has been my theme. Accomplishment has been the measure for how I value my days. But You call me to be still, to wait, to receive. Help me so to do.

Help me to feed upon Your word to nourish me for the day. Help me to drink the living water of Your presence to cleanse and refresh me. Help me to be open to the empowerment of Your Holy Spirit that I may be ready for the activity to which You call me.

For, Jesus, I cannot be what You would have me be without this equipment. I am weak. I am flesh. I am mentally distracted without Your Spirit recreating mine. But just as the disciples were new persons when they were filled with the wine of Your Spirit, calm me now and enable me to receive anew.

FEBRUARY 24

"Whoever does not receive the kingdom of God
like a child shall not enter it."
– Mark 10:15

From Fern:

Jesus, I want to speak to You today about children. I am concerned
for them. We are leading them astray. We are anxious for them to
grow up, to have the advantages of every aspect to life, to fulfill for
us what we missed. They are pressured. They have no time to be
children.

*Child, be still. I know. You have read enough history to know the plight of
children in all ages. But you are all children. What is your age in years related to
eternity? When I spoke of the children, I was speaking also in spiritual terms: the
dependence of a little child, the trust ("Blessed is the man who trusts in thee"); the
curiosity of a child ("Blessed are those who know they are poor in spirit")—those
who seek to grow; the easy forgiveness of a child (seventy times seven). Mary's
gesture of pouring out expensive ointment was typical of a child who comes to
express love without counting the cost.*

*These are the kingdom's doors. Remember your need to grow. Approach this and
every day as a child. Use your opportunities to better the situations of all God's
children, young and old.*

FEBRUARY 25

"For as he thinks in his heart, so is he."
– Proverbs 23:7

From Cat:

When I first started my company, Cat Cosmetics, I included a small Mylar piece in one of my make-up kits that read, "You are what you think, so think great things." It was my way of reminding you, and me, that today's thoughts actually determine what our lives are going to look like tomorrow.

I want you to check in on your thoughts every few minutes today, a simple, random, "What am I thinking right now?" Whatever you're thinking, jot it down. No editing for now, and no selective perception—include your thoughts during the best, the worst, and the most seemingly mundane moments throughout the day so that you can take an accurate look at your mental habits, and at what kind of tomorrow you're creating for yourself.

If you're happy with the portrait your thoughts have drawn at the end of the day, of yourself and your tomorrow, good for you!

If that portrait looks pretty negative, dark, dreary, and not the kind of future you can look forward to, it's still good news—you can do something about it, starting right now, and change it fairly easily:

From this day forward, every time you catch yourself thinking something unkind about yourself or someone else, cut yourself off with a (silent) loud, firm, "Stop that!" and start teaching your mind that unkind thoughts are unacceptable from now on.

Words like "stupid," "ugly," "loser," "can't," "idiot," "fault," "just my [bad] luck," "try," "can't help it," and "failure"—again, about yourself or anyone else—need to be weeded out of your vocabulary and immediately replaced with words like "bright," "pretty," "winner," "can," "smart," "forgive," "just my [good] luck," "*will*," "can do something about it," and "winner." Don't ever trick yourself into believing that cruel, petty, insulting remarks aren't damaging if you keep them to yourself. The power of your thoughts is as real as the air you breathe, and they're guaranteed to do more good, or more harm, to you than to anyone else—the choice is yours.

And by the way, if there's someone you dislike—and all of us know people we dislike, just as all of us know people who don't like us—who tends to trigger some of those off-limits words in you every time they cross your path or mind, ask yourself this simple, logical question: "If I don't like them, why am I giving them even a millimeter of my valuable head-space to begin with?"

Again—you are what you think, so starting today, train your mind to think nothing but great things, and then take a bow as you become the incredible person God created you to be in the first place.

Dear God, I thank You today for helping me
turn this mind You gave me
from my worst stumbling block
into my greatest, most positive asset. Amen.

FEBRUARY 26

"I have learned, in whatever state I am, to be content...
I can do all things in Him who strengthens me."
– Philippians 4:11

From Fern:

My child, let's consider the subject of priorities. Seek first the kingdom of God. First, before all else, seek God and God's kingdom; for within it is righteousness and justice, and love for one another. When you have sought and found it, all else will fall into place—like pieces of a puzzle in confusion until they have found the place where they precisely fit.

For life has many illusions: power seems impressive, success lifts certain persons above others, wealth appears to give security, popularity is reassuring. None of these last. All are temporary. Only God's kingdom offers transportation from the physical realm to the spiritual. Only God's kingdom has the lasting values of love, joy, peace, patience, kindness, goodness, faithfulness, gentleness and self-control.

When these pervade your life, outer circumstances matter less and yet they, too, fall into perfect place. Gone is chaos and confusion. Gone are uncertainties and insecurities. Power is God's and you are God's. Success is then permanent and secure.

Wealth is the riches of heaven, and popularity is with the angels, God's glorious messengers.

FEBRUARY 27

"The Lord hates...haughty eyes, a lying tongue,
hands that shed innocent blood, a heart that devises wicked plans,
feet that run to evil, a false witness...discord..."
– Proverbs 6:16-19

From Fern:

My child, I want to speak to you about pride. It kept Satan from his God-designed place in contrast to Jesus who demonstrated the opposite qualities of humility and service. Pride is self-centeredness, a distortion of values and priorities. Pride creates separation between persons and from God. Living in harmony with one another requires being in tune with the Lord.

There cannot be two centers in a whole person. Joshua said, "Choose you this day whom you will serve." Elijah, "Don't go limping along with two opinions." Moses spoke for God saying, "I have set before you life and death...choose life." Jesus said, "No one can serve two masters."

Only in full commitment to the way, the truth, and the life can humankind be whole, undivided, complete. God has left a cavity within each life which only God can fill. Until then there is an emptiness, and no matter how a person may try to fill it with another satisfaction, there is no true contentment until God is there, at the center.

God, who is love, longs for you as you long for God.

FEBRUARY 28

"Many signs and wonders were done among the people
by the apostles...More than ever believers were added to the Lord...
The people also gathered...bringing the sick and those afflicted
with unclean spirits, and they were all healed."
– Acts 5:12-16

From Fern:

My child, let us consider health. Health is wholeness and sciences are now learning that spiritual, mental, and physical aspects of health are all intermingled. They affect each other.

Health is dependent upon the center. Recall that healing is from the inner to the outer. The supreme health derives from Christ centeredness, while persons who are self-centered are prone to ill health. The mentally selfish, physically indulgent, spiritually lost are in a maze of false concepts. The inner condition soon manifests itself in outward display. Physicians treat symptoms, but health comes from God.

Be in health! It is God's desire for you. He created a perfect world and a perfect you within it. Your freedom to choose has filled your body, mind and time with less than God chose for you. But you can remedy that by restoring your relationship.

Remember that the greatest healing is death. All physical and mental imperfections slip away. Your citizenship is in heaven, at home with the Lord.

MARCH

MARCH 1

"...in thy book were written, every one of them, the days
that were formed for me when as yet there was none of them."
– Psalms 139:16

From Fern:

_____ (your name), *the day before you is as a blank sheet of
paper. Actually the plan is there, written in invisible ink. It is a combination of
my plan for you and the continued unfolding of consequences of what you have
done, and how you have responded. Let all that you do today be done in honesty.
Allow others to be themselves and do not accommodate your personality to
associations or situations. Remember my saying to Peter when he was curious
about John, "What is that to you? Follow me!"*

*Do not compromise your integrity. A reputation built during a lifetime can be
destroyed in an instant. I referred to myself as Truth and as surely as truth is
within you in my Spirit, it will always be available to you. Love life, for it is God
given. Love friends, for you were made to live in community. Love your enemies,
understand why they are your enemies, and pray for them as I taught you to do.*

*Be available when I call you to respond to an opportunity, for many you do not
presently see will come throughout the day. I will be with you to guide and direct.
These things I have spoken to you that my joy may be in you, and your joy will be
full.*

MARCH 2

"'I know the plans I have for you,' says the Lord,
'plans for welfare and not for evil, to give you a future and a hope.'"
– Jeremiah 29:11

From Fern:

How marvelous, O my Lord, to know that You know me and have a plan for me!

How beautiful life can be when I sense that in every moment and in every experience I can walk with You, hand in hand.

Dear Lord, I pray that I may know—not according to someone's interpretation of You, not as an image I have created in my own mind—but I seek to know You as the true God, Father, Son, and Holy Spirit.

I seek to know You as mercy and justice, love and wrath; and to worship You in awe as well as friendship.

I pray, Lord, to be drawn to Your height, and not reduce You to mine. I pray to be lifted to those plans You have for me and not ask that Your divine will be accommodated to my puny plans. I ask it all in Jesus' precious name.

MARCH 3

"...As the outcome of your faith..."
– 1 Peter 1:9

From Fern:

Dear Jesus, faith has many outcomes, hasn't it? You told ones You healed that it was possible because of their faith. Those of Your hometown did not see miracles because they lacked faith. Peter said that salvation is obtained through faith.

My Lord, faith is a gift. It is not something I can make up my mind to have, but it is like a seed that You have planted in me. The more I cultivate it, the faster it grows, or perhaps it is like a muscle that is strengthened by exercise.

I know that Your words are true. I can depend upon them, not as acknowledgement that all of this happened in Biblical times; but that, as I apply them, I shall see them coming to pass before my eyes, in my own life.

Today, Jesus, I step out in faith. I shall not be anxious. To whatever happens I will apply Your promise and have confidence that all things work together for good for those who love the Lord and are called according to Your purposes.

MARCH 4

"Abide in me, and I in you. As a branch cannot
bear fruit of itself unless it abides in the vine,
neither can you, unless you abide in me."
– John 15:4

From Fern:

Precious Savior, guide my hand and my thoughts this very moment
and throughout the day. You have given me this day and the energy
to meet its challenges. You have given me many gifts, associates, and
a work to do, and I give them all, in turn, to You.

You direct my day and use it to Your glory. *You* be in my relationships
and in my work, for unless it is to Your honor and glory, it is for
naught. Unless it is done for eternity, it is in vain. Eternity—beyond
what eye can see or ear hear or the heart imagine—beginning now,
continuing forever.

Lord, do not take Your presence from me! Increase my awareness
that You are near; that You are, this moment, not only knowing my
thoughts but inspiring them. For thus from You comes life to me,
and I return it to You. You are the trunk and I a branch. My very life
essence is from You!

MARCH 5

"Prayer is talking to God face to face
as a man speaks to his friend."
– from Exodus 33:11

From Fern:

Jesus, there are so many fine lines. How far shall I go and how much shall I "wait on the Lord"? How much shall I take charge and how much shall I "let go and let God"?

My child: you know the answer. We are not separate. As my Spirit becomes your spirit, so your will is in accord with my will, and we act in a unified way.

You have committed your life and have asked for direction. Will I not, then, give it? You have said that whatever I want you to do, you will do. Will I not, then, communicate to you what that is?

Note the verses from Exodus: "The Lord will fight for you, and you have only to be still...Tell the people to go forward." (14:14-15) This is the proper order. Be still, consult, seek direction; then advance, go, move. Take the obvious first step and the next will be revealed. Waiting for the Lord does not mean inaction but consulting, knowing I AM God.

MARCH 6

"In these days He went out into the hills to pray;
and all night He continued in prayer to God."
– Luke 6:12

From Fern:

O God, to love You with the love You have given me! To follow
Jesus, the Example whom You sent! To accept Him totally as my
Savior and Lord, moving forward, growing continually, "going on to
perfection," this is my goal.

"My Father, who art in heaven," not confined to the world, yet caring
for it; knowing what lies ahead and behind—the cause, the act, the
consequence all in one; and loving more in spite of than because of.

Help each of us and in total to know and experience the feeling of
the everlasting Arms, the waiting Shoulder upon which to cry; the
Ear, eager to listen to our joys.

You are God, and what is eternal life but to know that? To know
You not simply as acknowledging a reality, remote and unattached,
but as a Friend, Redeemer, Example, Counselor, Comforter.

Thank You for giving me a life, a work to do, a contribution to make,
family and friends to love, and Your divine Self, my Guide in the
wilderness.

MARCH 7

"Worry is the greatest thief of joy."
– Unknown

From Cat:

Don't let it enter your mind that I'm going to tell you that your exercise for today is to stop worrying. I'm an optimist. I believe enough for all of us in God's power to help ease our burdens. But I'm also a realist. Life on earth can be rough. Of course we worry, about everything from our health to our loved ones' well-being to covering next month's bills. On the plus side, worry can keep us vigilant and alert us to a need to seek out solutions. On the minus side, it can absorb every happy, positive, productive thought we have until we're focused on nothing but fear and hopelessness. It can even become a habit, so that we actually look for things to worry about because it feels so comfortably familiar. As hobbies go, though, worrying is among the least likely to get us where we want to go.

Today I want you to set aside ten minutes of quiet time, just you and God. Grab a piece of paper and a pen and write today's date at the top of the page.

Now, make a list, one by one, of everything you're worried about. Don't overthink it and start making things up, just list the worries that are genuinely on your mind today, from the most important to the pettiest, from needing a job to not being happy with your hair.

Begin each new entry with the words "I'm worried about..." and then write down whatever it is.

At the end of each entry, write the word "so..." followed by absolutely everything you can think to do about that particular worry. Don't jump right to, "Not a thing." Really throw your shoulder into it, and start training yourself to associate worry with taking action— your message to yourself that you're not going to tolerate one more day of worrying for the sake of worrying without doing everything you can to find a solution.

Just looking at them in the form of a list, rather than a dark knotted mess in the pit of your stomach, is bound to make them seem a bit more manageable.

Once you've finished, I want you to fold up the paper(s), seal it/them in an envelope, and put the envelope into this book at whatever date is exactly three months from today. Don't even peek inside that envelope again until that date arrives.

I feel pretty safe in predicting that when you read that list three months later, you're going to find it fascinating. For one thing, you'll be able to grade yourself on how good a job you did at being an activist on your own behalf—how many of those possible solutions you did something about and how many you didn't bother to try so that you could keep right on worrying instead.

For another thing, you're very likely to be amazed at some of the items on that list that either worked themselves out on their own or weren't worth spending a minute of your time worrying about in the first place. I've done it, and I've lost track of the number of times I gaped some of my entries and said, "Seriously...?!"

Again, none of us will ever have a worry-free life. So if we're going to be doing it anyway, the least we can do for ourselves is learn to be effective at it.

Dear God, I know beyond a doubt
that You and I are in this together.
Today, and always, help me remember to
share all my worries with You
and, at the same time, never forget
to hold up my end of our divine partnership. Amen.

MARCH 8

"To each is given the manifestation of the Spirit
for the common good.
To one is given...wisdom...to another faith..."
– 1 Corinthians 12:7, 9

From Fern:

_____ (your name), *let us think about faith. Beware lest you conjure up an idea of God and of the promises, and believe in what you have created. Do not reverse the roles. God created* you, *not vice versa. The promises to you are conditional. If you fulfill your part of the covenant, they prove true in your life. But faith is not of your making. It is something God effects in you. As fruit ripens, flowers bloom, seeds grow and mature, not of their determination, but because of their waiting before the Lord, what is natural for them is accomplished in them. It is natural for you to have faith. God has given to each a measure. Fruit ripens, flowers bloom, seeds grow into plants unless conditions prevent it. Your faith grows unless it is blocked.*

You cannot make a seed. You cannot make your own faith. Something you make and call a seed will not perform. Faith of your own conjuring will not produce the faith Jesus commended, the faith by which miracles occur. Ask the Lord who gives faith as a gift, then live it. Nurture it in the soil of God's word. Receive the blessed rain which accomplishes the purposes of God.

MARCH 9

"The genealogy of Jesus Christ..."
– Matthew 1:1

From Fern:

Divine Parent, we have only to read through the Bible's genealogies to realize that You did not use perfect human beings to convey Your truth: Noah did Your will and saved a remnant but in his latter days was a disgrace to his sons. Abraham, Your friend, lied, as did Isaac, to save their lives. Moses, who led the Israelites from slavery, had earlier fled from Egypt as a murderer. David, Your beloved choice for king, lusted after Bathsheba and arranged her husband's death.

Women mentioned were likewise not exemplary: Tamar deceived her father-in-law and became the mother of his child, Perez. Rahab, who saved Your people, was a harlot; and Ruth was a Moabite which nation, according to the book of Deuteronomy, was excluded from the assembly.

It is also obvious that You did not embellish the accounts, omitting these aspects of their lives. We have the whole truth. Thank You for using us ordinary people to do Your extraordinary work! Help me never to use my weaknesses as an excuse for not attempting great things for You.

MARCH 10

"It was not you who sent me here, but God."
– Genesis 45:8

From Fern:

Father, a reason the Bible remains current is that human nature has not changed. Jealousies, resentments, partialities are illustrated every day as they were in the life of Joseph. It is understandable that the son born to Rachel would be Jacob's favorite. He dressed him in a garment that distinguished him from the others, and aroused their resentment. Joseph was gifted to interpret dreams, which set him further apart, causing his half-brothers to plot against him. He was sold into slavery in Egypt, falsely accused, put in prison, forgotten by one who promised to use his influence on Joseph's behalf.

But, Lord, through it all You were with him. Abandoned, ill-treated by all around him, You remained. You gifted him with wisdom and managerial abilities so that, at age thirty, he became governor of Egypt. It was then, because of a famine, that he and his family were reunited. Joseph excused his brothers, seeing Your hand in the entire process.

O Lord, help me to see life in such a way that I discern Your presence and guidance in all situations and events. Help me to see beyond the moment and trust Your unfailing ability to bring good in every circumstance.

MARCH 11

"I will turn aside and see this great sight."
— Exodus 3:3

From Fern:

Dear God, there have been rare moments in my life when everything stood still, like a freeze frame in a movie. Your nearness was so evident that it enveloped all that was happening. Jacob had such a moment, initiated by a dream of a ladder that reached from earth to heaven. He awoke and said, "Surely the Lord is in this place; and I did not know it." Moses had such a moment when, in the conduct of a normal day, he beheld the abnormal: a bush that burned and was not consumed.

Lord God, these episodes happened as persons were going about their lives. They were not seeking an experience. It was Your interruption in their daily affairs. I see, also, that the experiences were for a purpose. In each case You gave these men a message that spoke of their call. This was true for Isaiah and his wonderful vision of You and the realm of heaven. You asked, "Whom shall I send?" He answered, "Here I am; send me."

Savior, keep me from fascination with "experiences," wonderful though they might be. Let me never be so preoccupied with a present occupation that I fail to see *my* burning bush, which will help me discern Your will for my life.

MARCH 12

"Who will say to Him, 'What doest thou?'"
– Job 9:12

From Fern:

Lord, some of Your servants felt close enough to You that they dared to argue with You: Abraham was appalled at Your plan to destroy Sodom and Gomorrah. He questioned You again and again. Moses used every possible excuse to dissuade You from choosing him to lead Your people. Gideon asked for a sign to prove that he was Your elected to deliver Israel from the Midianites. He must have questioned Your wisdom in cutting his army to three hundred men. Job declared his wish to confront You in a court of law. Jeremiah cried out against Your unfair treatment of him.

Master, I often pray to be more submissive but in these accounts there is a relationship I admire: courage to confront You when life seems to be unfair, honesty in stating specific feelings. There is a warmth about that. When I have this kind of honesty with a friend, it means we have broken through the surface politeness and are willing to risk exposing our deeper selves.

Lord, I want to yield my life to You, but I sense that You still want me to be me. You love me as I am, as well as for who I am becoming. Thank You, Father!

MARCH 13

"Let my people go..."
— Exodus 8:1

From Fern:

Dear God, there are certain refrains that run throughout the Bible. You intervened when Your people were slaves in Egypt. You empowered Your servant Moses and his brother Aaron to appeal successfully to the Pharaoh, and he released them. You gave Cyrus, king of Persia, a mind to free the exiles to go back to Jerusalem to rebuild the temple and walls.

There were many ways and times in which You said, "Let my people go!" You want Your people free. You desire that so much that You made the ultimate sacrifice of Your only begotten Son that we might have eternal life. Jesus came as truth that sets us free.

Lord, we keep falling into slavery—to passions, to habits, to false goals and concepts—in summary, to Satan. We become bound, which You do not want for us. You desire that all be saved and come to the knowledge of the truth. As heavenly Parent, You desire for Your children abundant life and that all may go well in body and soul.

Jesus, help me to declare with Paul in his letter to the Romans that he would not be enslaved by anything, but accepting Christ Jesus as my Lord and Savior, help me remember I have been set free!

MARCH 14

"Never diminish yourself with the words 'I'm only human.'
Use those words to elevate yourself, because humans
were the last and the best of all God created."
– Reverend Billy Graham

From Cat:

Today is a day for celebrating yourself.

Whether or not you think you deserve it, I'm sure of it enough for both of us.

Even if you're in pain, or sad, or disappointed, or scared, or frustrated, or lonely, or confused, I'm here to remind you, and *promise* you, that you are the child of the most high God, the Divine, the Creator. Your birthright is no less than sacred royalty. Be peaceful. Hold your head high and know that you are loved with the greatest Love there is. You always have been, and you always will be. With that Love, and the gifts He gave you, there's nothing you can't see your way through.

How do I know that? Because you're here, reading this right now, which means that you've already seen your way through a whole lot.

Look what you've survived to get to this moment, from infancy to today.

Some of you have horror stories, some just incredible stories of beating the odds, some not quite so dramatic but challenging nonetheless. And here you are. You made it! Whatever's next, lurking around the corner, you're living breathing proof that you can beat it.

You were born to do great things, however you define them. Greatness is accomplished every day, in the smallest, simplest, quietest lives, and if no one else knows about it but you and your Father, that's enough—it's yours to be nourished by and be proud of and aspire to again tomorrow.

You are the great I AM.

You've faced mountains before and, with all the faith, courage, and hard work it took, you moved them.

You will move them again.

90

Say it out loud if you need a reminder: "Mountain, MOVE!"

Now, look in the mirror, give yourself a grateful smile, and go have a joyful, fearless, blessed day.

Dear God, I especially thank You today
for creating the unique, capable, mountain-moving person I am,
so able to overcome all the challenges I've faced so far
that there's no one else I'd rather be. Amen.

MARCH 15

"I will not be enslaved by anything."
– 1 Corinthians 6:12b

From Fern:

My child, I would speak to you about time. There is no such thing as time as you know it. It is an illusion—an artificial division of night and day for the convenience of humankind.

It is useful and there is need to be attentive to it for respect of one another and of your own self. It is a reminder for, without an awareness of it, days can slip into more days and goals to be reached are lost.

But in the plan of God is eternity, which has to do with being rather than doing. It is not divided into segments but is a continuous flow. Think of an orange cut in half and the segments being as the face of a clock. Then think of it in juice form—the same orange, the same elements, in different form.

Just so, beyond this life the segments of days and nights disappear and life proceeds in a constant flow. A bad orange will not become good because it is juice. A good orange will not become better in its changed form. What it has been affects what it shall be.

So pay responsible attention to time segments but do not become their slave. Use time, but do not allow it to use you.

MARCH 16

"Choose...whom you will serve."
– Joshua 24:15; 1 Kings 18

From Fern:

Dear Lord, poet John Oxenham's words come to me about some who choose the high way and some the low, while "in between on the misty flats, the rest walk to and fro."

God, keep me from the misty flats! Give me always a passion for serving You. That will protect me from the emptiness that attracts the unclean spirits. Every gift You have given, You expect us to exercise, including our right to make choices. Joshua said, "Choose." Elijah said, "Choose."

Dear Lord, what a hilarious scene that must have been on Mount Carmel when the priests and prophets of false gods accepted Elijah's invitation to prove their powers. When nothing happened, he taunted them, "What's wrong? Where's your god? Off somewhere contemplating life? Maybe on a journey? Maybe it is nap time." When, finally, they had exhausted themselves, You demonstrated your power. Elijah's prayer, as mine: "Let this people know, O Lord, that Thou art God."

Master, this is not an issue about which we can be indecisive. As to Your disciples, so to us, You ask, "Who do you say that I am?" As never before this moment I can say, "You are Christ. I choose You, You only to serve!"

MARCH 17

"...Take possession of the land
that the Lord your God gives you to possess...
flowing with milk and honey."
– Joshua 1:11b, 5:6

From Fern:

Lord, as Canaan was the promised land for Your chosen people, the
kingdom of heaven is Your choice for all. Israel had to fight to obtain
her land, for it was already occupied.

This speaks to me, for although I desire to live within the kingdom,
wishing does not make it so. It says that I do not wander in or
happen upon it. My life and mind are full of distractions. I must
attend to the discipline of keeping the place You desire for me.

Dear God, I see this relating to the David and Goliath story. The ten-
foot-tall giant of the Philistine army called for an Israelite to meet
him in battle, "winner take all."

Only the shepherd boy David had courage to respond. In gratitude,
Saul offered him the king's armor. What a sight that must have been!
The slightly built David in the armor of one who stood head and
shoulders above the rest! David refused it, put his confidence in You
and won.

God, thank You for the warning. If today I may meet a giant
temptation that has the potential of enslaving me, I shall not depend
on my own armor or that of another, but on You to give me victory.

MARCH 18

"(God) saw (wisdom) and declared it; He established it."
— Job 28:27

From Fern:

God, I have read that the longevity of ancient Bible characters may have been to provide opportunity to observe the rhythms of the earth and perceive their constancy. Their ability astounds me! Mathematics can soon become too advanced for me, astronomy and other fields of science are beyond me. To realize that someone first perceived that two plus two equals four, *always*; that someone observed the courses of the heavenly bodies and interpreted them for their use is amazing!

But, Lord, there is another aspect of their perception, perhaps even beyond that; for knowledge, wonderful as it is, is not as great as wisdom. You wove into the pattern of the universe the natural laws. Every advance from the beginning of time has been made because those laws are unfailing. But wisdom is another matter. Wisdom defines the right use of natural laws; the right use of our bodies, minds, spirits, of our time, abilities, and energy. Wisdom directs our attention to the spiritual laws revealed in Your world and Your Word. They are as reliable as Your natural laws.

Father, intellectually I have limitations; spiritually, I may have none. Increase my wisdom for the living of this day.

MARCH 19

"I know that my Redeemer lives."
– Job 19:25

From Fern:

Dear God, what a marvel You created when you made our minds! We are still discovering their structure and how they function. The multitude of events that happen every day are somehow filed for future reference. Occasionally one is accompanied by such strong feelings that it affects us for life. I am remembering nearly ninety years ago when I eagerly accepted the Santa Claus concept with all the attendant stories. Come Christmas seasons, he was always present, just beyond my sight. He was watching and listening, "making his list, checking it twice" to reward or punish according to whether I had been "naughty or nice." Then suddenly he was eliminated. This one who was as real as any person I knew was obliterated, and I was teased for ever having believed.

O, Father, has that affected my concept of You? Can I say without fear of future developments, "I *know* my Redeemer lives!"? Help me, Lord, to know that I know You, not as an extension of childhood fantasy, but You as ultimate truth and love. Help me lose all doubt that I have wished You into being but to know with Paul that I now see in a mirror dimly, but some day face to face.

MARCH 20

"The Lord God said, 'It is not good that man should be alone.'"
— Genesis 2:18

From Fern:

God, I thank You for arranging Your world in families. Thank You for giving me the privilege of motherhood, for thereby You have shown me something of Your kind of love. You knew the pain and risk of loving. Mothers know that, too. You made yourself vulnerable to the whims of Your created, to the possibility of unreturned love, of disappointment. Mothers know that, too.

Father, the story of the prophet Samuel's childhood touches me deeply. Like Abraham, Samuel's mother Hannah was willing to give to You the most precious gift she had to offer. What sacrificial love was involved when, as soon as he was weaned, she gave Samuel to You, to grow and serve in the temple. How it tugs at my heart to read that each year she made him a little robe and took it to him there.

Dear Lord, I pray for young mothers in this complex world. I pray for the kind of love in them and in me that knows when to hold and when to let go, when to shelter and when to push children from the nest. In love, You gave us freedom to decide, to err, to learn, to grow. Help us mothers of all ages to have that same kind of love.

MARCH 21

"Sometimes the only thing we can change
is our perspective."
– Yours Truly

From Cat:

What a weird day I had a few weeks ago.

It started with an unexpected glitch on a business matter before I even left the house at 8:00 a.m.

But no time to dwell on it—I was off to the airport for what should have been a breeze of a nonstop flight to Texas.

I arrived at the airport two hours early to find literally hundreds of people in line at the curb. The terminal itself had been closed, it turned out, because the lines inside were even worse.

Several hundred of us missed our flights and couldn't get on the next flights' standby lists because they'd all been overbooked to begin with.

My luggage was on that standby flight. I waved good-bye to it from yet another line and pouted.

Sometime during all this my cell phone died. I bought an airport-overpriced charger before going through security, and then discovered that my shiny new expensive charger didn't work. Since I'd already gone through security, going back and returning it wasn't an option.

AAAARRRRRRRGH! Calgon, take me away!

I won't torture you or myself with more of this nonsense. You get the picture.

At each and every ridiculous turn, like everyone else around me, I was getting more and more frustrated. I scanned the crowd and found a sea of people spinning out of control, yelling at overwhelmed skycaps, screaming at equally overwhelmed ticketing employees. I admit it, I wanted to scream and yell too, maybe even roll on the floor and throw a good old-fashioned tantrum as a lot of the under-fives were doing.

Then, somehow, I managed to take a breath, do a quick retrospective on similar situations in the past, and remind myself that

98

getting in people's faces has never worked to my advantage. And fair enough—people who get in my face when I'm doing the best I can tend to walk away disappointed too.

So I allowed myself to feel every bit of the anger and frustration I felt entitled to, decided it wasn't a good look for me and wasn't likely to inspire a lot of cooperation, or change one bit of this mess...and stepped back for a wider look at things.

Let's see...Was I flat broke? No. Was I homeless? No. Was I physically challenged? No. Was I employed? Yes. Was I healthy? Yes. Were my loved ones healthy? Yes. Perspective. Perspective. Perspective.

Praise God, I was finally learning to focus on what's right, even if it took me awhile.

I told my increasingly bad mood to get lost and forced my mouth into a smile. What do you know, smiling actually made me feel better, and nicer. As an almost immediate result, the people I was dealing with were nicer to me in return. I became a ray of sunshine in a sea of dark, rumbling thunderclouds, and it was so effective I held my own private pageant and trounced the competition for the LAX Miss Congeniality tiara.

I even dipped into my savings and invested in another airport-overpriced phone charger. It worked! Bluebirds sang. A rainbow draped itself around my shoulders.

I credit this "roll with it" attitude with getting me the very last stand-by seat on another flight to Houston a mere five or six hours later. Okay, it wasn't nonstop, like the flight I'd originally booked, but what better opportunity to explore the Austin airport, where I'd never been before? (Seems nice, lovely people, by the way.) And in the end, I leapt joyfully off the plane in Houston more than twelve hours overdue and thrilled to be there, enjoyed a heartwarming reunion with my luggage, and headed on to my hotel—beyond grateful to myself that I'd chosen to spend that seemingly endless day in a good mood rather than enraged, despite all temptations to the contrary.

All of which is to say, when a day seems to be conspiring against you due to circumstances beyond your control, give your anger a quick nod, tell it to take a hike because it's going to accomplish nothing but make you and everyone around you miserable, and focus your energy on this question: "Doctors' offices are filled with people whose anger and resentment have given them a wide variety of illnesses. Do I really want to be one of them, for *this* nonsense?"

When all you can change about a situation is your attitude toward it...

Take a deep breath...

Relax...

Say, "And so what?"...

Remind yourself what's right with your life...

Smile at someone...

And let it go.

The day will change, because you do.

Dear God, when it looks as if a ridiculous day
might get the best of me,
please help me remember that I can make the choice
to turn the tables
and get the best of it instead. Amen.

MARCH 22

"Prayer is not effective
until we want to hear what God has to say."
– Anonymous

From Fern:

Kneeling, I ask Jesus, "What is the message for the day?"

His answer:

Go forth from here with head held high. Go out to contend with life and, in the contending, win a few for me. For it is not only in the church where souls are won. It is not in the saying that persons are gained for the kingdom. It is in the being.

BE my ambassador.
BE strength.
BE integrity, and your faithfulness to me will show through.

Face the day unafraid, confident that you are prepared. You have walked steadily toward it. The experiences you have encountered have made you ready.

And I will be with you. What can man do to you and to your plans when they are grounded in me? I will not leave you or forsake you. My faithfulness does not waver; what is there to fear? The stage is set. The cast is ready. The day has begun. Go forth in my name.

MARCH 23

"The Lord is a stronghold in times of trouble."
– Psalms 9:9

From Fern:

Lord, I am brought down. How I loved freedom from restrictions and pain, being energetic, eager to tackle each day's opportunities and challenges! Then an accident that took a moment in time will require weeks of incapacity. It has hardly begun and I am tired of hurting, frustrated by awkwardness.

Father, You have shown me that from the right perspective, everything has a purpose. I ask You to so bless this. I look to You for strength. I ask for patience, and acknowledge that it was impatience and hurry that caused me to fall. I seek the attitude of Paul, "Give thanks in all circumstances," yet he suffered so much more than I, that I should not mention us in the same breath.

I do thank You, God, that my injury is not worse than it is. I thank You that you put healing properties within our bodies. I thank You for friends who offer to help. But it is really hard to thank You for the accident itself. Help me to do so.

Child, you were going too fast. Don't attack life. Flow with it. Already you are realizing that there are persons who live in discomfort and pain every day, who must adjust to permanent incapacities. You have greater empathy for them. Take this time for the quieter activities. Be still. Allow your body to heal. Rejoice.

MARCH 24

"A little leaven leavens the whole lump."
– Galatians 5:9

From Fern:

God, You warned Israel against associating with the Canaanites when they came into the Promised Land, lest their hearts be turned from You to other gods. You told them You were jealous for them. You wanted so much to bless them with abundant life, but that would be impossible if their hearts were turned another way.

We have the account of Samson. He seems so foolish. We want to cry out, "Can't you see that Delilah is using you? Isn't it obvious that her love is for her own people, not for you? You had marvelous potential at birth, Samson! Angel visitation, parental dedication—you squandered it with the result that your life was filled with intrigue, deceit, revenge, and death. The Lord wanted so much better for you!"

But, God, Samson is a type, isn't he? This is more than his story (history), it is the story of all humankind. I know him well, for I, too, have fallen for what is cheap and tawdry. I have given my loyalty to that which is shallow and undependable. That, like Samson's enemies, blinded my eyes. His going round and round, grinding at the mill like an ox, makes me wonder about my "daily grind."

Forgive me, Father. Help me to have learned my lessons in order that my life will not end as his, in death, but in Your promise of eternal life.

MARCH 25

"The donkey saw the angel of the Lord..."
– Numbers 22:23

From Fern:

Lord God, I am fascinated by the activity that goes on beyond physical sight! Elisha's servant was terrified until You opened his eyes to see that mountain full of chariots and horses. Unclean spirits were visible to Jesus and they recognized him. Throughout the Bible persons saw and talked with angels. But the account of Balaam's donkey seeing the angel whom Balaam was unable to see presents a hilarious scene. This diviner, called by the king of Moab to put a curse on the Israelites, was detained because the animal he rode refused to go forward. Finally, You opened the donkey's mouth to explain, and Balaam's eyes to see.

Lord, there is a line of a hymn, I ask "no sudden rending of the veil of clay."* There must have been a reason why You dropped a veil between the realms. Paul said that Christians look not to what is seen but what is unseen. Help me to obtain the fine balance that acknowledges there is the other realm, while not becoming preoccupied with it. If it was important for Jesus to come here to serve, I shall know that is my place now. Reveal to me as much as I need to know, for what You would have me do, I pray.

* United Methodist Hymnal #500

MARCH 26

"Be faithful unto death and I will give you the crown of life."
– Revelations 2:10

Jesus, there are so many tension points in Christian living.
How much shall I do and how much shall I entrust to You?
I want to accept the responsibility for living out my convictions, but
where is the balance point that will prevent
Christian living from becoming mostly activity?

From Fern:

_____ (your name), *you have committed your life to me. You take seriously that I asked, "What more are you doing than others?" and "Him to whom much has been given of him will much be expected." You have been about what you perceive to be the Father's business. What is the balance point? God. Keep God central. Center all activity in the Father. Evaluate all busyness in the light of God-love.*

Your world has become complex. Why? Because the tendency has been to shift the center, to compromise divine law. It operates only when it is accepted and lived literally. The promised blessings were founded on that interpretation. For many, money and what it can buy, the power and prestige it can assure, has become the center. To so live is to base a life on the formula that two plus two equals five. Nothing will then come to a correct result.

MARCH 27

"Unless one is born anew he cannot see the kingdom of God."
– John 3:3

From Fern:

How vividly I remember the spirit of wildness that for years ruled my life! Psychologists would identify it, I suppose, tracing it back to being a long-awaited, pampered, only child when my parents were affluent. Then came the Depression, other siblings, contending for a position I had somehow lost, not knowing why. I came from that, needing to be not one of the crowd but its leader, for good or bad. There was a curious mixture of both. Headstrong living set me on strange paths, all with dead ends. I affirm what Paul says of sins of the flesh. Finally, completely broken, the good that had been in my life became a beacon. I wanted to take that outstretched hand and totally accept Jesus as Lord of my life.

I identify with what Jesus said to Peter, "When you have turned again, strengthen your brethren." I admit to moments of envy of those whose lives have gone along steadily. However, my own far from exemplary beginning gives me a way to empathize with others of similar nature. Any moment I am tempted to be judgmental, I am reminded of an experience incredibly like the one at hand. No holier-than-thou attitude is possible for me. I feel akin to Paul whose zeal Jesus turned from "against" to "for." He found me, too, and saved me. I am eternally grateful!

MARCH 28

"It's not the critic who counts.
It's not the man who points out how the strong man stumbled.
Credit belongs to the man who really was in the arena,
his face marred by dust, sweat, and blood, who strives valiantly,
who errs to come short and short again,
because there is no effort without error and shortcoming.
It is the man who actually strives to do the deeds,
who knows the great enthusiasm and knows the great devotion,
who spends himself on a worthy cause, who at best,
knows in the end the triumph of great achievement.
And, who at worst, if he fails, at least fails while daring greatly,
so that his place shall never be with those cold and cruel souls
who know neither victory nor defeat."
    – Theodore Roosevelt

From Cat:

I once had the honor of working with a remarkable young man named Cameron Clapp.

When Cameron was fifteen he was living on the central coast of California. He was a popular high school student, a model, a surfer, had an identical twin and, sadly, was on his way to becoming an alcoholic.

One night he was trying to get a nice wide view of the 9/11 memorial that he and his family had erected in the front yard, backed up onto a railroad track, and was so drunk and loaded that he didn't hear the oncoming train.

Within seconds, he was mowed down by the freight train, with no one there to help save what was left of him.

When Cameron didn't come home, his twin brother finally went to look for him and found him horribly injured and broken, lying there on the tracks. He was rushed to the hospital, where both of his legs and one arm were amputated. It was a miracle that he survived at all.

Several days later, he awoke to learn that he'd lost three of his limbs and knew his active, athletic life had been irreversibly replaced by a future of learning to walk without legs or being confined to a wheelchair. His emotional adjustments were even more of a challenge than his physical ones, especially as he struggled to come to terms with the fact that he was now living with the consequences of no one's actions but his own.

His doctors told him he might as well invest in a good wheelchair and make himself comfortable, because he wouldn't be a candidate for artificial limbs—his legs had been amputated above the knees, and his arm above the elbow.

Cameron refused to accept those limitations, or to be defined by his losses. Instead, he learned how to walk on his stumps, and he began to build his strength and try swimming and surfing again, rebuilding his life literally from the ground up.

He insisted on finding a way to reclaim as much of his old self as possible...which, unfortunately, included drinking.

Then the unthinkable happened.

Cameron's identical twin died from an accidental combination of alcohol and drugs.

Cameron finally hit bottom, and hit it hard.

He never had another drink. He doubled his efforts to regain his strength and mobility, driven to make sure that his life and his brother's were remembered for more than just a couple of alcohol-related tragedies. He was eventually fitted with artificial limbs and committed himself to the difficult challenge of learning how to use them.

By changing his mind, he changed everything.

Today Cameron Clapp is somewhat of a "bionic boy" and is an advocate for Hanger, the company who created the state-of-the-art limbs he's mastered.

He works with soldiers who come home from the war without the limbs they left with. He acts as their living proof that not only can they reclaim their lives, they can also reclaim the peace and joy they've more than earned through service to their country.

He speaks to high school kids about choice and consequence, about living life to its fullest potential without letting drugs and alcohol rob them of it. He teaches them about transforming obstacles and pain into power, and he does it with a wonderful sense of humor that prevents him from ever, *ever* sounding or acting like a victim.

He's acted on TV shows, dived off cliffs, snow skied, run marathons, and found a beautiful, talented girlfriend named Nataly, who happens to be crazy about him.

When I met him, he told me he had to literally be hit by a freight train and lose a brother to wake up and find his purpose.

He suggests, and I agree, that you find an easier way to do it.

What obstacles are you facing today, and which choice will you make—to lie down and let someone else define your limitations, or to shoulder through those limitations and use them as tools to make the masterpiece of your life that this man has made of his? Cameron's a wonderful example of why I chose hypnosis and hypnotherapy as a profession—I love helping to guide people to a better way of thinking, one that works for them rather than against them, one that wakes them up to the endless possibilities that are sleeping inside them.

We can die without actually exiting this planet. Giving up, and turning our backs on our potential joy and service, and letting our spirits wither away from malnourishment amount to a far worse death than the one that will end our lives on earth.

God bless you, Cameron. It's an honor to know you and to share your magnificent story. Someone needed to hear it today, and I needed to tell it.

Dear God, please help me today
not to just be inspired, but to inspire as well,
as an example of a child of Yours
who, no matter what my obstacles
or how hard I have to fight,
refuses to let my spirit be diminished. Amen.

MARCH 29

"Jesus also suffered outside the gate
in order to sanctify the people through his own blood."
– Hebrews 13:12

From Fern:

_____ (your name), *it is hard for you to understand the basis
of sacrifice. Know that before the spiritual, comes the physical. A little child must
come to know the intangibles by what is tangible. Love cannot be perceived except
by demonstration. Truth moves from a philosophical concept to reality through
life's experiences.*

*God, loving Father, showed by sacrifice atonement for sin. First it was necessary
to identify sin, and thus the commandments were given through Moses. Obedience
is the formula for blessed living. Disobedience constitutes sin. It breaks the
relationship God desired to have with the created. When it is broken, a sacrifice is
necessary, for it is serious. You cannot know how serious or how widely the impact
is felt. It is like a pebble dropped into the ocean. You do not know where the effect
ends. It influences others and becomes a power over you, thus requiring the pouring
out of the essence of life in redemption. I came to conquer sin, to redeem
humankind at the cost of my life.*

MARCH 30

"If you have raced with men on foot, and they have wearied you,
how will you compete with horses?"
– Jeremiah 12:5

From Fern:

Dear Lord, thank You for answers revealed in this verse about why
You do not make easier a life given to You; why, in fact, Your chosen
are often given incredible burdens. Jeremiah is only the immediate
example: lonely, beaten, imprisoned, ignored, labeled; he is typical of
the prophets' fate.

But, God, You tell me through this verse that there is a purpose, that
You are preparing us, strengthening us for what lies ahead. Like a
runner daily demanding more of his body than was possible the day
before, You continually equip us for greater mission.

If with You nothing is impossible, if, in Your Spirit, we will do
greater things than You did in Jesus, You must ready us for unknown
demands.

You tell me in this verse that every day I need to attend to spiritual
disciplines of study and prayer in order that I may be in position to
carry out faithfully what You have for me to do.

Father, though the way is sometimes hard, thank You for preparing
me for the opportunities You give!

MARCH 31

"If they had been thinking of that land
from which they had gone out..."
– Hebrews 11:15

From Fern:

Timeless God, Your truth stands forever and the Biblical accounts
are but illustrations of that truth. In Abraham's day the wickedness in
Sodom and Gomorrah was so great, they had to be destroyed.
Abraham pleaded for them, but You could find no goodness therein,
except for Abraham's nephew, Lot. Angels warned him to gather his
family and leave; but his wife looked back, and was turned into a
pillar of salt. Even today the salt-encrusted rocks near the Dead Sea
are called by her name.

O God, You would have all of us flee from wickedness. How many
opportunities You gave to me! I do not know the number of times
You called before I heard; for, like Lot's wife, evil intrigued me.
That's where my friends were. That's where fun was, and laughter
and hilarity. The pious seemed stodgy and holier-than-thou.

Thank You, Lord, for continuing to call until I heard, turned and did
not look back. Your Spirit helped me to see unholiness for what it
is—shallow and destructive. You gave me new values, a new life, and
a depth of joy in the heavenly city You prepared.

APRIL

APRIL 1

"The steadfast love of the Lord never ceases."
– Lamentations 3:22

From Fern:

Loving God, Your book illustrates many kinds of love: indulgent love like David's for his son Adonijah; self-sacrificing love like that of Hannah for Samuel, or Esther for her people; loyal love like Ruth's for Naomi; brotherly love as between David and Jonathan; lustful love of David for Bathsheba, or Amnon for Tamar. The latter, when passion was satisfied, turned to hate that was stronger than love had been.

Father, we have one word in English that records all of these and other situations. Clarify for me what You mean when You command that I love You, my neighbor, and myself.

Child, the only love not centered in self is sacrificial. The answer is not in words, but in Example—in Jesus who said, "Love as I loved." He said, "When I am lifted up, I will draw all to me." Jesus drew persons. He did not compel them. He lifted them from where they had been to a new status. They were made whole, given sight, and fed. You can do this. Think about it. Apply it today. Care. Go in peace.

APRIL 2

"...The wall fell down flat."
– Joshua 6:20

From Fern:

Dear God, there is a word missing from the scriptures. When You commanded one of Your obedient chosen, they did not ask, "Why?" I ask it: Why did the Jericho walls fall down? Why did the water rise up in the city of Adam that Your people could cross on dry ground? Why did the sun stand still while the Israelites avenged their enemies? How can such things be?

Father, You give me two answers: First, You tell me that this is evidence of my pride, my desire to control; for as long as there are situations I cannot explain, questions I cannot answer, I realize that I am not in command. Help me accept that and simply trust. Help me, in fact, to live in a state of awe, being willing to acknowledge that Your power, knowledge and wisdom are as far beyond mine as potter to clay.

Second, You remind me that I need to live in an attitude of unquestioning obedience, for You know and I do not what is in store this very day. This day walls may come down that have separated me from another or blocked a path. This day You may part waters that seemed to impede me, or give me moments when time stands still.

God, You are with me, Your miracles all about me, *now!* Help me to see!

APRIL 3

From Fern:

Lord, I picture the Israelites in the wilderness, on their way to the Promised Land, hearing the report of giants they will have to overcome, and in contrast, feeling like grasshoppers. I am at that point. You have freed me from the past that enslaved me. You have set me upon the right path and assured me. You have given me evidence of Your faithful guidance. But life seems at times to be a wilderness of unanswerable questions. When I try to project what may lie ahead, it does appear like giants to be contended with and I am a grasshopper.

Thank You for the Caleb-thoughts which assure me that I will be able to overcome. Thank You for the experiences that have shown me that You do not forsake Your own. To every doubt, every fear, You say, "But I will be with you."

No, I cannot in my own wisdom and strength defeat the giants; but You give the undated, unspecified promise, "My grace is sufficient for you, for my power is made perfect in weakness."

Holy Spirit, stay close! Give me courage to face whatever is ahead. Make me strong in *Your* strength, and in *Your* wisdom, wise.

APRIL 4

"Courage is fear holding on a minute longer."
– George S. Patton

From Cat:

I'm usually a resilient woman, good at bucking up and facing things, quick to pull up my Big Girl pants and keep moving.

In 2013, due to circumstances beyond my control, I lost those gifts in the darkness for a while. Grief grabbed me by the throat, and I wondered if I would ever take a happy breath again. It felt so foreign to me that I couldn't recognize myself.

In a nutshell—on the heels of losing my beloved vibrant, sassy, sometimes bitchy, incredibly funny ninety-one-year-old mom to a longtime illness, my precious pet goose Buddy Boo, whom I'd raised from an orphan hatchling, was senselessly killed thanks to some careless, cruel-minded people I've since banished from my life.

I went into a tailspin of rage and sorrow I could never have imagined, and I had no idea what to do with those feelings. My heart was truly broken. I curled up in a ball and cried and cried until I couldn't cry any more, begging God to take my pain as soon as possible so I could feel normal again, until I realized that, all things considered, what I was feeling *was* normal. My new normal? This? Please, God, no.

Within a few weeks, this woman who helps people overcome fears and phobias for a living found herself afraid to leave the house. I developed a terrible dread about leaving our central California ranch, not to mention leaving my animals in the care of even the best, most dependable people. I vented my tears, my fear, my grief, and my anger on social media, and God help anyone who told me to get over it and turn that frown upside down. My husband was wise and loving enough to be there for me without once trying to "fix" me, just standing back and letting me heal. It was a terrible situation for him, too, since the people who'd cost Buddy Boo his life were family members, but he kept his emotions out of it and focused on what had happened and what was *right*.

No doubt about it, grief is a process, and you can't rush it or postpone it. You just have to feel those feelings, painfully and completely, not running from them but leaning into them until you eventually re-emerge and reunite with your thinking mind. And as the late Sylvia Browne used to say, grief is really very unapologetically selfish. I knew my dear mom and my dear pet were whole and healthy and blissfully happy in heaven. I wasn't crying for them. I was crying for me. I wanted them back, and I wanted them back NOW!

I'd committed to a trip to Los Angeles, but I kept putting it off, overwhelmed by my ongoing fear. Finally, when I couldn't postpone it any longer, I got up, took a deep breath and a leap of faith in the spirit of "don't think about it, just do it," climbed into my car, and drove away from the ranch, after taking every precaution that my animals would be cared for this time by good, responsible people who'd love them as much as I do.

It was a long, slow, frustrating four-hour drive that demanded too much of my concentration to let me focus on how frightened and homesick I already was. I'd barely limped inside the L.A. city limits when I felt an almost urgent need to pull over, get out of the car, stretch my legs, and regroup.

I wasn't familiar with the neighborhood I'd randomly landed in, so what a nice surprise to find myself in front of a store window full of my preferred style of clothing: bohemian and easy and almost never "dry clean only." There were some beautiful pieces in the window, so purely for the distraction, I wandered inside.

The owner of the store walked over to greet me, and we must have looked like twins as our jaws dropped open in unison at the sight of each other.

We'd known each other in New York, when she'd just arrived from Sweden to launch her designing career. She was a very quiet, very kind, very talented girl, and we'd lost track of each other fifteen years earlier, during which, it turned out, she'd moved to Los Angeles, become a very successful designer, and opened her own shop that happened to have an available parking space in front of it at exactly the right time on exactly the right day.

We hugged, we almost cried from the surprising joy of it, and for the first time in longer than I could remember, I laughed. I completely indulged in the amazing "coincidence," trying on clothes, catching up on her life, catching her up on mine without sinking back into the grief part, and insisting on a selfie of the two of us—I had to capture on film the event that, without a bit of planning on my part, began my healing.

I was bolstered enough that I headed straight from there to my mother-in-law's house. I'd missed her and wanted to see her, but not until I had more to greet her with than wracking sobs and a dark, angry silence. I was able to burst into her bedroom with a genuine smile, and she gave me one right back. More healing. We sat and talked about Everything Else, and I drank it in, so grateful to be gently, hilariously lured outside of myself to just relax and play for the second time that day. And believe me, no one has more stories to tell and no one can tell them better than my husband's mother, Debbie Reynolds, who's become not just my mother-in-law but my second mom.

The moral of this story?

If you or someone you love is in the vice-like grip of grief, please know that I'm so terribly, genuinely sorry for your loss.

Curl up in your Father's arms, feel every bit of the pain you're feeling and cry every tear you have in you for as long as you can take it.

To those who don't understand, or want you to hurry up and get over it because you're making them uncomfortable—buh-bye, at least for now.

To those who do understand, God bless them for their patience and their respect for the process they can neither fix nor go through on your behalf, no matter how much they wish they could.

Impossible as it is to believe right this minute, there really will be a day when you laugh again, and start to recognize yourself again, and begin to heal.

That day will be a gift from your friends, your real friends, who know how to love and be fun and just be there with no demands or expectations while you put the pieces of yourself back together. When you can't cry or rage any more, reach out to your best friends and be available to the ones you weren't expecting. The best ones, the ones you deserve, will be there with whatever you need, no questions asked, both of you secure in the knowledge that you'll do exactly the same for them someday.

119

❤ ❤ ❤

Dear God, I especially thank You today
for loving surprises, for unexpected fun and for
the healing, unconditional love of real friends. Amen.

APRIL 5

"Fear not...It is the Father's good pleasure
to give you the kingdom."
– Luke 12:32

From Fern:

Dear Father, to live the life You would have me live, to be humble
and obedient to all You would ask me to do, help me.

I thank You for placing me in a position of service, for planting in
my heart a desire to respond to need; but I know my tendency to do
for instead of *with*, to send off a check instead of involving myself.

I like what I am doing, but I need You to assure me that I am not
doing what I like to do, assuming it is Your will. I pray to know what
is Your will and do those deeds whether or not I like to do them.

*My child, I have put my Spirit within you. The Spirit and I are one. The Spirit
is the Spirit of Jesus who chose to do the Father's will. Will my Spirit who has
become your Spirit not take delight in doing the Father's will? Do not think you
must suffer through distasteful work. Do not believe it is the Father's pleasure
that you be miserable.*

APRIL 6

"And the whole city gathered together
about the door. And He healed many who were sick
with various diseases, and cast out...demons."
– Mark 1:33-34a

From Fern:

Thank You, dear Lord, for giving me a ministry! Thank You for
friends with whom I can quietly share my faith. No sermons from
pulpits, no reaching others through great music or literature—but
through a handshake, a touch on the shoulder, You have allowed me
to express the love You have given me to others. No one shall seek
me out today, God, to serve on a mission field, but a friend who has
a need may call and I will respond. That is my ministry. Thank You
for it!

Such did Jesus do, O Lord. Being available, people came to Him. He
healed physical problems and You have not given me that gift—but
sometimes You have allowed me to help those deep hurts of the
spirit. He brought sight to the blind and I cannot do that—but
sometimes You have given me opportunity to help another to see
from a different point of view. He went about doing good. I can do
that! Help me so to associate with others that wherever I go,
situations, moods and outlook will be better, more hopeful, than
before.

APRIL 7

"Whatever is true...honorable...just...pure...
lovely...gracious...if there is any excellence...
anything worthy of praise, think about these things."
– Philippians 4:8

From Fern:

Lord, I accept these words as my own assignment. Help me regard them as applying not to some vague future or an indefinite overall; but this very day, let this be my task:

1) To love more dearly all who sweep across my path and mind. Help me see them anew with Your eyes of love, of understanding, of tenderness. Help me to realize that love doesn't just happen but is an intentional attitude.

2) To help a wandering child to find the way. O, my God, how many years I fumbled and bumbled along life's way before I found the joy and peace of surrender! Without denying another's free will, without forgetting Your divine timetable, may I help someone this very day to find the way that has given me life in fullness!

3) To ponder noble thoughts, and pray. Whatever happens to me, dear God, I am in charge of my thoughts. I can fill my mind with whatever I will. Help me always to seek the highest and the best. No garbage, no waste, just noble thoughts which in themselves constitute prayer.

APRIL 8

"This is the day which the Lord has made;
let us rejoice and be glad in it."
— Psalms 118:24

From Fern:

Father, I thank You for this day, this glorious segment of life—with blood coursing through my veins, with my mind ready to concentrate on challenging work to do, my energy at a peak to be expended in glorious activity for You. You have gifted me with all of this and I pray to use it to Your honor and glory. Of my own self my work is for naught. My own ideas are immature and not worth sharing. But as I open myself to Your inspiration, there are beautiful results. Words flow from thoughts beyond myself, and I praise You for the gift.

Be my guide and inspiration, Lord. Direct my thoughts, my hands, my feet. Let every word that proceeds from my mouth be words of love, forgiveness, and peace that You have given me to share. Help me to encourage and construct rather than their opposites. Help me to think of others more than of myself. All of this can come about only as You are my close companion.

APRIL 9

"I have called you by name, you are mine."
– Isaiah 43:1b

From Fern:

My God, in the quietness of this moment, I bow before You. I listen for Your gentle voice and know it is within me. I know that we commune spirit to Spirit and I attune to thoughts of love and high desires, so may I come into the realm of Your habitation. And I find, to my surprise, that You are not just waiting there but You are reaching toward me, coming more searchingly to me than I to You.

O God, thank You for this love that includes the promise of waiting for my readiness, that includes forgiveness and gifts of peace and comfort, the undergirding of the everlasting arms. Thank You for the inner security of realizing that better than anyone else knows me, You know. You know my innermost feelings, doubts, disappointments, and triumphs—You know better than I *why* I am as I am, what motivates and stimulates me, what differentiates me from others. For that reason, when I come to You, I can come in confidence! I can come in the security of Your understanding. I stand before You stripped of any pretense—the two of us—Your Spirit and mine united.

May I catch some gleam of radiance from Your Spirit to sustain me this day?

APRIL 10

"Behold, I stand at the door and knock;
if anyone hears my voice and opens the door,
I will come in to him and eat with him, and he with me."
– Revelations 3:20

From Fern:

Lord God, help me to fling open the door of my heart and to ask You in the whole way. Are there areas of my life I have kept closed? Rooms for my private resentments and hurts where I go for self-pity from time to time? Are there places I keep my treasures—special keepsakes that take precedence over my worship of You—money that represents my security? What about relationships and conversations? Have I kept You out of them?

O my God, yes! I know that is true and I would not have it so! Help me to open every facet of my life in order that awake or asleep, in sickness or in health, in sorrow or in joy, in need or fulfilled, You shine into every corner of my "house."

My life belongs to You more fully now than when I knelt here minutes ago. My heart and mind are more open to Your divine inspiration, my dedication to You is stronger; but of myself I cannot carry through my convictions. Come in, Lord Jesus, in Your Holy Spirit, and take charge.

APRIL 11

"Become the person you want to attract."
– Unknown

From Cat:

I know. We've all heard that quote so often that it's started to register as white noise, but since it's inventory day again, let's take a good long look at it and see what happens.

I counsel a lot of people who feel as if the best things in life are eluding them, and they don't understand why. They're either unemployed or they hate their employers or employees. They're disillusioned by a series of unsuccessful relationships, or surrounded by so-called friends who are much more interested in taking than they are in giving. They're fresh out of energy from the hamster-wheel they feel trapped in, and they're fresh out of ideas about what to try next. The good news is, they've finally admitted to themselves that what they've been doing isn't working, which is why they found their way to me.

One of the most fascinating, enlightening exercises we tackle during our time together, if those are the issues they're struggling with, is to ask them to make a detailed list of the qualities they're looking for in their ideal employer/employee, partner, or friend. Those lists invariably bear a strong resemblance to each other and tend to include most or all of the following (in no particular order):
smart
reliable
responsible
compassionate
hard-working
kind
patient
would rather solve problems than complain about them
honest
financially sensible
good sense of humor
clean and sober

personable
respectful
open-minded
values integrity
practical
spiritually grounded
useful in a crisis
doesn't mind admitting when they're wrong
eager to grow and encourage growth in others
a healthy outlook on life
puts reasonable effort into their appearance, hygiene, and home
willing to give as much attention as they ask for

Now, before we go on to step two of today's inventory exercise, grab a pen and a piece of paper—or better yet, a journal—and make a list of the qualities *you'd* find in your ideal employer/employee, partner or friend. Don't take it lightly. Throw your shoulder into it, be thorough and take your time.

****

(long, quiet pause)

All done?
Good work.
On to the probably predictable step two:
Review the list you just made and, gently, lovingly and honestly, ask yourself the following question:

"How many of those qualities apply to me?"

Sometimes the most effective gift you can give yourself is the ability to step outside of yourself (i.e., tell your ego to go wait in the car for awhile) and see yourself in the third person. If you were a boss, would you want to hire you? If you were an employee, would you want to work for you? If you were a potential partner, or a potential friend, would you want to invest in a relationship with you?

Thinking we can't change our lives and that change is dependent on the people around us are illusions. It takes work, and it can be painful. But isn't it thrilling to know that we can do it, that we can make that choice, once we get it through our heads that "like attracts like"? I'm a huge fan of shining a spotlight on our shortcomings and weaknesses so we can see them clearly and delighting in the fact that, until the day we leave this earth, we're all works in progress. Believe me, I'm not wagging my finger in anyone's face—been there, done that on so many levels when it comes to that list, and in the end, excruciating as it sometimes was, I learned to love who I became through a whole lot of hard work and *therefore* who I learned to attract.

Put it any way that resonates in your soul: "become the person you want to attract," "you get back what you give," "what you sow, you shall reap." Just don't think of it as a theory of how the universe works. It's a *law* of how the universe works. It's a fact. Start living it.

Dear God, my ever-present co-pilot and guide,
I turn to You with all my imperfections,
past mistakes and wrong choices
and thank You from the bottom of my heart
that starting today, with Your help,
I'll make it my business to *become*, rather than look for,
that person who's been missing from my life. Amen.

APRIL 12

"Beloved, you are God's child *now!*"
— 1 John 3:2

From Fern:

Child of the King! You have been baptized in the name of Jesus and have gained fulfillment of the promise to receive the gift of the Holy Spirit. All who are led by the Spirit of God are children of God. When you say, "Abba! Father!" it is the Spirit bearing witness with your spirit that you are a child of God and heir of God, fellow heir with Christ. Anyone who is in Christ is a new creation. The old has passed away, behold, the new has come. Therefore, put off your old nature which belongs to your former manner of life and be renewed in the spirit of your minds. You did not receive the spirit of slavery to fall back into fear. God did not give you a spirit of timidity but a spirit of power and love and self-control.

Put on the new nature, which is being renewed in knowledge after the image of its creator. Put on, as God's chosen, compassion, kindness, lowliness, meekness, and patience. Be gentle and ready to forgive as the Lord has forgiven you. Above all, put on love which binds everything together in perfect harmony. Whatever you do, in word or deed, do everything in the name of the Lord Jesus, giving thanks to God the Father through Him.

APRIL 13

"Naaman was angry and went away..."
– 2 Kings 5:11

From Fern:

Father, I chuckle at the account of Naaman. This Syrian army commander, favored by the king for his success in battle, accustomed to barking an order and having it obeyed, the portrait of a man in control—until he became leprous. He heard of the prophet Elisha, went through the chain of command, then, fortified with money and a letter of introduction, he arrived at Elisha's door; but he could not accept the simplicity of the prescription. "I thought he would surely come out to me, and stand, and call on the name of the Lord his God, and wave his hand over the place and cure the leper."

Dear God, suddenly You show me that Naaman is not a stranger. You hold up the mirror and I see the times when I, too, have been in charge. All was going as I ordered it, until...I tried the world's answers, and they did not suffice.

Teach me the Naaman lesson that healing, health, and wholeness are available. It is Your desire for me and all who call upon Your name. It comes from obedience to Your instruction. It comes through yielding to You, accepting Your divine wisdom which may differ radically from my expectations. Instill in me the humility to submit rather than to question.

APRIL 14

"Remember..."
– Psalms 105:5

From Fern:

Jehovah God, throughout the Bible the history of the Hebrew people is told and retold. It is true particularly in regard to their release from Egypt—how You accomplished that and led them during the wilderness years into the land of Canaan. Though centuries passed, all Your promises were fulfilled because You are steadfast in your love and faithful to Your covenant.

Lord, thank You for this reminder; for often, in the midst of a problem, I fail to sense Your nearness and direction. I cannot see, then, what good can possibly come of it. But then I remember...Thoughts of Your goodness come flooding in. I recall the dangerous paths You have led me through, the crises You have resolved, the errors You have forgiven. I praise You for these blessings!

You have allowed consequences and I thank You for that, for they helped me to learn. And You endured them with me. You gave me strength to see them through. When darkness hides the path, and I do not sense You near, thank You for the gentle whisper, "Remember that I have never forsaken you in your need, nor shall I now."

APRIL 15

"You can be very sure that God will rescue the children of the godly."
– Proverbs 11:21 (Living Bible)

From Fern:

Thank You, God, for this marvelous proverb! Whether these sayings are from Solomon to whom You granted wisdom, or a collection of sayings among Hebrew people, I rejoice in this verse! I claim it as a promise!

For many of us are concerned for our children. We did not experience the world in which they live. I know the feelings of rebellion, the determination to find my own way, scoffing at the warnings of "old people." But there were not the dangers there are now—or the serious consequences possible today.

Father, I do pray for our young people generally and my own children specifically. May their angels be close by and watchful! May my prayers be a hedge against the pressures put upon them. On the basis of this proverb, strengthen me that I may qualify for "godly." This proverb gives another motivation for walking in the light of Your wisdom and love.

I cannot do this independently. I lean more and more upon Your Holy Spirit. Thank You for the unceasing provision for me. Help me grow in godliness with this new sense of purpose.

APRIL 16

"With the Lord on my side I do not fear.
What can man do to me?"
– Psalms 118:7

From Fern:

Father, how can I ever be fearful when You have given such examples as Gideon? When life overwhelms me and I feel powerless to change what is, I can think on the desperate situation of Israel, harassed by the Midianites. Whenever they planted crops, the Midianites came and destroyed them. Their plight finally became so grave that they sought refuge in dens and caves in the mountains.

God, You made a surprising choice through whom to rescue Your people. From the weakest clan You selected the most insignificant person, Gideon, on whom to bestow Your Spirit. He prepared to lead the Israelites in battle but You said, "You are too many," and cut the number by 22,000. You cut the size again until only three hundred were to go against a multitude of combined enemy forces, and through Your Spirit, You gave them victory.

O Lord, when the complexities of life and a multitude of sorrows come upon me, remind me of Gideon, the least of the least, who, empowered by Your Spirit, overcame. "Not by might, not by power, but by my Spirit, says the Lord of hosts." (Zechariah 4:6)

APRIL 17

"I the Lord do not change."
– Malachi 3:6

From Fern:

Father, help me be warned by the life of King Saul. In the time of Samuel the Israelites asked for a king. He protested, but You encouraged him to listen to the people, warning them of the dangers. You chose tall, handsome young Saul whom Samuel was to anoint. This he did, and told him the signs by which he would know that this was the will of the Lord. Among them was that Your Spirit would come upon him, and turn him into another man. You gave him a new heart. Samuel's instruction was, "(Then) do whatever your hand finds to do, for God is with you."

But Saul was not obedient to Your Spirit or to tradition. He assumed a right that was not his. He did not handle well the power You had given, and what he had was taken away. You removed your Spirit from him, and an evil spirit tormented him.

O Lord, I pledge myself anew to whatever You direct me to do, confident of Your nearness and guidance. You have given even me a power of influence. Help me to handle it responsibly, and to know the parameters beyond which I must not go. Take not Your Holy Spirit from me, I pray!

APRIL 18

"What's your sign?"
– Pretty Much Everyone

From Cat:

Every one of us has an invisible sign that we wear around our necks. That sign indicates what impression we're projecting about ourselves to the world around us, whether we mean to or not, and obviously influences how the world around us responds.

We're all living, breathing force fields, giving off and absorbing energy from each other, both positive and negative. Our invisible signs simply define that energy.

Don't believe me? Think about the last time you were at the grocery store, or a restaurant, or anywhere else where you're surrounded by strangers. Would you have any trouble at all choosing signs for each of them to wear purely by glancing at them—from "needy" to "drama queen" to "a legend in his/her own mind" to "entitled" to "I am loved" to "I'm a lot of fun" to "bad boy" to you-name-it? And if it's true for everyone around you, it's true for you too.

For much of my adult life my sign was: "I trust no one." It was my invisible shield, my defense against getting hurt and, of course, it said more about me than it said about the people in my life—my inner "knower," my antenna, wasn't serving me well. My emotions were more in charge of me than I was of them, so if I took a position of mistrust across the board, that should pretty much cover it, right? Not until I devoted a year of my life to self-examination and my ongoing studies of how the mind works did I really get it that it wasn't everyone else I didn't trust. It was *me*. It was my ability to make wise choices for myself, to both find and attract the best and walk away from the rest, so that I could change my sign from "I trust no one" to "Too smart for fools, I am loved, I forgive myself, I am ready to receive the good now!"

Unfortunately, by the way, the toxic people of this world, those emotional vampires we all run across, are very adept at reading our signs, too, and using them to their advantage. They're drawn like magnets to signs like "Needy" and "Vulnerable" "Insecure Pushover."

136

If some variation of those is the sign you're wearing, you might as well shorten it to a simple "Use Me."

I'm sure it goes without saying that once we've chosen our sign, we back it up with our behavior sooner or later. Usually sooner. Todd and I recently needed an extra crewmember or two to help with preparations for the third and final Debbie Reynolds Memorabilia Auction. A young woman showed up to apply for the job with a huge neon "Victim" sign around her neck. Oh, well. That happens, that's a shame, and no way would we turn someone away without giving them a chance.

I was about to start interviewing her when it became apparent that she had her own agenda—she immediately launched into an endless monologue about how she'd earned that "Victim" sign and how attached she was to it as the shining star of her identity. She was so busy telling me about every bad thing that had ever happened to her, through no fault of her own, of course, that she never got around to mentioning what a hard, reliable worker she was or why we should hire her, unless we did it out of sympathy, apparently. I found out later that, in the course of wandering around the auction site, she'd cornered everyone on our crew she could find and delivered the same sob-story monologue to them.

She finally walked away without a job, and I'm sure she added us to her long list of those who'd been unfair and unkind to her. Whatever! Forget wanting to work with her eighteen stressful hours a day; by the time she left, we were all virtually hiding from her!

The Reverend Billy Graham, who is one of my heroes, told a wonderful story at a celebration of his ninetieth birthday, about Albert Einstein, the brilliant physicist whom *Time* magazine named "Man of the Century." Dr. Einstein was traveling by train one day and, when the conductor came down the aisle punching the passengers' tickets, realized he'd misplaced his. He looked in his vest pocket, his trouser pockets, his briefcase, the seat next to him, but his ticket seemed to have disappeared.

The conductor stepped up beside him, sensed the problem, and said, "Dr. Einstein, I know who you are. We all know who you are. I'm sure you bought a ticket. Don't worry about it."

Einstein thanked him, and the conductor moved on, only to turn around a few minutes later to find Einstein on his hands and knees, searching under his seat for the missing ticket.

The conductor rushed back to him and said, "Dr. Einstein, please don't worry, it's no problem. You don't need your ticket, I know who you are."

To which Einstein looked up and replied, "Young man, I, too, know who I am. What I don't know is where I'm going."

Reverend Graham then went on to say, "See the suit I'm wearing?...I bought a new suit for this luncheon and one more occasion...This is the suit in which I'll be buried. But when you hear I'm dead, I don't want you to immediately remember the suit I'm wearing. I want you to remember this: I not only know who I am...I also know where I'm going."

Now, *that's* a sign!

Take some time today to give some serious thought to the sign around your neck—not only what it says, but also how that's working for you. If you're happy with it and it's taking you where you want to go, good for you! If you want or need to change it, choose carefully what you want it to say, put it around your neck where it belongs, and make it your business to grow into it.

Yes, you can!

Dear God, please help me be mindful today
of the way I'm presenting myself to those around me
to make sure my sign honors both You as my Father
and me, Your treasured child. Amen.

APRIL 19

"Abide in me, and I in you. I am the vine. You are a branch.
He who abides in me and I in him, he it is that bears much fruit
for apart from me you can do nothing."
– John 15:4-5

From Fern:

In me you are strengthened with might through my Spirit in your inner being. In faith I dwell in your heart and the roots go down deep into the ground of love. When I abide in you and you in me, you are constantly being filled with all the fullness of God. In this process you are being changed from one degree of glory to another. You resemble more and more the One you worship. You love indiscriminately not because of who the beloved is, but because of whose you are.

Your mission is to express good news to the poor, release to Satan's captives, recovery of sight both to those physically and spiritually blind. You set at liberty the oppressed.

In this state of mind you give food to the hungry, drink to the thirsty, welcome to the stranger, clothing to the naked, healing to the sick in my name. Their worthiness to receive will be no more pertinent than that I died for you while you were yet a sinner.

The kingdom is not earned. It is your Father's good pleasure to give it. Salvation is not your own doing. It is a gift of God's grace. Go, serve in this attitude.

APRIL 20

"Even Satan disguises himself as an angel of light."
— 2 Corinthians 11:14

From Fern:

Jesus, Lord and Savior, it is interesting that sometimes Your Spirit is recognized more readily by persons outside than within the faith. When You walked upon the earth, demons identified You when persons did not.

In the days of Daniel, the queen of the kingdom in which the Jews were exiled pointed him out as one in whom was "the Spirit of the holy gods." She recognized that by this Spirit Daniel had light, understanding, and wisdom. This was genuine, exceeding the abilities of Babylonian wise men, astrologers, and enchanters, and by this Spirit Daniel was able to interpret the handwriting that had appeared on the wall. In the days of Moses, when the Israelites were in exile in Egypt, the Lord's miracles were imitated by those of the Pharaoh's wise men, sorcerers, and magicians.

Lord, there is the real and there is the imitation. There have always been false prophets. O, let me have the true Spirit! How much I need light for understanding and wisdom, for the living of these days! This day I want to walk by the light of Your Spirit, making decisions according to Your guidance and direction, in harmony with Your divine will for my life.

APRIL 21

"No man can say 'Jesus is Lord' except by the Holy Spirit."
— 1 Corinthians 12:3

From Fern:

Dear God, even though the Holy Spirit is Your Spirit, and You do not change, I perceive that there is a before and after, a B.C. and an A.D. in the distribution. In Old Testament times, You gave Your Spirit to select persons, called to perform special tasks. Prophets and deliverers were spirit-led, as were the writers of our Bibles; thus the many books have a conformity and continuity, even though they represent the work of many authors over centuries of time.

Twelve centuries B.C., in Moses' day, when the burden of leading the people became too great for one man to bear, You took some of the Spirit which You had put on him and supplied seventy men that they might assist him. Jesus did the same when He sent the disciples on before Him, to heal the sick, raise the dead, cleanse lepers, and cast out demons.

Lord, this speaks to me in several ways: 1) To do Your work I must be equipped by Your Spirit. You will even give me the words to say. 2) This truth and these promises are present as well as past tense. Today I will go forth to do Your bidding, empowered by Your Spirit.

APRIL 22

"God...gives His Holy Spirit to you."
— 1 Thessalonians 4:8

From Fern:

Dear Lord, help me think this morning on the difference between the old and the new. John the Baptist represents the old. His was a fine message of repentance and fair treatment of others. He baptized those who came to him to be cleansed from their sins. But he acknowledged that the One for whom he was preparing the way would have for his followers a different kind of baptism. They (we) would be baptized with the Holy Spirit and with fire.

Thank you, God, for this new baptism that not only cleanses, but burns away the old me and makes way for new growth. It is a refiner's fire. In Christ I become a new creation! The old has passed away, the new has come!

This is the new wine that bursts old skins. For the old skins, old concepts and ideas, are dried and brittle. There is no flexibility, no receptivity for the new me to grow. Paul told me that my part in this process is to accept what You have for me, put off the old and put on the new, which is in Your likeness. I have the baptism! I am new! Life begins again! Hallelujah!

APRIL 23

"The unspiritual man does not receive the gifts
of the Spirit of God, for they are folly to him."
– 1 Corinthians 2:14

From Fern:

Lord Jesus, what a marvelous surprise You have for us when we say
"yes" to you! Your Spirit has been lying dormant in our lives until
that moment. You do not force Your way in. You stand at the door
and knock. For one reason and another, mostly the fear of what we
will have to relinquish, we hesitate. Finally we yield. We say as clay to
the potter, "Mold me and make me after thy will." And You recreate
us. You give us a new mind, a new understanding, new priorities.
You make all things new! It is a divine secret. The unspiritual person
does not understand. He has not the gifts that You give through
Your Spirit.

Lord, You did this for me and I want to tell others. I want to invite
them that they may share this unutterable joy, this peace of mind that
passes all understanding. Even when life comes at me from every side
and the rug is pulled out from underneath, You sustain me. I feel the
support of Your everlasting arms.

Father, I lift to You these for whom I care, asking that You touch
and call them that they, too, may know You in this way.

APRIL 24

"And they were all filled with the Holy Spirit."
— Acts 2:4

From Fern:

Dear God, I love Your church! With all our faults and weaknesses, our failure to understand what we are really about, it represents good in our world. We may bicker as family members are inclined to do, but we are, each in our own way, a worshipping community, serving You, seeking good.

A great teacher once observed that a plan or undertaking of men will fail; but if it is of God, it will not be overthrown. Your church has lived more than 2,000 years because it is Your institution, founded by Your Spirit, comprised of persons filled with Your Spirit, gifted by Your Spirit, directed by Your Spirit.

O Lord, Your task has not been easy in this regard. The church continues at least as much in spite of as because of Your people. Your vision of us as Christ's body in the world, carrying forward His work in the world, has not been fulfilled. His prayer that we all be one has not come to pass. It must begin with a single flame and spread outward. Let it begin anew, with me, today, I pray.

APRIL 25

"To think is easy. To act is hard.
But the hardest thing in the world
is to act in accordance with your thinking."
– Johann Wolfgang Von Goethe

From Cat:

Several years ago, while I was still living in New York, I decided to try my hand at stand-up comedy, partly because I've always admired it as a performance art and partly in my ongoing effort to conquer my lifelong battle with stage fright. (More about that on another day.)

Some very gifted stand-up comedienne friends were generous enough to work with me until we finally decided I was ready to give it a try in front of a live audience. I was terrified, but I got through it and continued to leap at opportunities to book myself into comedy clubs all over the city. The more I performed, the more I caught on that the raunchier my material, the easier the laughs, and laughs were what I was after, right?

At the same time, the more I performed and the raunchier my material became, the more separated I began to feel from myself, from the woman I was finally learning to love and be proud of. But I'm no quitter, so maybe I could find a way to get over it...?

One night, at about 12:30 a.m., I was walking home from a performance. I'd been anxious—not stage-fright-nervous, but *anxious*—all evening, and I'm sure it showed, because I certainly hadn't done my best. Even at my raunchiest and bawdiest, the laughter sounded polite at best.

The last thing I was expecting, or even in the mood for, was a conversation. But suddenly, clear as a bell, I heard God's quiet but perfectly audible voice in my heart, starting a dialogue that went exactly like this:

God: What are you doing?
Me: I'm walking home.

God: No, I mean what are you *doing*? I gave you all these gifts, I gave you all these opportunities to use them, but here you are getting up on a stage telling off-color stories, using profanity...What's that about?

Me: (after a long thoughtful pause) Well, now that you mention it, I'm not enjoying myself, this isn't really me.

God: You know I'm in the front row of everything you do, so make me proud.

Those words were still ringing in my ears when I arrived at my building, walked up the stairs and into my apartment, went to bed, and never set foot on a stand-up comedy stage again.

Of course, now I'm doing two hundred stage hypnosis shows a year all around the country, and I take a lot of heat from the Christian right for it, too. But frankly, I couldn't be more proud of what I do. I don't just make people laugh, and laugh hard, but I empower them. I relight fires in them. I help them believe in themselves, believe they go out there and do anything they set their minds to, because they *can*.

Always, at every show, I bring God into the equation. This is my ministry. I take joy in serving Him and sharing that joy with every audience I meet. And since that talk with Him on a New York street in the middle of the night years ago, I've been mindful of the fact that no matter where I go or what I do, onstage and off, I have the honor, and the obligation, of knowing that God's in the front row, cheering for me to make Him proud.

Who's in your front row, and how are you feeling about your performance so far? If your answer is "Not so great," take it from someone who's been there: Doing something about it, refusing to embarrass your Creator ever again or to disrespect the gifts He's given you, will add a whole new depth to your life that you'll be grateful for as long as you live.

Dear God, my Father and most loyal, loving Fan,
I thank You for expecting nothing less than my best
from me, and for Your eternal patience
as I try with all my heart to find my way there. Amen.

146

APRIL 26

"In the world you have tribulation; but be of good cheer,
I have overcome the world."
– John 16:33

From Fern:

*The ruler of this world opposes good. I created perfection. I completed the world
and called it good, but he chose to compete with me. His aspiration was, "I will
make myself like the Most High." By that same enticement he invited Eve,
"When you eat of (the fruit) your eyes will be opened and you will be like God."
And she ate and gave some to her husband and he ate, and the consequences were
separation from God and expulsion from the garden.*

*Everyone who makes the choice to cling to the world and be ruled by its standards,
whose god is the belly, whose mind is set on earthly things, is doomed to
destruction. Such persons soon fade like the grass and wither like the green herb.
They are the chaff to be separated from the wheat, goats from the sheep.*

*But I overcame the world and provided a way for you. I know the rigors of
temptation. I was there. I became the way of salvation. I do not wish that any
should perish but that all should reach repentance. I freed you from your sins by
my blood. I paid the price for your soul. Your true home is not the world but
heaven.*

APRIL 27

"Martha, you are anxious and troubled about many things."
– Luke 10:41

From Fern:

I once had a vivid dream I have never forgotten. Thinking about it brings back the feelings it aroused. Jesus was coming to town! We knew it ahead of time. We planned an outdoor dinner. Oblong tables and folding chairs had been set up to accommodate the crowd. Suddenly, there He was! But just as I caught a glimpse of Him, someone upset a bowl of salad on the ground. Although it wasn't my salad, I thought it should be cleaned up. I got down on hands and knees and tried to scoop it back into the bowl, but it came alive. It turned into crawling shellfish that began going every which way. The more I tried to contain it, the more it escaped. Jesus did not wait. I saw His back as He walked away, surrounded by the crowd. He turned and looked at me, but went on.

I might get "Brownie points" for taking care of the mess, just as Martha earned points for taking care of Jesus' physical needs. The bottom line was that I in my dream, as Martha in the kitchen, missed being with Jesus.

I still remember the look in His eyes as he glanced over his shoulder at me, while He led the crowd down the street. Luke 22:61 says that He turned and looked at Peter. I wonder if it was the same look.

APRIL 28

"Mary has chosen a good portion."
– Luke 10:42

From Fern:

Am I a workaholic? I don't know. I do know I regard time as a sacred gift, and to waste it, a sin. But what is "waste"? I know my need to be productive, to end each day able to define what I have done. That Jesus commended Mary in this story says to me that I need to seek a balance. This time I have set for meditation, prayer, worship in the morning is my Mary time to prepare me for the Martha hours the rest of the day.

I learned a great deal about worship from my friend Pat with whom I was sitting one morning at a church service. We had just read the Psalter and sat down. I closed my book and was ready for the next order of service when I noticed that Pat continued to read. That was all. Suddenly I knew an important difference between us. I had followed instructions. I had sung when told to sing, read when told to read, bowed my head when told to pray; but I had not worshiped. I had gone with my Martha-mind and it was busy with many things.

How differently I attended church from that time forward. No longer were the minister, organist, choir performers, and I their audience, and therefore their judge. I became part of a worshiping community. That experience changed me from observer to participant in worship!

APRIL 29

"Not everyone who says to me 'Lord, Lord' shall enter..."
– Matthew 7:21

From Fern:

At the foot of the pyramids I had an unpleasant experience with a very aggressive young Egyptian vendor who insisted on a larger tip than my lady friend and I chose to give for a service neither asked for nor wanted. This led to a serious conversation with a more mature vendor who said, "You Americans are all millionaires—you have freedom." In ensuing years that statement has lingered longer than almost any other part of our tour. He is right. We do not know what we have when we have freedom, or what it has cost us to have it. But I *do* know that I have much that he did not have and more than I need of clothes, comfort, conveniences, conveyances, and home. I give, but not sacrificially. I share, but not threateningly. I deprive myself of nothing. I know how my life looks to people of other countries. How does it look to my Lord?

Nothing is more important to me than to live in the kingdom here and hereafter. I know I do not earn it. Jesus accomplished it for all who will accept. He said eternal life is believing in God. Paul told the jailer, "Believe in the Lord Jesus and you will be saved." But many verses say that what we have done with our salvation figures into the equation.

APRIL 30

"We who are strong ought to bear with the failings of the weak."
— Romans 15:1

From Fern:

A fascinating phenomenon occurred when it was said that there were
no undiscovered lands to explore, then scientists found an
unexplored area within our own bodies: the brain. The complexities
are enormous. The challenge is for each of us to explore our own and
reassess our attitudes in that light. For example, it has been
discovered that there are right- and left-brain influences. Persons
who function primarily by right-brain are imaginative, creative,
worshipful; while those by left-brain are practical, analytical, logical.
How helpful it is to know that as we relate to one another. Another
aspect of the studies is that the chemical make-up of the body
influences our thinking, our responses to life, even our behavior.

When we know this we can obey Jesus' command to judge not. We
can follow Paul's suggestion to help the weak. We can join John
Wesley, who remarked when he saw a drunk, "There but for the
grace of God go I."

I lived a lot of years thinking mine was the way everyone thought, or
should think. "It takes a heap o' livin'" to realize how narrow that is.
Jesus saw the crowds but also individuals within the crowds and His
heart went out to those who were not in the main stream. He knew
then what we are beginning to know now.

MAY

MAY 1

"To Him who...is able to do far more abundantly
than all we ask or think..."
– Ephesians 3:20

From Fern:

Many situations in life call for radical adjustment. I had entered the
business world after my husband's death only because I was willing,
rather than claiming any expertise. I knew nothing about auto parts.
My only contribution was that I knew the basic function of a
successful business: purchasing, selling for a price sufficient to pay
the costs of operation, and leaving a return on the investment. I
found, of course, the necessity to make dozens of decisions for which
I was not qualified. Much as I tried to study the trade papers and
books, even the terminology was strange.

One morning I felt utterly defeated. How could I possibly go on? I
maintained a time for prayer at the beginning of each day and on that
particular morning, I felt urged to read Paul's letter to the Ephesians.
I read woodenly. The words had no meaning until I came to 3:20.
There is a Power at work in the world and in my life! Sorrow,
loneliness and misfortune do not have the last word! The Power of
goodness, of wisdom, and love is purposeful, moving toward a life
far more abundant than all we could ask or think! Those words saved
that and many days. Those years gave me more than I invested. I am
very grateful that I felt the urge to be involved.

MAY 2

"Make time for the quiet moments,
for God whispers and the world is loud."
– Unknown

From Cat:

I believe that inside each of us is a Wise One, a Wise One we're either in touch with or denying. As a result we're either feeding or starving our spirit, and a starving spirit shrinks to the point of disappearing. We become all too human and subject to all-too-human emotions—fear, anxiety, uncertainty and hopelessness—because without the guidance of our spirit, our Wise One, we're trying to navigate without a compass.

How can any of us move our lives in the right direction without that compass, when the voice of our inner Wise One is being drowned out by the noisy, chaotic, negative tapes that play over and over in our heads?

Today you're going to learn to quiet those annoying tapes and meet your Wise One. It's easier than you think, and all you need is a candle, a pen and paper, and ten uninterrupted minutes to yourself (no matter what you have to do to claim them) in a place in your house or yard where you feel most peaceful, your new sacred space.

Why a candle, other than the fact that they're pleasant? I've read that the spirit world (the spirits of our loved ones in heaven) can see and are drawn to candle flames. I have no idea if that's true, but I'm perfectly happy to hedge my bets and light a candle in case it is.

Mornings are best for my Wise One and me to meet, to set the tone for the day and make sure this special time doesn't get trampled on as the day's inevitable busyness takes over. Settle into your sacred place with a cup of coffee or tea or whatever non-alcoholic drink you enjoy first thing in the morning—we want these ten minutes to become a part of your routine, not a disruption of it, so make yourself comfortable.

Light your candle and sit back to focus on the flame. Stay focused on it while it begins to relax you and clear your mind. When your eyes begin to get heavy, let them close, and as you do, take a

155

nice deep breath and let it out slowly. If a thought enters your mind, don't try to block it and fall into the "for the next five minutes, don't think about elephants" trap. Just let that thought pass right on through like an unwelcome visitor. This is *your* time, alone with your Wise One. Do Not Disturb.

With your eyes still closed, feel your shoulders and your neck relax and let the peace of being alone with yourself settle over you like a calming, soothing veil.

Once you're fully aware of that welcome peace, it's time to call upon your Wise One, which takes nothing more than a silent openness. Ask the questions you need answered. Ask for solutions to your problems. Describe your greatest goals, allowing yourself to visualize your life with those goals achieved. Ask for clarity. Ask for direction. Ask for the wisdom and patience to see, hear, and feel your Wise One listening to every word with unconditional love.

Continue to relax, focused on the quiet, until your eyes want to open again. Now, put your pen to paper and, without letting your conscious mind interfere, begin writing. If the pen seems to write on its own, don't be surprised, it's just your peaceful mind receiving what your Wise One has to say.

Allow that pen to continue writing for as long or as short a time as it chooses. When it's finished, take another nice deep breath, exhale...and don't forget to say, "Thank you."

Now, put the pen and paper down, blow out the candle until tomorrow and go on with your day. When you look later at what was written during these quiet minutes, as I always do, you may find that it seems to have been written by Someone Else. And who's to say it wasn't?

I promise that if you make this simple exercise a priority for just a week, seven days in a row, you'll find that those ten short minutes alone with your Wise One, your subconscious mind where your spirit and your divine birthright live, have become blissfully essential. They've made a treasured difference in my life, and they'll do the same for you if you'll just give them, and your Wise One, the peaceful attention they deserve.

❤ ❤ ❤

Dear God, please remind me every day of my life
to stop looking for You "out there"
in all that noise and chaos
and look "in here" instead,
where You're waiting, my Wise One,
with all the answers I need. Amen.

MAY 3

"I stand at the door and knock;
if anyone hears my voice and opens the door,
I will come in to him and eat with him and he with me."
– Revelations 3:20

From Fern:

I prepare a table for you. I invite you to my banquet, a marriage feast, and will send my servants to get you. I want the wedding hall filled with guests. Why do you resist? Why does my invitation go unaccepted? Here you find love of a quality unequalled. There is no greater love than I have shown—greater love has no man than this, that a man lay down his life for his friends.

Here you will find peace that passes all understanding. Here is all you have searched for by other means: joy, patience, kindness, goodness, faithfulness, gentleness, and self-control as fruits of my Spirit. Here is total acceptance, for I show no partiality.

What enticements does the world offer that keeps you from my feast? With what attraction does it compete for your life? The world is glitter without substance. It is here today, gone tomorrow. The world enslaves you; I offer freedom. The world entices you to "eat, drink and be merry for tomorrow you die"; but I tell you that you were not made for death but for life. Those who come will receive manifold more in this time and in the age to come eternal life.

MAY 4

"The cup of blessing which we bless, is it not
a participation in the blood of Christ?
The bread which we break,
is it not a participation in the body of Christ?"
– 1 Corinthians 10:16

From Fern:

_____ (your name), *do not pass thoughtlessly over the invitation to participate. Participation is partnership and I have always invited followers to participate in my life and ministry. I did not only teach and invite others to listen, or do miracles and invite them to watch. I first sent my disciples to practice what they had seen me do. Then I gave the Spirit to all followers with the promise that they would do all that I did, and more.*

But it is not only participation in ministry. It includes my life, for unless you have a part in my joys and sufferings, my motivations and goals, you will be going through the motions but not truly participating. For this you need the fortification of my body and blood. I had one goal, to do the Father's will; one purpose, to give glory to the Father; one motivation, love for the Father, and for all life. I invite your participation. I choose you to participate in the work that remains to be done, to be my helpmate.

MAY 5

"God is at work in you."
– Philippians 2:13

From Fern:

Jesus, what a divine provision You made for us who believe in You to Peter's reply to those who asked what they could do to rectify the wrong that had been done. He said, "Repent and be baptized every one of you in the name of Jesus Christ for the forgiveness of your sins; and you shall receive the gift of the Holy Spirit." He immediately applied the promise to the future as well as the present.

Your Spirit drew and still draws followers into the fellowship of the church. Many signs and wonders were done in the body, and in individual believers then and now.

Your Spirit pours your love into my heart, teaches me to pray, intercedes on my behalf, equips me for participation in kingdom work, empowers me to do far more than I would otherwise be capable of doing, fills my life with qualities I had long sought from other sources: love, joy, peace, patience, kindness, goodness, faithfulness, gentleness, self-control. Thank you, Jesus, for this wonderful gift!

MAY 6

"Not everyone who says to me, 'Lord, Lord,'
shall enter the kingdom of heaven,
but he who does the will of my Father who is in heaven."
– Matthew 7:21

From Fern:

Jesus, I love You so much! I love Your servants. I want to spend
eternity with them and with You. Such a warning as Matthew quotes
startles me, for *You* said that not everyone who utters Your name
shall enter the kingdom. Activities, even if done in Your name, are
not the qualifications for entry. Only doing what our Father wills
provides the key.

Lord, it is not only difficult to *do* Your will, but to discern it in the
complexity of living out these days is also difficult. Amidst all the
noises and voices it is hard to hear the still, small one within. In all
the traffic involved in fulfilling my responsibilities, it is a challenge to
still myself and know what You are calling me to do.

Only by Your Spirit does it become possible. Left to my own
initiatives, I reiterate Paul's remark: "I do not do the good I want, but
the evil I do not want is what I do." But the same Spirit through
whom Jesus declared, "Not my will but thine be done," lives in me,
motivating me to join Mary in saying, "Let it be to me according to
Your word." Help me so to live!

MAY 7

"If we live by the Spirit let us also walk by the Spirit.
Let us have no self-conceit, no provoking of one another,
no envy of one another."
– Galatians 5:25-26

From Fern:

Thank you, Lord, that You not only give purpose to Your children's lives but You equip us to fulfill it. My "yes" to You has called me far beyond myself and my capabilities, but You say to me as You said to Paul that my weakness is opportunity for Your strength. You gift each of us with abilities, not as reward, not as favor; but in order that Your body can function as an effective whole. All of this You do by your Spirit! How could we, how *can* we, presume to function as Your body in your world without giving credit to Your Spirit who empowers us to do it?

O Lord, thank You for Your Holy Spirit! Help me to have the proper attitude toward the gifts and abilities, to exercise my own without envying those of someone else. Help me not to rank the gifts, giving higher place to those in which persons are more visible, but to know that the person at the sink and in the pulpit are equally important as they apply the gifts You have given. The ultimate test: Does whatever we do bring glory to Your holy name?

MAY 8

"All who are led by the Spirit of God are sons of God."
– Romans 8:14

From Fern:

Lord Jesus, how wonderful to have the love the Father has given us, that we should be called children of God. It does not yet appear what we shall be. We are being changed from one degree of glory to another.

This is totally beyond my doing. I depend on what happened to the disciples: They had been with You for three years. They watched You teach, heal, restore sight, and even raise the dead. They experienced Your crucifixion-resurrection. They heard You say, "Go, make disciples."

Jesus, I would have been so eager! I would have been devastated by loss at Your death, then overwhelmed with joy at Your reappearance! I would have wanted to tell the world, but You said, "Wait! Wait until you are clothed with power from on high!"

They did, and the power gave boldness to those who had hidden for fear of the Jews. It gave stability to Peter, motivating him to stand before the assembly at Pentecost and deliver the first sermon of what would be the church. It gave to John and James, who had sought honor, maturity to be servants. Give me patience also to wait to be molded and led by Your Spirit.

MAY 9

"Sometimes walking away is a step forward."
– Unknown

From Cat:

Whether it's a personal situation or a professional one, if we've invested a lot of time, money, effort, trust, and heart into it, whether or not to walk away when it seems to have played itself out can be one of the hardest decisions we have to face. Unless we're masochists, we tend to put up a fierce struggle against feeling like a failure, or a quitter, or a loser. We've got our pride, after all, and when we sink our teeth into a longtime dream, we believe in staying in it to win it, no matter what—right, team?

Well, not necessarily, as most of us have had to learn the hard way. Sometimes that dream turns out to have been more of an unrealistic fantasy. Sometimes our dreams change as we learn more about ourselves and the world. Sometimes we hang onto a bad situation because we'd rather be right than happy. (I personally think "I was wrong" can be a great show of strength, but for reasons I'll never understand there are people who can't seem to get those words out of their mouths.) Sometimes, even if what we're struggling with isn't a dream but a matter of practicality (a paycheck is a paycheck, after all) or familiarity, we realize that it's too financially, physically, or emotionally expensive for us to continue. And if a job, a relationship, or a friendship is eroding any aspect of our well-being, it's definitely time to either change it or move on.

It's also definitely time to think it through thoroughly, exhaust every opportunity to make it work, and give feedback as you go along (think "cautionary suggestions," not "complaints") for the peace of mind of knowing you played fair every step of the way. And don't forget to own up to your share of the responsibility for the situation, since very rarely is it 100 percent the other person's fault. (I happen to be a fan of Judge Judy. She'll listen without expression as a plaintiff tears apart the "lazy, cheating, deadbeat" ex-husband/ex-boyfriend/baby's father defendant, then respond to the plaintiff with a simple, "You picked him." It makes me smile every time.)

Several years ago, a client of mine fulfilled his longtime dream of buying a hair salon in Manhattan. He invested a great deal of money, time, energy, and passion in it, and hired a talented battery of hairdressers.

Within a year the salon had begun to drain his finances, his joy, and his life force, mostly because his employees revealed themselves to be an entitled bunch of divas, disrespecting both my client and the integrity of the business itself, and none of them would own up to it when he tried discussing it with them. In fact, he was astonished to discover that by the end of that first year, everyone in the salon was making money but him.

And God bless him, as he was quick to point out when he came to me, "I'm the one who hired them." No blame-shifting there.

He struggled terribly about whether to give up on that dream or hang on and ride it out. Hanging on would have meant starting over with a clean slate—firing his employees, finding new ones and spending time training them, only to run the risk that nothing had changed but the faces. He could do it, but was he up to it?

The more we talked, the more apparent it became that his dream was lost in the relentless stress it was costing him. After three sessions with me it was clear to both of us that he was over it. His one major hesitation was that he'd be losing every dime he'd invested, and it was a lot of dimes! I asked him which was more important in the end: money, or being reunited with his health, his peace of mind, and his joy.

Money came in a distant second. He closed the salon and never looked back. It took him a long time to repay his business loans, but that was a pleasure compared to walking through those doors every morning with a knot in his stomach to face another day of resentment, disloyalty, back-biting, Attitude, and unreliability.

He called six years later to check in and report that he eventually started a new business that in every way exceeded his highest hopes for the salon he'd left behind.

His dream came true by letting go of a dream that wasn't worth it.

If you feel the same thing might be happening to you in some aspect of your life, you can make the decision a bit easier by asking yourself three questions (and as always, I recommend writing down the answers during those ten-minute sessions with your Wise One we've talked about):

1) What's the best thing that can happen if I change or let go of this situation?

2) What's the worst thing that can happen if I change or let go of this situation?

3) Whatever I've defined as the worst—can I live with that?

Now, take a long, well-deserved breath, think about anything else for awhile since you've probably worn yourself out thinking about this, and trust that God's already provided the solution and is just waiting for you to catch up.

Dear God, I'm especially listening for Your voice right now
and waiting to feel Your definitive nudge,
since You've given me all the signs that it's time to move on
to the far better dream You've arranged for me. Amen.

MAY 10

"Be zealous to confirm your call and election."
– 2 Peter 1:10

From Fern:

This is a divine appointment. You have been chosen and destined by God the Father and sanctified by the Spirit for obedience to Jesus Christ and for sprinkling with His blood. You are not your own; you were bought with a price. The price was the lifeblood of your Savior who paid the ransom for your soul.

Make every effort to supplement your faith with virtue, and virtue with knowledge, and knowledge with self-control, and self-control with steadfastness, and steadfastness with godliness, and godliness with brotherly affection, and brotherly affection with love.

These are not gained by your own effort. They are fruits of the Spirit, and if they are yours and abound, they keep you from being ineffective and unfruitful in the knowledge of your Lord Jesus Christ. They keep you from abandoning the love you had at first and the works you did at first. They keep you from indifferent acceptance of blessings which attitude causes you to be neither hot nor cold but lukewarm.

Rejoice in what you have been given. Rejoice always! Like Peter and John, never cease to tell others what you have seen and heard. You are to be my witness to the end of the earth.

MAY 11

"How much more will the Heavenly Father give
the Holy Spirit to those who ask Him."
– Luke 11:13

From Fern:

Dear God, I remember when I sought to understand Your Holy Spirit. I attended course after course of study. I had many questions: What is the baptism? Must it be emotional with extreme physical manifestations? How do I know if I have the Spirit? Should I be saying "He" or "It"?

Father, You must have smiled at my naïveté. Now I have come to know that Your Spirit is not to be comprehended but experienced. If someone else had my spirit, she/he would think like me, approach and interpret life like I do, have my drives and goals.

I recall a Sunday school teacher who believed there should be a carry-over from the Sunday lesson into service during the week. She was unable to motivate any of her class members, until suddenly she became ill and died. Then her spirit seemed to be dispersed through all her pupils and their desires came to be precisely what hers had been.

Lord, when I am filled with Your Spirit, I want what You want. I hunger for more of You, more of Your word, more communion in prayer, more expression of the life You lived in Jesus. Simple as that.

MAY 12

"Those who live according to the Spirit,
set their minds on the things of the Spirit."
– Romans 8:5

From Fern:

Father, I had a question: Why do we who are filled by the same Spirit often disagree? And You have begun to show me: 1) that You consistently give us freedom to choose. You made us as individual as snowflakes and fingerprints, and we maintain that uniqueness even as You remake us by Your Spirit. Thus the impetuosity of Peter, the zeal of Saul, were not extinguished but redirected. 2) That in order for us to be the whole body You meant your church to be, we need differences. Paul noted that we cannot all be eyes or ears, hands or feet—some have one purpose, some another. But all are appointed, equipped, and sent by the same Spirit. 3) That You chose disciples with a variety of personalities, and in teaching them You did not make them carbon copies of You or of one another.

Lord, thank You for helping me see this truth. I am too inclined to decide what another should think or be or do. Help me respect the individuality of another's call and response and to see that I have challenge enough in attending to my own.

MAY 13

"I will pour my Spirit upon your descendants, and my blessing."
— Isaiah 44:3

From Fern:

Dear Lord, Father, Son, Holy Spirit: You are God, changeless throughout the ages, desiring the best for Your children, that we might all be saved and come to the knowledge of truth. To this end You came in Jesus, and for this purpose You come to us in Your Holy Spirit, who abides with us and lives in us.

In the days before Jesus, You sent the Spirit to give to specific people abilities to perform what You designated as their tasks. But prophets discerned a day would come when there would be liberal outpouring of Your Spirit upon all flesh. "Your sons and daughters shall prophesy, your old men shall dream dreams, and your young men shall see visions."

Thank You, Father, for giving me the privilege of living in this day; for the Spirit is at work in and around me. It is an awesome day because once You make us aware that the spirit world is real, we come to know that many spirits contend to dominate our souls. John warned us to test the spirits.

God, I have made my choice. I want only Your Holy Spirit to direct my life. Help me to live this day.

MAY 14

"(The prophets prophesied)
by the Spirit within them" – 1 Peter 1:10-11

From Fern:

God, throughout the Bible, the account of the exodus from Egypt, the wilderness years, the entry into the promised land of Canaan, is told and retold. It is always a reminder of the faithful leading through Your Spirit. Isaiah said that You put into the midst of them Your holy Spirit and Your Spirit gave them rest. Ezra reminded the Israelites after the Babylonian exile how You provided Spirit and sustenance to their ancestors.

Father, help *me* to be encouraged, in the midst of a dilemma, by how You have been present and have seen me through situations in the past. Help me to stay aware of Your Spirit's activity in my life, for I easily fall into the trap against which Moses warned those he led, who would enter a land already developed, "Take heed that you do not forget the Lord who brought you there."

When I have "eaten and am full," my tendency is to feel self-sufficient and I do forget. I need Paul's words, "Let anyone who thinks that he stands and takes heed lest he falls." Thank You for your faithfulness in spite of my forgetfulness!

MAY 15

"We teach people how to treat us."
– Dr. Phil

"'No' is a complete sentence."
– Unknown

From Cat:

I almost hate to bring up this woman's name in a positive, God-centered, hopeful book, but since she can help illustrate a point...Like millions of you, I watched every minute of the Jodi Arias trial. There was something so creepy and disturbing about that entitled, narcissistic woman, loving the spotlight, justifying her way through the vicious murder of Travis Alexander, by all accounts a wonderful man without a clue whom he was dealing with.

One of about a thousand outrageous details of that trial that stayed with me after the "guilty" verdict was the story of Jodi, uninvited, for no other reason than because she felt she had the right, crawling into Travis' house through his dog door. I can honestly say that nothing short of a serious emergency, like someone and/or their animals being trapped in a burning building, would send me plunging through a dog door. And unless I've specifically asked someone, for reasons I can't imagine and no matter how I felt about them, to stop by and please come in through my dog door, I promise you they wouldn't be staying, unless it's to wait for the police to get there.

Don't let it enter your mind that I'm blaming the victim for putting up with that behavior, let alone for the hideous death it led to. But it was a *way*-over-the-top trigger for a lot of self-examination on the subject of boundaries, or, as I prefer to call them, "house rules."

Like a lot of other people-pleasers, I've struggled with house rules over the years, based on the theory that everyone would rather hear a "yes" than a "no." Well, in the bigger picture, that theory is wrong. I've said "yes" when I really meant "no" more times than I can count, and ended up feeling resentful and taken advantage of. So whose fault is it, really, when people take my "yes" for an answer and proceed accordingly? What kind of favor am I doing them when I'm

172

too insecure or eager-to-please to be clear about how I expect to be treated and what I will and won't tolerate? I love clarity! I don't like breaking anyone's house rules because I have no idea what they are, and then finding out later that they resent me for breaking them—which means it's a safe bet that most other people appreciate, and deserve, that kind of clarity, too.

Today I want you to think seriously about and write down your own personal house rules—and "house rules" in this case refers to you as well as your home. Yours may be different than the few of mine I'll list as examples, but we all need to keep some conditions in mind about these rules: they need to be reasonable; they need to be consistent; they need to be rules we're willing to follow ourselves (no rule about never forgetting our birthday, for example, unless we can promise to never forget anyone else's); and probably most important and hardest of all, they need to be *enforced*. They don't mean a thing if you're just making noise.

Here's a handful of the house rules on a list I finally became confident enough to demand, to give you the idea:

* My home and I are safe places for me and the people I care about (whether they're there or not) and for my animals. There will be zero tolerance for disrespect toward any of us in my presence or you'll be shown directly to the door.

* Lie to me, steal from me, deliberately deceive me, and/or talk badly about me behind my back while pretending to be my friend, and I'll wish you a nice life and send you on your way. (Doesn't it mystify you that there are people who conduct their lives on the premise that none of the rest of us talk to each other?!)

* This is a no-gossip, no negativity, no-manufactured-drama zone.

* The Twenty-Minute Rule: Twenty minutes is as long as I'll sit by myself in a restaurant without an apologetic update phone call. At the twenty-one-minute mark, I'll be headed home with a doggie bag and not very likely to make another restaurant date with you.

* If I inadvertently offend you in some way—and it happens to all of us—call me on it right then and there so I can

173

clarify what I meant and/or apologize. I don't want to hear about it for the first time weeks, months, or years later.

* Stopping by without the courtesy of a phone call first? No. Just no.

Like I said, those are some of mine. Yours may look completely different. But make them, and insist on them. You'll be doing a huge favor to yourself and to the people in your life. It's their choice whether or not they like the house rules, and if they don't, they're more than welcome to spend their time elsewhere.

Dear God, thank You for helping me find
the self-confidence it takes to teach people
to treat me with the same clarity, fairness, and respect
I'm ready and willing to offer them. Amen.

MAY 16

"The days are coming when I will make a new covenant."
– Jeremiah 31:33

From Fern:

There was a day when I gave my law, the directives for how to live the blessed life I desired for my people. I wrote it on tablets of stone. It was the covenant with my people Israel. But there came a time when I declared to my servant Jeremiah, "The days are coming when I will make a new covenant. I will put my law within them, and I will write it upon their hearts; and I will be their God and they shall be my people."

The first covenant was sealed with the blood of sacrificed oxen. The new covenant was sealed with the blood of the sacrificed Lamb, my own blood poured out of the human body of my Son, Jesus. The first ceremony was officiated by Moses. For the second, Christ was the High Priest. He entered once and for all into the Holy Place, taking not the blood of goats and calves but His own blood, thus securing an eternal redemption. The first covenant was affirmed as an annual memorial. The new covenant observance was instituted by Jesus as a Passover meal during which He revealed that the bread was his body and the cup his blood. Thus my people will continue to gather to reinforce and celebrate the covenant in remembrance of me, proclaiming all that is meant by the death of your Lord.

MAY 17

"The blasphemy against the Spirit will not be forgiven."
– Matthew 12:31

From Fern:

Thank You, Lord, for giving Your children glimpses into the future realm. You have told us in Your word that what You have in store for those who love You is beyond what eyes can see, ears hear, or the heart imagine; that You desire that *all* be saved and turn from his way and live. You have promised eternal life to those who believe in the Son. There will be an accounting. Books will be opened and how we have lived will affect our eternity.

Father, I long to hear, "Well done, good and faithful servant; inherit the kingdom prepared for you." But the above verse gives me pause. One sin is unforgivable. Let me not commit that sin!

You have called to my attention the "if's" of the Bible. *If* I obey the commandments...but if I do not, there are consequences. *If* I love You, I will obey You. *If* I forgive, You will forgive me, but if not...I perceive that these are little doors that I open or close. The main doorway is the Spirit. If I rebel against Your Spirit, I shut out the blessings You long to give.

O God, help my channel to be open to receive You fully into my heart!

MAY 18

"When He comes He will convince the world of sin
and of righteousness and of judgment."
– John 16:8

From Fern:

Jesus, when Simon Peter first perceived Your deity, he exclaimed,
"Depart from me, for I am a sinful man." When Isaiah beheld a
heavenly vision, he cried, "Woe is me! For I am lost; for I am a man
of unclean lips, and I dwell in the midst of a people of unclean lips."
Visionary Ezekiel fell on his face as he perceived Your glory, and
Your Spirit revealed the transgressions of the people to whom he was
to speak.

Lord, there are moments when we automatically examine ourselves.
In the presence of spotlessness, we are aware if we are dirty. When a
companion is impeccably dressed, we are embarrassed if our clothing
is inappropriate. Our lives may seem acceptable when measured by
the culture in which we live, but when we are filled with the Spirit of
the Sinless One, we see how poorly we have followed His example.

Thank You, Father, that you do not leave us there. When we pray the
sinner's prayer, "Be merciful to me, a sinner," we know that if we
confess our sins You will forgive and cleanse us. You are true to
Your promise. You free us from guilt and guide us to a better life.

MAY 19

"He has put His seal upon us and given us His Spirit
in our hearts as a guarantee."
– 2 Corinthians 1:22

From Fern:

Lord of hosts, King of glory: You have put Your seal on me! Not a
"Good Housekeeping Seal of Approval" but the King's seal! All
other guarantees are of limited duration, based upon a company's
integrity, which may vary with the administration. But Yours is a
permanent stamp in which I have absolute confidence for now and
eternity.

A king's seal is authority, it indicates ownership. A king seals what he
treasures. I dare to think You treasure me as Your very own child! I
dare to come in the Abba Father relationship.

O dear Lord, what a difference this makes! How it brings me from
years of believing You were "out there," distant, barely approachable
by one so unworthy! I had to try hard, work hard for "Brownie
points" to win Your favor. Now I know that You initiated the love.
My acceptance is not earned but is because of Your grace. I have
heard the word of truth, the gospel of salvation, and believed. I am
sealed with the Holy Spirit, the guarantee of my inheritance. It
behooves me to live accordingly.

MAY 20

"Do not quench the Spirit."
– 1 Thessalonians 5:19

From Fern:

O God, what a glorious month You have given me, immersed in your Spirit! You are nearer to me now than ever before. You have changed me from "one degree of glory to another." May I never quench Your Spirit when You give as lavishly as You give all Your gifts!

You have impressed upon me my complete dependency upon Your Spirit. It is through Your Spirit that I become aware of our separation, which brings me in the spirit of the prodigal son, to ask if I may come home. You welcome me and confer upon me the symbols of membership in Your family. The Spirit pours Your love into my heart, recreates me, and gives me capacity to see life and persons through Your eyes.

Jesus, You said that we who believe in You will do even greater works than You, which is not possible except as Your Spirit gives the ability. You said we must be perfect in the image of our Father. Only by the power of Your Spirit is it possible. What inexpressible gratitude I feel for the gift that makes us one, You in me, as I go to meet life. Thank You, Father! Amen!

MAY 21

"...How much he must suffer for the sake of my name."
– Acts 9:16

From Fern:

For many years, my concept of God kept me from giving Him my life. It seemed that suddenly He would notice, and then what? Abraham's test was to give up what he loved most. And Job was doing fine until the Lord gave Satan permission to test him. He lost everything he had—wealth, family, and health.

Jesus, God's beloved Son, went through His ministry with nowhere to lay His head. He was not understood or accepted, finally being executed in the most tortuous way. Mary, whom God chose to bear His Son, surely suffered all that her Son experienced as she stood helplessly by. Mothers do that.

I was utterly perplexed that those in the early church rejoiced to suffer, counted it a privilege to endure what their Master had endured that they might be glorified as He was glorified. It has come to me slowly that suffering is another example of the values of this world being turned upside down. Renouncing all that is important here is rewarded by receiving all that is important in the kingdom.

Why does God not coddle those who give Him their lives? Because the coddled are not strong. God is preparing kingdom people whose qualities of faith and love will endure.

MAY 22

"Miriam...spoke against Moses because of
the woman whom he had married."
– Numbers 12:1

From Fern:

Lord, this morning, throughout the day, throughout my life, help me
gain victory over my critical nature and my wagging tongue. How
well James knew us when he wrote that we can control horses with
bits and ships with rudders; but no human being can control the
tongue.

Father, there is a Miriam-spirit within me and around me. For at least
three thousand years, that same spirit has prompted humankind to
find fault, to presume to judge that the choices made by another
person are inferior to those we would have made in the same
circumstance. I know that You have given each of us a role and a
purpose; but I, like Miriam, have often challenged that of others.
"Has the Lord spoken only through Moses...not through us also?"

Miriam became leprous, and even though the results of my disdainful
attitude may not be outwardly evident, I know it taints my soul in
Your sight.

Father, forgive me, cleanse me, restore me to wholeness. Place within
that clean heart a new capacity for acceptance, that I may concern
myself with my own cross, not that of others.

MAY 23

"Whatever we plant in our subconscious mind
and nourish with repetition and emotion
will one day become a reality."
– Earl Nightingale

From Cat:

One of many reasons I became determined to study hypnosis, starting in my forties, is the direct access it provides to the subconscious mind, where we hold the "truth" that propels us toward or away from our dreams. Our conscious minds base their marching orders on the powerful beliefs of the subconscious, programmed from the day we're born. Want to change your life? Change those subconscious beliefs.

It hurts my heart to hear some of my clients tell me about the destructive programming they were subjected to as children by the adults in their lives—"You're an idiot." "You'll never amount to anything." "You're just like your loser (mother, father)." —and the list goes on and on and on. Life is tough enough without those subconscious "truths" acting as your guide.

And to complicate things, the subconscious is like a sponge, absorbing information but not necessarily interpreting it correctly. One client, when she was a freshman in high school, found herself on the receiving end of a crush by a senior who happened to be a popular star athlete and homecoming king. She was thrilled. Her parents weren't having it—the age and experience differences were too great as far as they were concerned, and there was no way she'd be allowed to go out with him. At some point she overheard a discussion between her parents in which her mother said, "What's wrong with him that he'd even be interested in her?" What she meant, of course, was, "What is a high school senior doing pursuing a freshman girl in the first place?" But what my client's subconscious heard was, "My own parents think a cool guy like him must be crazy to want to go out with me." She went out with her share of "cool guys" in the next several years, but it took her a long time and a lot of work on herself to get past being braced for the day when they'd come to their senses and dump her.

There's a lot of great news in whatever negative subconscious "truth" we picked up as children from the grown-ups around us. For one thing, now that we're grown-ups too, we have the perspective of knowing that those authoritative, all-knowing adults were just as flawed as we are now, hopefully doing the best they could but just as likely as we are to be wrong from time to time. For another thing, there's a statute of limitations on everything but murder, so a point really can come when we can declare that negative programming expired, "expunge" it from our "permanent records," and make our own decisions about who we are and what our full potential really is.

Of course, we all do our fair share of negative programming to ourselves, too. When I first decided in my forties that I wanted to go back to school to learn everything I could about hypnosis and the way our minds work, I immediately wondered if I could overcome a "fact" about myself: "I'm not a good student."

I'm sure any number of my high school teachers would back me up on how disinterested I was. I never thought of myself as stupid; I was (and still am) just a dreamer, with *big* dreams that I knew wouldn't require me to know the main export of Chile or the square root of 144. (I guess I was out sick the day they explained that the main point of school was essentially learning how to learn.) I was "different," a bit of an outcast and a drama nerd (which, in our high school at the time, put you just a notch above the ROTC boys), and I couldn't wait to graduate so I could get out of Dodge and get on with that wonderful life I saw in my dreams.

Luckily, that "I'm not a good student" thing wasn't quite as much of a fact as the fact that I was really, really curious about hypnosis and the mind. So I held my nose and dived into those classes, and what do you know? It turns out I'm a *great* student, eager and attentive and stimulated and everything else I'd always believed I academically wasn't, when it's a subject I'm passionate about and I understand why it's to my advantage to learn what I'm being taught. I even jump at the opportunity to study new hypnosis techniques every year so that I can broaden my skills...and if you'd told me during my teenage years that I would ever, in a million years, hungrily sign up for more school, I would have laughed in your face.

183

Today, maybe while you're having your quiet time with your Wise One, I want you to dig deep and write down every negative "fact" your subconscious mind is holding onto about yourself, no matter where it came from or how long you've believed it.

Then, today and every day for as long as it takes, I want you to look at every "fact" on that list and say, with absolute certainty, "That's not true," followed by its exact, most positive opposite. "I'm a loser" can and will become "I'm a winner" if you say it often and sincerely enough. "I'm fat" can and will become "I have a beautiful body." "I'm stupid" can and will become "I'm as smart as I need to be." "Nothing good ever happens to me" can and will become "Great things are happening to me," because they are, right now, thanks to the wonderful work you're doing on yourself.

Remember, every negative thing you believe about yourself is there because it was programmed into your subconscious. So, since you're living proof that programming works, don't doubt for one minute that you can start reprogramming yourself today for the great life you're capable of and absolutely deserve.

Dear God, I'm so grateful for Your help
with clearing out the negative myths about myself that have
been taking up precious space in my subconscious,
to make room for the exciting, positive truths about myself
I'm filling it with from this moment on. Amen.

MAY 24

"Thy kingdom come.
Thy will be done, on earth as it is in heaven."
– Matthew 6:10

From Fern:

The prayer is often on your lips. Am I your King and you a loyal subject? Contemplate the total authority of a king to call upon his subjects as an officer commands his soldiers. Realize the total commitment of the soldier. No soldier on service gets entangled in civilian pursuits, since his aim is to satisfy the one who enlisted him.

What is my kingdom? A state of being...a set of the mind...a condition of the heart. The kingdom is not coming with signs to be observed; the kingdom is within you.

The kingdom comes as you relinquish your own will in favor of doing the will of the King. Thereby you live in the kingdom which is a treasure worth all a man has, the pearl of great price. You do not come on it all at once but, like leaven, it increases every day.

Lift up your heads, O gates! and be lifted up, O doors of your heart, that the King of Glory may come in. Who is the King of glory? The Lord, strong and mighty, the Lord mighty in battle! Lift up your heads, O gates! and be lifted up, O ancient doors! that the King of glory may come in. Who is the King of glory? The Lord of hosts, He is the King of glory. Enter His gates with thanksgiving and His courts with praise!

MAY 25

"...When they had come down from the mountain..."
– Luke 9:37

From Fern:

I am inclined to pray elaborately, "O God, take my life, take all of me. Use me however You will. Thy will be done." One day such a prayer was interrupted by words that came in a powerful thought: "You wouldn't even give a cup of tea!" I was startled back to reality. It may have been, to some degree, a parallel to when the disciples saw the transfiguration of our Lord, then came back down the mountain to face a desperate need.

I quit drinking tea for several years but then began to realize—or to rationalize?—that there was a far deeper lesson than is contained in a tea bag, a lesson that says it is much easier to be elaborate than specific in prayer. The lesson tells me there may be excusable inactivity when the problems are of gigantic proportion: world peace, pollution, destruction, and/or abuse of species of God's creation. What can I do about that? But it is not excusable if focusing on broader situations takes my mind off problems that I *can* do something about, right before my eyes or in my own heart. There is a lesson of looking beyond myself into the life of another person and judging precisely what she/he should do or be, without having "walked a mile in their moccasins." God gives mountaintop times, but calls us to descend again.

MAY 26

"It is good...to declare thy steadfast love...and thy faithfulness."
— Psalms 92:1-2

From Fern:

There have been occasions when God has spoken directly to me
through the Bible. One time, those who foresaw a devastating
earthquake for California became specific, narrowing predictions to a
certain week. Both my children lived there, and it was much on my
mind and in my prayers. One morning, the thought came to turn to
Psalm 46, which assured me that there is no need for fear. "Though
the earth change or the mountains shake, God is our refuge and
strength, present in trouble."

Again, the wisdom of a planned trip to Africa was in question.
Colonel Qaddhafi's terrorist forces were active. Flying into the
Libyan area seemed questionable. A daily reading led me to Isaiah 43
and I accepted God's promise, "Fear not, you are mine. When you
pass through the waters I will be with you, when you walk through
fire, the flame will not consume you. I am the Lord. You are precious
in my eyes. I love you."

I do not see these as happenstance. How I wish those who have no
time for spiritual disciplines would know that such experiences are a
reward. There is little possibility of finding a needed reference, little
benefit from prayer, if reserved for times of panic. There is the
serendipity of gaining an extended, caring "family" in church
involvement. Count them all joy!

MAY 27

"But I say to you..."
– Matthew 5:22

From Fern:

Lloyd C. Douglas' "Magnificent Obsession" awakened my awareness that there are two sets of laws. Just as God created humankind with two natures—physical and spiritual—so He wove into the universe laws which govern nature and upon which all technology is built, and another set equally available, equally reliable, which are spiritual laws.

The widow of a good friend discovered that her husband had been responding to need by giving large sums of money. He demanded secrecy. He did not allow repayment, for, he said, he was using it. His diary revealed that he had found the principle in the Sermon on the Plain (Luke 6). What an exciting life when we come upon these treasures and have faith enough to apply them! "Give, and it will be given to you...The measure you give will be the measure you get" is both promise and threat depending upon whether we send out good or bad, the positive or the negative.

"Forgive," for unless we exercise the capacity to forgive, we have no capacity to receive the Father's forgiveness of us. "Love God, your neighbor, yourself" in such a way that you "turn the other cheek, go the second mile; lend, expecting nothing in return." There is an adventurous life for all who take Jesus' laws seriously, and apply them every day.

MAY 28

"In the net which they hid had their own foot been caught."
— Psalms 9:15

From Fern:

I well remember the beginning of the end of an era. I was on a bus returning to the town where I worked. I had been home for a weekend. My parents had lovingly said good-bye. They believed in me and only I did not. I felt that only I knew the real person I was, and I was sick of that person. I began to cry. In the back of a nearly empty bus, I lost all control. I tried to regain it but my tears continued to flow and my body to heave with sobs. A lady sitting on the opposite side, several rows ahead, turned to look. I knew she desperately wanted to speak to me, to comfort me; but how grateful I am that she did not. It was a part of a cleansing I needed.

It was a lesson I should have learned that has not always stayed with me, for I am an active person. "What can I do to help?" springs out of my mouth involuntarily. There are times when persons, like myself, do not want help; times when they must work something through for themselves. Other times, the best to do is listen. A friend, Jessie, had this beautiful quality. She never tried to help with the problem. She listened. She might sympathize or empathize, but when we left the real problem somehow was clearer. There is a time to speak and a time to be silent.

MAY 29

"Judge not..."
– Matthew 7:1

From Fern:

The times the Lord has spoken to me directly have been rare. I recognize them because there is no hesitation between my thought and the answer. It is reflex action. My thought goes out, the answer is there. One of those times was when I was preparing a message for a lay-speaking engagement. I wanted to use, "No one comes to the Father but by me." I was thinking in terms of heaven and wondered who will be there. Immediately came the reply, "You're not on that committee." Isn't that delightful, and isn't it a wonderful committee not to be on?! And aren't we glad there will not be a committee deciding for us when the books are opened and we will be judged according to what we have done?

Someone has conjectured that if Jesus had depended on a committee to choose His disciples, they would still be meeting. We can trust judgment to Him who looks not on outward appearance, but on the heart. I appreciate the interpretation of this verse by William Barclay in which he did not see it as exclusive. Instead, Jesus was the One who brought the concept of God as loving Father. He had been regarded as Creator, Judge, King, Divine Ruler of the universe; but Jesus said, "When you pray, say, 'Our Father.'"

MAY 30

"The universe doesn't give you what you ask for with your thoughts;
it gives you what you demand with your actions.
In essence, you don't get what you WANT, you get what you ARE."
– Dr. Steve Maraboli

From Cat:

I don't claim to be more than a kindergartner when it comes to
my knowledge of the universe. Brilliant minds have devoted their
lives to studying it for thousands of years, and they're still trying to
figure it out. But I'll tell you one thing I do know about the universe
with more than a fair amount of confidence, based on personal
experience and decades of observation and faith:

The universe only knows to give back what we consciously or
subconsciously put out to it, and it's a very literal listener.

It's easy to fall into the habit of starting declarations to that great
power with the words "I wish" or "I want" or "I need." That might
be very effective if the universe were, in reality, our fairy godmother.
But when the universe hears "I wish" or "I want" or "I need," it
essentially responds, "Okay! Got it!" and gives back exactly what we
just communicated: a perpetual state of wishing, wanting, and
needing.

Starting today, it's time to give up wishing, wanting, and needing
and tell the universe in no uncertain terms, "I HAVE" and "I AM."

It's hard to wrap our earthly minds around this, but there's no
such thing as time in the universe. There's no past, there's no future,
there are no hours or months or years. There's nothing but *now*, and
the more we can get in step with that concept and stop making our
happiness conditional on some future partner, job, situation, or
accomplishment, the richer the *now* we'll get back from the universe.

An easy example: I often hear a friend or client say, "I want to *be*
somebody!" All together now: You already *are* somebody! No need to
waste one more bit of time or energy trying to be what you already
are, for heaven's sake! And if you have a misguided concept of what a
"somebody" is that you haven't achieved yet, don't confuse a dream
with a fantasy. I recently counseled a young woman whose "dream"

191

was to be married, which was her idea of reaching "somebody" status. She had the wedding planned in exhaustive detail, from the designer of her gown to the number of bridesmaids to the specific flowers in her bouquet, and the itinerary for the honeymoon cruise was all mapped out. The problem was, not once did she ever mention a groom. That's called a fantasy, not a dream—or, to put it another way, missing the point. On the other hand, if you equate "somebody" with wealth or fame, talk to some lottery winners or former reality show stars and get back to me. Again, you *are* somebody, right this minute, so say "thank you" and move on.

The partner you've been searching for? You already have him/her. He/she is already headed your way, the circumstances just aren't perfect quite yet for the two of you to get together. How's that news for saving you a whole lot of "impulse shopping"?

That job, or situation, or accomplishment you've been wanting? Already yours—you and the universe just have more work to do to properly prepare you for it, and watch how easily it falls into place when you're genuinely ready. A good reminder for all of us: God and His universe are much wiser and better at orchestrating our lives than we are, if we'll just get out of our own way and stop trying to force the issue. (I shudder to think of the universe we humans would have created if it had been left up to us. We'd probably still be sitting in the middle of a black hole trying to organize ourselves into committees. We're blessed every minute of every day with this miraculous, breathtaking world God created, but we think we know better than He does what should happen in our lives and when? Seriously?)

Again, it starts today. The universe is waiting to hear from you about *you*. Not about what you want. Not about what you need. But about what you *have*, and who and what you *are*. Then just keep on working and learning and growing and being grateful and getting ready every day of your life. The rest is already on its way.

Dear God, I thank You,
with more gratitude than I can express in words,
for all I am
and all You and Your glorious universe
have prepared for me to claim
in the only time that really exists—*now*. Amen.

MAY 31

"My Father is working still, and I am working."
– John 5:17

From Fern:

"Work"—one of the most used words in your vocabulary. It consumes your time, characterizes your days, becomes your very identity. But Jesus said to those who stood around Him, "Do not labor for the food which perishes, but for the food which endures to eternal life." They asked, "What must we do, to be doing the works of God?" Jesus answered them, "This is the work of God, that you believe in him whom he has sent." This may not change your employment but it will characterize your attitude toward and your deportment during your employment. It will become your identity.

When you believe in me you will love me with all your heart and soul and might. You will see beyond this day and life into eternity. You will not work to lay up for yourself treasures on earth where moth and rust consume, and where thieves break in and steal, but you will lay up for yourself treasures in heaven. For where your measure is, there will your heart be also. When you truly believe in me you will dedicate your life to me. You will know that I am with you and you will do what is pleasing to me during work or leisure.

193

JUNE

JUNE 1

"Your brother came with guile. He took your blessing."
– Genesis 27:35

From Fern:

Lord God, how can You have woven into the framework of creation the rules for life that are still valid? Deceitful Jacob seemed temporarily successful, but he met his match in his father-in-law. The story evokes both laughter and sympathy.

With the help of Rebekah, Jacob tricked his father, whose eyesight could not distinguish between his sons, and he received the blessing that should have gone to Esau. He fled to his mother's country and served her brother Laban, who had the same trait. Jacob fell in love with Laban's younger daughter, Rachel. They contracted that he would work seven years for her hand in marriage. It is hard to imagine his shock, after the wedding night, to discover Laban had substituted his older daughter Leah for Jacob's beloved.

O Lord, thank You for the lessons to be learned: the one which Jesus stated as "The measure you give is the measure you get," and His admonition for us to live innocently but wisely. I shall meet many people this day. Help me in every instance to deal with understanding and integrity, for that is the way of my Master.

JUNE 2

"Esau despised his birthright."
– Genesis 25:34

From Fern:

Creator God, You have made millions of persons individually. You gave me children as different from one another as could be. I thought I treated them the same, for I loved them the same; but they responded differently. You remind me of this as I read about the twins born to Isaac and Rebekah. One was a skillful hunter, a man of the field; the other a quiet indoor man. The outdoorsman lived by his "gut feelings," his immediate physical impulses, while his brother contemplated the future.

Lord, the scene that reveals this is vivid. Esau returned from the field famished. He smelled the food Jacob was cooking. His immediate need overcame him and he traded his birthright for a meal. I know people like that.

My God, I *am* people like that! All humankind is represented by Esau, for you made us in your image, after your spiritual likeness. This is our birthright as your children. But our inclination is to follow our Adam nature and satisfy the immediate physical desires, oblivious of the outcome. Yes, I am Esau and Jacob, physical and spiritual. Help me to be aware that in each decision, this is the choice I have to make. Give me wisdom to make the right choice.

JUNE 3

"Then Abraham fell on his face and laughed."
– Genesis 17:17

From Fern:

Dear God, You demonstrated to Abraham in several instances that there are no restrictions of time in Your plan. You told Abraham the land of Canaan would belong to his descendants, but it would be over four hundred years before they could claim it. You promised Abraham that he would have descendants who would become a great nation, but he was nearing one hundred years of age, Sarah was ninety, and they had no child. It was Your reassurance that the promise was still valid that caused Abraham to fall on his face in laughter.

But God, You did open Sarah's womb. You gave them a son. You gave him descendants who became a great nation. It reminds me of my need to persist. It speaks to me of how often I discontinue a prayer after awhile, thinking it is ineffective, that You are not responding. It also calls to mind my contrasting unfaithfulness to responsibilities that I accept with a zeal that flags after the first excitement has passed.

God, whom James called Abraham's friend, help me learn from Your dealings with him to persist and to trust; to persist in prayer and patiently wait; to trust that good will ultimately prevail, for it is Your divine will.

JUNE 4

"God tested Abraham."
— Genesis 22:1

From Fern:

Dear God, reveal the truth of the Abraham story for this day. It is obvious that You challenged his obedience. Was it sufficient to give You his most precious possession? He passed the test.

But, God, Jesus said that Abraham foresaw this day. Is it more than coincidence that Isaac foreshadows so much of Your life on earth: the place of sacrifice, Mount Moriah, which is in Jerusalem; the willingness of Isaac, so like Your saying, "No one takes (my life) from me, but I lay it down of my own accord"?

Isaac carried the wood as You carried the cross. Then, at his question, his father answered, "God will provide himself a lamb for the offering."

God, You did provide yourself. In Your Son You became the Lamb for the offering. I am in awe!

Father, I've known the Abraham story since childhood, but You have shown me new levels. Through it You call me to faith that is expressed in obedience. Here is an inducement to mine beneath the surface to find golden nuggets of truth. Here is the continuity of life, a signpost to Jesus two thousand years before You came. Oh, may I, too, be a signpost that points the way, that others may find You.

JUNE 5

"All scripture is inspired by God
and profitable for teaching, for reproof, for correction,
and for training in righteousness."
– 2 Timothy 3:16

From Fern:

Father, You have never left us without direction. Even as I have tried to instruct my children, so You have done for us. You desired for us a life that would be harmonious with You and with the universe. You gave us the rules condensed into Ten Commandments, and said, "Oh that they had such a mind to fear me and to keep all my commandments, that it might go well with them and with their children forever!" You gave us the Books of both old and new covenants, which contain examples of those who lived accordingly or defiantly and the consequences of each.

Dear God, I have done my share of defying Your word, to my own harm and shame. You have taught me that it is unbreakable. Those who try are left broken physically, emotionally, spiritually. You carved your law in stone, and it has borne the test for thousands of years.

I have come to know and love You, and to appreciate Your truth. I have prayed and continue to pray for Your forgiveness, and that I may apply and share what I have gained to Your praise and glory.

JUNE 6

"Love and appreciate your parents.
We are often so busy growing up,
we forget they are also growing old."
– Unknown

From Cat:

In September of 2013, I lost my mom due to a longtime illness brought on by a series of strokes.

She was ninety-one and in a lot of pain, but to the very end she kept her vibrant, sassy spirit and her sense of humor. She lived in Florida, a continent away from my home in California, but we were very much a part of each other's lives. Todd and I even live-streamed our wedding in December of 2012 so that Mom, who was too ill to travel, could share it with us as best she could.

Like most mother-daughter relationships, we went through phases when we drove each other nuts. She and my father divorced when I was five, and Mom was a strict, tough single mom. My curfew on weekends during my high school years was 11:00 p.m. If I came home at 11:01, I'd find the house locked up tight and have to spend the night sleeping outside on the wet grass. It taught me to be on time and be respectful of rules and boundaries—none of which I appreciated as a willful, fiercely independent teenager, believe me. She wasn't easy and neither was I, but oh, my God, did we love each other and become great pals as "one of us" became enough of an adult to realize how amazing she really was under less than ideal circumstances.

I was on a seven-week tour shortly before she died, and I loved hearing her laugh when I regaled her with stories about being on the road with my pet chicken, Henny Boo Boo. Every phone call started with her asking, "How's the chicken?" Only those who know and love me would understand why on earth I would choose to drive across the country for seven weeks with a chicken, and she knew, loved, and got me completely.

She even waited to let go until my tour was finished and she knew I was home safely. My last words to her were, "I love you, I love you, I love you, I love you." I guess that was all she needed to hear. She passed away that night in her sleep, just as she'd prayed she would.

As many of you know, when a loved one is ill and dying over an extended period of time, it's hard on them and hard on us—it's so painful to know they're ready to leave their "human suit" and move on to their spiritual life but can't make that exit until they're called. When they finally do get to go Home, it leaves us sad and relieved at the same time, and the sadness lingers long after the relief is over. I'm so blessed to have her as long as I did.

To this day I catch myself thinking, "It's getting late on the East Coast, I'd better call Mom..." and then remember that the time change from here to Heaven is a whole lot less than three hours. I go outside and talk to her, and it's instantaneous—if I stop and quiet my mind, I can feel her presence in my heart, and she feels good there. She is now happy and healthy and part of the great "I Am," at one with everything and present everywhere in my life. She lived long enough to see me accomplish my goals, dream new dreams, and marry a great man I adore, and that's as it should be. This life I love only exists because she brought me into this big world in the first place and helped me learn, the easy way and the hard way, to really live it instead of just coasting through it only half alive.

Enjoy Heaven, my Angel. I love you, I love you, I love you, I love you.

Today I want you to do what I can only do in spirit: I want you to say "thank you" and "I love you" to someone who's earned those words for as far back in your life as you can remember. If you still have living parents, this is the day to surprise them with a phone call or an e-mail or a letter telling them what you might not tell them often enough—how much emptier your life would have been without them.

Some of you, I know, weren't blessed with parents who've earned those words, and I'm so sorry. But this invitation is for you too. Think back. There was someone in your childhood—a family member, a foster or adoptive parent, a teacher, a pastor, a priest, a nun, a mentor, a friend's parents, *someone*—to whom it would mean the world to hear that you've never forgotten, and never will, the difference they made just by making sure you knew you were special and you were loved.

I don't care if it's been thirty minutes or thirty years since you were in touch with them. Find them and tell them they mattered. It will make their day, and yours, too.

Dear God, please grant all of us
the blessed peace You gave me,
of never sending a loved one into Your arms
with an unspoken "I love you" on our lips. Amen.

JUNE 7

"For whoever would draw near to God must believe
that he exists and that he rewards those who seek him."
– Hebrews 11:6

From Fern:

*Believe in me. Believe that I am in the Father and the Father in me. Believe not
only with your mind but in faith. Without faith it is impossible to please me. If
you believe in me, you have hope in God. You forget not the works of God but
keep his commandments.*

*If you believe in me, you will love me, and if you love me, you will keep my
commandments. If you love me, you will have peace of mind because you accept my
promises. What no eye has seen, nor ear heard, nor the heart of man conceived,
God has prepared for those who love him. In everything God works for good with
those who love him, who are called according to his purpose. Whoever believes in
me has eternal life, and this is eternal life: that they know the only true God and
Jesus Christ whom God has sent.*

*When you have glimpsed eternal life, your values change. You no longer look to
the things that are seen but to the things that are unseen, for the things that are
seen are transient, but the things that are unseen are eternal. When this happens,
you will know that the One who raised the Lord Jesus will raise you also with
Jesus and bring you into his presence.*

JUNE 8

"Teacher, I will follow you
wherever you go. And Jesus said..."
— Matthew 8:19-20

From Fern:

Heavenly Lord, how perceptive You are! How able to read hearts and discern our true nature, which sometimes contradicts our words.

I have seen persons who, at great personal cost, have responded to Your call, relying, in faith, on your provisions. Others, like me, enjoy our comfort and the routine of our lives and hope that is acceptable to You.

O God, search me and know me. Cleanse me of self-centeredness and help me be available to Your call.

What did You have in mind for me as you formed the clay into this body and blew into it the breath of life?

I do not want to stand before You, finally, and realize that this lifetime has been wasted in fruitless living.

How I long to hear, "Well done, good and faithful servant." I desire to spend eternity in Your divine presence. I know the way. You told us the way: "Believe in the Lord Jesus."

JUNE 9

"When Jesus had spoken thus
He was troubled in spirit."
— John 13:21

From Fern:

Jesus, this morning I am troubled in spirit. I have no cause to the
degree that You had. In fact, mine is obscure. I do not know why I
am troubled except that much around me seems chaotic. Persons for
whom I am concerned seem headed for calamity—but that is just a
feeling, nothing definite.

My own deportment has been less than I wish these past days. Hurry
has made me careless. I have fulfilled obligations, attended all the
right meetings, the worship services; but I have not participated. I
have simply filled a chair. I have not been moved.

O, my Lord, help me! To do what? To get hold of myself, or to allow
You to get hold of me?

Help me to immerse myself in prayers for these for whom I care. I
cannot change them. I can stand by and catch them if they fall.

I want to be Yours, Jesus, every day in all the ways there are. I renew
my commitment to be what You would have me be, to live for You
and in Your loving care.

JUNE 10

"It is required of stewards that they be found trustworthy."
— 1 Corinthians 4:2

From Fern:

My Lord and King, You possess the treasures of the world, the lands and oceans, the gold, the jewels, the all. You have made humankind Your stewards, and myself a steward of a portion. I must be worthy of Your trust to care for it. It has additional preciousness because it belongs to the Master I love.

But there is another area of responsibility; for the invisible kingdom of which Jesus spoke is also a treasure. Over it I have a degree of mastery as well. It is available for me to live within it. Its qualities are those that Paul listed as fruits of the Spirit: love, joy, peace, patience, kindness, goodness, faithfulness, gentleness, and self-control.

Jesus, You called it precious, a pearl of great price. I must so regard the stewardship of it. It is fragile and needs my daily attention. It must be at the forefront of my mind continuously. My Lord has entrusted it to me.

But, dear God, You did not intend that I hoard it. Part of my stewardship responsibility is to tell others as well. Increase my confidence, I pray.

JUNE 11

"Thou hast drawn me up."
– Psalms 30:1f

From Fern:

O Lord, I sing Your praises with the Psalmist; for You have healed me. You have restored my life. No, the healing is not physical. My abilities are not restored. But this morning I sense You are saying, "Look ahead, not back. Take your mind off what happened. Evaluate where you are and what can be made of this situation. Plan. Concentrate on what *is* rather than on what is not."

Praise You for this time that we can be together! Praise You for making Yourself available to us not only in our need, but in our joys, our exhilarations, and our triumphs. Praise You for giving us something beyond the physical, and for making that something the most important part. "Sing praises to the Lord, O you His saints...Weeping may tarry for the night but joy comes with the morning...Thou hast loosed my sackcloth and girded me with gladness." Thank You, Lord, for showing me the bright ray of sun beyond the clouds. You have not left me alone to deal with my problems. You have come to me, blessed me, encouraged me to look beyond the problem to victory!

JUNE 12

"Whoever would draw near to God
must believe that He exists."
– Hebrews 11:6b

From Fern:

A very productive time in my life was when, at my request, my name
was removed from a church roll. I had received a letter that every
Finance Committee can probably recognize, the one that attempts to
remind members of responsibilities that attend their relationship to
the church. No matter how carefully worded, hurt and anger usually
result. I had replied, "Remove my name." Until then I had given my
membership little thought, but this left me with a peculiar sense of
being set adrift. I had a sense of aloneness that nagged at me, and I
shall not forget the day when it climaxed. I was washing dishes at the
kitchen sink, and suddenly, in panic, I thought, "I don't even know
what I believe!" Just as suddenly, the answer came in the form of the
Apostles' Creed, memorized decades earlier because it had been a
part of the worship ritual in a church I attended. What peace to
declare, "I believe in God, the Father Almighty," and the rest.

This experience and others have convinced me of the value of
memorization. It has been discouraged as of no value without
understanding. In this case, the understanding came with experience
and years, as deeper and deeper understanding of all spiritual matters
comes with maturity.

JUNE 13

"Do not be afraid; our fate cannot be taken from us; it is a gift."
– Dante Alighieri

From Cat:

We all go through life with our own unique set of fears. Some of them, the ones that have to do with self-preservation, are just plain healthy, depending on how you handle them. If you're afraid of earthquakes or tornadoes, for example, and you make sure you're well-prepared and take shelter when and if the time comes, good for you. If you spend your life huddled in a doorjamb or the southwest corner of your basement (both of which turn out to be safety-precaution myths, by the way), your fears own you instead of the other way around, and you're so afraid of dying you're forgetting to *live*.

Then there are those fears that stand in our way, hold us hostage, and keep us separate from our greatest potential. Almost all neuroses, and negative thoughts and behavior, are fear-based, so we owe it to ourselves to get to the bottom of what's scaring us, face it squarely in the eye and then decide whether to co-exist with it or send it on its way.

One of the first steps to bringing self-destructive fears into perspective is to think of the word "fear" as an acronym: **F**alse **E**vidence **A**ppearing **R**eal. It's an unfortunate fact of human nature and our overactive imaginations that when we anticipate a possible change in our lives, or a risk we're considering taking, or anything unknown or unfamiliar, we rarely imagine the best possible outcome. Instead, we scare ourselves half to death with the worst scenarios we can think of, complete with Dolby sound and a lot of hideous close-ups, so that even taking a first step toward a potentially wonderful dream feels like much too big a risk.

Believe me, if I hadn't been there, done that and owned the t-shirt to prove it, I wouldn't feel nearly so qualified to help walk you through the process of staring down your fears. Years ago, when I became obsessed with the idea of becoming a stage hypnotist, I came very close more than once to stopping before I started, due to an overwhelming, paralyzing terror of being onstage alone, with a live audience and the unavoidable demand that I'd have to improvise my way through a whole show.

Thank God (literally), my desire to perform comedy hypnosis (I'd already become a certified hypnotherapist) was just as overwhelming as my stage fright, and with no conscious game plan or awareness at the time that I was doing it, I started attracting and saying yes to experiences that would propel me over that one terrifying hurdle.

I was playing that wicked bitch Lindsay Rappaport on *One Life to Live* at the time, and the tragic heroine Fantine in *Les Miserables* on Broadway, which led to...NO!!!!!!...talk shows! No script, and a live audience?!?! Jesus, take the wheel!!! It was like an out-of-body experience. To this day, I have no idea what I was asked or what I said; I just remember hoping that my uncontrollable trembling didn't show.

And then, just when I thought it couldn't get scarier out there, I was invited to be the centerpiece of an off-Broadway show called *Pieces (Of Ass)*, in which eight beautiful women described in self-written monologues the way their beauty had both helped them and harmed them throughout their lives and careers.

My immediate reaction was "No way!" and I tried my best to convince myself that I was too busy, between the TV soap opera and running my company, Cat Cosmetics. And besides, I could just imagine how cheesy the show must be with a title like that...Oh, and by the way, the whole audience thing...

But *Pieces (Of Ass)* had become a hit within two weeks of opening, and I didn't want to be disrespectful, so I agreed to at least go see it before I officially turned it down.

It was fantastic—inspiring, funny, and incredibly touching to see eight brave women stand there in front of four hundred strangers and tell the best and the worst of what their lives had dealt them and how they'd handled it. I was on my feet with the rest of the audience for a long, well-deserved standing ovation, and I found myself wanting nothing more than to be part of it. At age forty-nine, I'd be the oldest cast member by far. I'd get to write and tell my own story, my way, and boy, oh, boy, did I have a story to tell. Stage fright? Hell, yes! But could I really let it stop me from an opportunity like this?

I didn't just do *Pieces (Of Ass)*; I also decided that if I was going to do it, terror and all, I might as well do it right and do it all. So on my first night, I stood there in front of a full house and, for the first time in my life, included in my story the fact that as a young girl, I was molested by our family doctor.

When I say "for the first time in my life," I mean I'd never told another living soul. My then-husband, Michael Knight, heard it for the first time sitting in the audience that night. It was a horrible event that created a deep-seated shame in me and followed me like a dark, threatening cloud since the day it happened. I was sure if people knew, they'd think less of me, no matter how many times I told myself it wasn't my fault.

I can honestly say I'd never received an ovation like I got that night when the show ended. Not only did those four hundred terrifying strangers not think less of me, they embraced me, even waiting by the stage door to meet me and shake my hand. It blew me away. But nothing shocked and humbled me more than the number of girls and grown women who pulled me aside to confide that something similar had happened to them—in some cases much worse. Like me, they'd never told anyone, and somehow my willingness to finally say it out loud with no shame and no apologies had helped them realize that they didn't have to keep that awful secret any more, either.

That audience I'd been so frightened of for as long as I could remember? I discovered that night that they wanted/needed to connect as much as I did, and they gave back more than I gave them—they helped me heal, a healing I'd been denying myself by keeping quiet about a hideous, tragically common experience.

From that night on, I've felt more excited than afraid about an audience and me spending time together. And you know what? It turns out that excitement and fear feel very much alike.

My fear could have cost me all that, and the stage hypnosis career I've fallen head-over-heels in love with and will continue to love for decades to come.

Thank you, God, THANK YOU for giving me an opportunity to experience the truth: that fear has no business in this world winning out over anyone's dreams!

I want you to sit quietly today with your Wise One, your candle, and your paper and pen and answer some questions. Dig deep, and don't turn away if an answer makes you uncomfortable—chances are the most uncomfortable answers are the most important ones. And remember, no one else but you will ever see what you write unless you want them to, so spill it and spill it all. The only wrong answer to any of these questions is "I don't know."

1) **What am I *really* afraid of that's been standing in way?**
(Be specific. It's impossible to win a battle against an enemy when you don't even know who or what the enemy is.)

2) **What's the very worst that this fear can do to me?**
(Go ahead, don't fight it, imagine it all, every awful detail of the very worst that could happen if you dive head first into your greatest dreams, no matter how hard your fear tries to talk you out of them.)

3) **Whatever that "worst" is, can I handle it?**
(Without even knowing you, I'm willing to bet you've already handled worse in your life than that "worst" you just imagined, and probably come away stronger and wiser than you were before, so look at it this way: If it doesn't kill you or land you in prison, why turn back now?)

4) **What am I *feeling*?**
(Time to feel more, think less, and shine a nice big spotlight on what emotions come up when you focus on something important you want to do that scares you. First, identify those feelings. Then, take a long, hard look at where any negative ones come from. Are they really what you know to be the truth? Or are they maybe other people and old programming who have no right and no authority to define you and tell you what you can and can't do?)

5) **Which fears am I really trying to overcome, and which ones might I be clinging to as part of my identity?**
(I once knew a woman who had a fear of getting lost. But rather than turn to a map, or a GPS, or Google, or ask a friend for

directions, she chose to sit in her house and say, "I can't go. You know me, I'm afraid I'll get lost." She was a very lonely woman, missing out on a whole lot of life.)

And finally, bearing in mind that fear is really nothing but **F**alse **E**vidence **A**ppearing **R**eal...

6) **Which is stronger, my fear or my desire?**
(Think about your greatest dreams, and how much or how little you're willing to expect of yourself to make them come true. Then, before writing anything, sit very still, close your eyes, open your mind, wait quietly and listen.)

God will give you the answers.

JUNE 14

"Am I not allowed to do what I choose with what belongs to me?"
– Matthew 20:15

From Fern:

This was my question to workers who had agreed to a wage but became disgruntled when they saw what others received. I put it to all who look enviously at others. Envy is a product of living by the flesh, not the Spirit. Envy causes separation: Miriam and Aaron became envious of their brother Moses, because I spoke to him face to face as to a friend. Envy caused Joseph's brothers to sell him into slavery. Peter became curious about what would happen to John, and I answered, "What is that to you? Follow me!" If your heart is free from envy and your mind is focused on what I have for you to do, you will have no time for wondering what I assign to others. If you do not, you are the pot calling the potter to account for why your vessel was made for one purpose and another for another purpose.

Envy separates, whereas the love I command rejoices at another's good fortune. This kind of love binds everything together in perfect harmony.

Trust in the Lord. Do good. Be still before the Lord, and wait patiently for Him; fret not yourself over him who prospers in his way. The Lord will not forsake His saints.

JUNE 15

"God is at work in you."
– Philippians 2:13

From Fern:

Dear God, my life is like a house in which I live. The plot of ground surrounding it represents me and my "turf." It is mine and I am in charge.

But I have given it to You and made You its master. Those to whom I might not have given entry, You have invited in; and I have found pleasure because of that. Activities I would not have been involved in have become part of the schedule and each one has been a joy.

My Lord, I affirm with Paul that You are at work in my life. You bring surprises and excitement, challenges beyond imagining. You are setting me free from limitations. You are raising my sights above fear of failure; for You have proven again and again that when I dare beyond myself and my capacity, You show yourself at work in me.

I sense You reminding me that what no eye has seen or ear heard or the heart of man imagined, You have planned for those who love You. I cannot imagine, God, where we are going or to what You will call me next. But I need not know, for each day has its own opportunity as You work in my life.

JUNE 16

"And Peter...with John...said, 'Look at us.'"
– Acts 3:4

From Fern:

Dear Lord, I think of the word and action "look." "Look at us—see us!" And when we truly see You in Your servants, and we take our eyes off ourselves and our afflictions, we can be healed, as happened to the cripple.

How many times do I pass a chance to *look* beyond my weaknesses, my problems, my limitations, and fasten my eyes and mind on You wherein lies no weakness, no limitation, and in whom all problems are solved?

How often do I fail to look at other persons, to *really* see them for who they are? When I do, I discover beauty and qualities I have not suspected were there! This, too, is healing.

My Savior, every day You reveal to me new truth! Every time I pick up Your book, I find a thought that expands my life. Words beckon to me, challenge me to leave behind what *was* a moment ago, to step out in bold faith to another plateau. Every new learning makes me more aware of how little I know compared to the expanse of knowledge beyond me. I want to be open to receive all that You have for me, heavenly Teacher.

JUNE 17

"Strive...for the holiness without which no one will see the Lord."
– Hebrews 12:14

From Fern:

O Lord, Your word is consistent. Jesus told us that the pure in heart will see God. How I live out my Christian convictions is important to You! I most often know better than I do and I ask for Your help.

Dear God, forgive my past errors, both known and unknown. Forgive the defiance of those years before I came to know and experience You personally in my life. I accept Your promise of forgiveness following my confession, and I pray that You, by your Holy Spirit, will enable me to begin anew. May I rise clean and fresh to begin my day, empowered to live the holiness You require of kingdom people.

And where shall I expect to see You, Lord? In something supernatural? Or are you more obvious than that? Yes! I shall expect to see you all day long—in Your faithfulness in the coming of the morning and in all of nature...in revelation as I read Your word...in Your love, expressed to Your created as I go about the day. Open my eyes that I may see You more and more clearly, more and more constantly, I pray.

JUNE 18

"Now to Him who by the power at work within us..."
– Ephesians 3:20

From Fern:

Dear God, so many wonderful things happen to me during prayer! I am remembering a few days ago when my morning had begun in confusion. I tripped, I spilled things, my thoughts were disorganized. I came in that mood to prayer; I left peacefully and the day proceeded in that mood.

I think of the times I come to prayer feeling as though a cold or headache might be coming on; and when I rise to go into the day, I am fine.

And Lord, I particularly am reminded by this verse of the day I wondered how I could go on—widowed, alone, in a life that in all respects was strange to me. How could I continue? Why should I try? Then You led me to this verse, this beautiful reassurance! I was and am not alone! Beyond that, the Presence is not simply *here* but is a power—a power to do, to be, to heal, to recreate; and the further promise is that what will be done, what will be, is more than we could ask or think.

You gave me courage that day and since. In the intervening time You have proven that promise to be true. Thank You!

JUNE 19

"...We have confidence to enter the sanctuary by the blood of Jesus..."
– Hebrews 10:19

From Fern:

Dear Lord, throughout the ages You have come by inspiration, by Your Spirit, and then by Jesus! You first transmitted the directions for constructing a tabernacle, "the sanctuary," as a visible location of Your presence. Into the inner court only the highest priests could go—a curtain closed off all the rest.

Then, dear God, came Jesus. By the blood of His sacrifice You have given entry to the most lowly, the most undeserving, the most unworthy. By Jesus' promise we can find forgiveness and be made new and whole. He gave passage through the curtain and we stand in Your presence as children of the Most High God!

My Lord, this truth overwhelms me! The realization that Jesus' death was to provide this for me is beyond my comprehension! Help me never to receive it casually, but to grow in awareness of what it means. Help me continually to evaluate my priorities and to take as my sole aim serving and obeying the One who sacrificed for me!

JUNE 20

"All the powers in the universe are already ours.
It is we who have put our hands before our eyes
and cry that it is dark."
– Swami Vivekananda

From Cat:

We've all heard that we're supposed to "own our power."

It sounds great, doesn't it? A terrific t-shirt and note card to keep on our desk and quote to friends whose self-confidence has taken a beating. Just one small problem—what on earth does it mean, and how are we supposed to go about that, exactly?

I got curious enough about it that I took a random poll among some of my friends. The question was, "What does 'owning your power' mean to you?"

Here are a few of their answers:

"Owning my power means that I'm self-assured in who I am, knowing what I want, knowing what I'm capable of and being self-confident." (male)

"Owning my power basically means I can do whatever I put my mind to. There are no limits. I am the boss of me. I totally believe I can do anything. If I want to do something I will, and if I don't I won't. Simple as that. No one can make me do something I don't want to do." (female)

"This is my life. Owning my power means anything is possible. I'm a risk taker and a rule breaker, and I love that about myself." (female)

"Owning my power is living life on my terms." (female)

"Owning my power is Presence. I realize that I am a presence, and when I walk in a room people see me. I'm special in the way that everybody is special. I hope everyone realizes that they're special." (male)

"Owning my power is not being afraid to be proactive. People hold themselves back because they've been told that they can't, or they shouldn't. I say, shake it if you've got it. Just because someone else hasn't done it doesn't mean you shouldn't." (male)

"Owning my power is just letting myself come through. Not worrying about what the world around me is expecting. Letting myself float to the surface and move straight ahead." (female)

"Owning my power means I know my positive streaks and use them to my advantage." (male)

"I build on my strengths. That's owning my own power." (female)

The point of asking wasn't to grade them or have an opinion about the answers. I really wanted to know, and it inspired me to start thinking about it for myself: What does owning my power mean to me?

My first thought was that I used to hand over my power like crazy, and almost at random. I might as well have been walking down the street passing out business cards that read, "Hi. I'm Catherine. Please decide for me what kind of day I'm going to have, what mood I'm going to be in, and what my opinion is of myself."

So much for what *not* owning my power was like—I know I'm done with that nonsense. Now, what *does* it mean to me?

It means freedom. And peace. I can just BE. It means knowing what I want, charting the path that will get me there and moving toward it, whatever it is—and getting it through my head that I already have it; it's simply a matter of being fully prepared to make the most of it when it and I meet. It means sharing, caring, loving, and saying NO without guilt when that's the honest answer. It means knowing *and living* what I stand for, keeping things simple, and honoring God in every breath, every gesture, every decision, every transaction, every relationship, every win, and every loss.

Today I want you to think about what owning your power means to you. It really is a valuable challenge, once you push past the fact that you've heard it so often it started to sound like, "Yeah, right, own my power, blah, blah." When you throw your shoulder into it and dig deep, you'll be surprised at how much more powerful you feel just by defining it for yourself and behaving accordingly.

Dear God, help me truly understand, deep into my soul,
that I am a part of the great "I AM."
I AM stronger than I ever believed I was.
I AM more courageous than I ever thought I was.
I AM worth loving in the best way possible,
and I start with loving myself.
Though my time may not always be mine,
my heart is mine, my soul is mine, and my mind is mine.
With Your blessing, I choose to follow them wisely,
and to honor my feelings.
Before me is the page on which You've drawn
a beautiful picture of my life.
My thoughts are alive
with who You're having me BECOME,
and what You've planned for us to create together,
step by baby step. Amen.

JUNE 21

"O taste and see that the Lord is good."
– Psalms 34:8

From Fern:

Come to eat what feeds the soul. Build in you an appetite for Christ. When my people came out of Egypt, having been accustomed to fresh and spicy foods— cucumbers, melons, leeks, onions, garlic, and meat—they complained about the bread I provided, although the psalmist called manna the bread of angels. They were not impressed by its miraculous qualities. In their preoccupation with the foods of Egypt, they forgot that I had seen their affliction at the hands of taskmasters and had heard their cry. I delivered them from their sufferings. They ignored the fact that I was leading them to a land of milk and honey promised to their ancestors.

Beware lest you be caught at the level of earthly food. Declare with Paul, "I will not be enslaved by anything. Food is meant for the stomach and the stomach for food—and God will destroy both one and the other." The body is meant for the Lord. Do you not know that your body is a member of Him who said, "Do not labor for the food that perishes but for the food which endures to eternal life, which the Son of man will give you?" The bread of God is that which comes down from heaven and gives life to the world. Hunger for this food.

JUNE 22

"Whoever does the will of my Father in heaven
is my brother, and sister, and mother."
— Matthew 12:50

From Fern:

Dear Jesus, this scripture reminds me of two truths: First, how bothered I have been by the preceding verses, to the detriment of the teaching verse. I was so busy with the less significant point that I missed the significant.

How often do I do that, Lord? How often do I so exhaust my energy in preparation for an event, that I have none left for the event? How often does Your body, the church, spend so much time meeting and planning to evangelize that we never get to actual evangelism?

We need Your help, O Lord!

The second truth is one of relationships. How close I feel to those of my same spirit! How united I am to ones who have the same priorities. We are truly "one in the Spirit, one in the Lord." There is mutual understanding and love that often surpasses those whose kinship is family blood.

But You have done something wonderful! You have united us by the blood of Jesus! He is our family tie. He is our unity and in His name we are family.

JUNE 23

"While we were yet sinners, Christ died for us."
– Romans 5:8

From Fern:

Savior, what limitless love You have for us! While we were yet sinners You gave Your life that we might live! But sin must be ugly to Your sight and a stench to Your nostrils. Yet You reached out to rescue us from its clutches, as You reached out and touched the untouchable, the rejected of the world.

Holy Lord, we have such distorted views. We spend so much time and attention on outward appearance to make ourselves attractive to our associates, but Your eyes see through all this directly into the heart, and it is the pure of heart who ascend your holy hill.

While we were yet sinners, yet impure, yet unlovely, You made the supreme sacrifice for our salvation!

O my God, I accept Your death for me. I take it into my awareness and my life.

I ask that You create in me a clean heart, a purity of mind and motives. Rearrange my priorities that I may focus on Christ who gave His life that I might live. Give me the intention to live this day for Him!

JUNE 24

"Is the Lord among us or not?"
– Exodus 17:7b

From Fern:

Dear Lord, I can relate to the Hebrews in the wilderness asking this question. There are days when I am overcome with what is happening in the world and I wonder, are You here? In my own prayer time, is it habit that prompts me to come? Is it my imagination that You hear and answer me?

My child, I know, but do you not go from these times refreshed? Do you not receive answers and healings? Nor is it only you who needs this time. As Mary knelt and received, I, too, received from her.

But God, what of the Marthas? Are there not persons incapable of perceiving what Mary perceived? Are there not those whose natures relate to physical instead of spiritual needs? Their love is expressed in this way, and it is genuine love of people.

Child, will you allow me to deal with that issue? Did I not create the Marthas as well as the Marys?

Be still and know that I AM God. I have told you that what I have prepared for those who love is beyond what eye can see, or ear hear, or the heart imagine. Quiet your concerns and be glad you do not have the responsibility of judgment.

JUNE 25

"He who sows sparingly will reap sparingly."
– 2 Corinthians 9:6

From Fern:

Divine Parent, thank You for giving us, Your children, a way to participate in this law, which is both physical and spiritual. It is true of the literal sower of seeds, but it is true as well for sowers of love and good deeds. For the one who fears to risk loving reaps a scanty love in return, while generosity pours a great return into the heart and hands of the giver.

Dear Lord, thank You for giving me time and experience to observe this for myself. There have been occasions when I have not obeyed the common sense that told me to stand aside and not get involved. I have responded to appeals for support that have bypassed my head and gone straight to the heart.

In every case You poured back an overflowing blessing! Regardless of what these gestures meant to the recipient, they gave to me an abundant harvest. Thank You, for by such experiences a life is made! *Life*, not existence! Not reluctantly leaving the bed each morning, facing another dull day, but rising in eagerness to see what the day will hold! That is a return You have given me for my investment.

JUNE 26

"My God will supply your every need."
– Philippians 4:19

From Fern:

Precious Lord, You will supply my every need, and I see my primary need is of You. That You supply my needs, not my wants, simplifies my life. As I look back over the years, I can smile at some of my wants, some so intense that I thought life was not worth living without them.

And then came a time to clear out the accumulated clutter. How cheap, how gaudy, how useless it all looked! None of those things brought lasting pleasure.

But You, dear Lord, supply the *needs* of my life. I need food, water, and air for my physical survival, but I have further needs for my spiritual well-being: I need *You* and an awareness of Your presence. You have provided prayer as a means to this end.

I need love, which You are, and the evidence and the exercise of it. I need peace and joy, which You have promised and given, as You have dwelled within my life in Your Holy Spirit.

Thank You, dear God. Thank You for the maturity and the growing tendency to eliminate clutter and focus more and more on You as the only true need of my life.

JUNE 27

"A merry heart does good, like medicine,
but a broken spirit dries the bones."
– Proverbs 17:22

I actually like *New Living Translation*'s way of saying it even better:

"A cheerful heart is good medicine,
but a broken spirit saps a person's strength."

From Cat:

I'm a comedy stage hypnotist. I hypnotize people and make them do outrageous things in front of a live audience—not to humiliate them, but to make them laugh and, more importantly, to show them the unlimited possibilities of their God-given gift of a mind. When people come to my show, they expect a funny evening. What they get is that...and sometimes so much more.

I recently did my show at the Delaware State Fair, which has become one of my favorite venues thanks to my precious, now one hundred-year-old great aunt I told you about, who lives ten minutes from the fairgrounds.

As always, at the end of the performance, once the laughter has finally subsided, I gave the people onstage what I call "The Gift." It's a blessing that lasts four minutes and goes by like a shot. It's an opportunity for my volunteers to see their lives in the future and imagine what they want that future to be. They get to imagine what they want to change, where they want to go, and *who* they want to be. I affirm that they have everything inside them to make anything happen, that they're loved, and most important, that they are blessed.

When I finished that night in Delaware, I walked off the stage and through the audience as I always do. A young man stepped up to me and said, "Do you remember me?"

I most certainly did. He'd been on my stage as a volunteer a few times, and I knew he was using hard drugs (I predicted crack). I can always tell by a person's skin and teeth, not to mention their

230

demeanor and attitude. I never allow anyone onstage if they're drunk or high, and I watch carefully for the signs.

This man was straight when he volunteered, but I could tell he was living a rough life. He had a very pregnant girlfriend, and they were just a couple of kids. I remember feeling concerned about their situation and what kind of life they were going to give to this child, and I said a prayer.

But this young man who asked if I remembered him was a different person. His skin and eyes were clear. His smile was genuine, and his demeanor was very soft.

He then said, "Do you remember my girl was pregnant? Well, here's our son." He pointed to a beautiful baby in a stroller next to his wife. The baby was otherworldly happy, bouncy, and active, and all smiles and giggles.

I gave him a big hug. "Of course I remember you!" I assured him, genuinely excited. "You did it! Look at you! You look so terrific and happy!"

"And guess who encouraged me," he said.

"Who?

"YOU!" he replied, with the most sincere, heartfelt look of gratitude on his face.

There isn't an Emmy or any other award on this earth that would mean more to me than a moment like that.

I often have people write me or come see me again the following year and wait for me after a show to tell me how their lives have changed. That's exactly why I love what I do—and all I'm really doing is reinforcing a feeling of love, safety, and belonging, something too many "authority figures" and "leaders" in our lives forget to pass on...or maybe never knew in the first place.

I'm sure that young man's life isn't all sunshine and rainbows. But he was clearly on his way to building a solid life, he was clean and drug-free and very much *with* his wife and child. He looked healthy, he looked responsible, and he looked at peace.

Every day—*every day*—I ask God to bring me people who need me.

He never fails.

Love does heal.

I am blessed. I am loved.

And so are you.
Will you receive that today?

If so, will you pay it forward?

JUNE 28

"Put off your old nature which belongs
to your former way of life and is corrupt,
and be renewed in your mind.
Put on the new nature, created after my likeness."
– Ephesians 4:22-24

From Fern:

When I created the world and humankind to care for it, I provided a way for them to live in love—love for me, for one another and for themselves; with no anger or quarreling, no wrath, malice, slander, no lying to one another, no division by race, religion, culture, class, or gender.

When strife seemed to be the inclination of my human creatures, I provided a way to overcome it—the Lord Jesus and the power of my Spirit through whom they may be made new.

Accept my Spirit and become the creature I predesigned you to be—conformed to the image of my Son. This is my Spirit within you, daily renewing you, changing you into my likeness from one degree of glory to another. When I call you to be perfect, do not protest that it is impossible; for nothing is impossible for me. Would I have given this directive if it could not be accomplished! When my Spirit is your motivation, my will is your will. You are then on your way toward perfection; for I, the Lord, am perfect.

JUNE 29

"Repay no one evil for evil."
— Romans 12:17

From Fern:

Lord Jesus, You set the example of forgiveness. You gave us the Holy Spirit who empowers us to forgive. But how unnatural this seems. The ego rises in protest when we have been diminished in someone else's or in our own sight. How badly we want to use the old adage "an eye for an eye, and a tooth for a tooth."

But Jesus, Your Sermon pleads with us to choose a better way. What is to be gained if we retaliate? Who shall break the cycle of vengeance for vengeance; who shall show love's way unless it is us, Your followers—unless it is *me*, your follower?

Holy Spirit, help me. Reveal to me those dark spots where resentment lies within me. Shine Your divine light into such recesses that I may bring it forth to ask forgiveness, to make amends, to humble myself by going to the offended and offending persons to right the wrongs.

As long as one brother is out of fellowship with me, I cannot come to the altar in good conscience. Help me, I pray.

JUNE 30

"I'll cast on Him my every care
And wait for thee, sweet hour of prayer."
– William Walford

From Fern:

PRAISE YOU, Eternal God, for the gift of prayer. How could it be that the almighty God chose to provide an avenue through which the clay vessels could communicate with the Potter? How could it be that the all-wise Master sought to converse with finite creatures? More than that, Lord, You give us power through prayer in elaborate promises that *nothing* we ask in Your name will be impossible.

Through Jesus, You gave the example of a prayerful life and a prayer for disciples to follow. Through Your Spirit, You even help us to know how to pray. Even more, Abba, Father, You do not require that we kneel in prayer as subservient slaves receiving daily assignments. You do not schedule us as subjects having an audience with a king. We come at Your bidding as trusting children to loving Parent. We come secure in the knowledge of being welcome at any moment.

We do not come to tell You what You do not know. You are not far from any of us. There is nothing in our lives or hearts that is hidden from You, nothing in our world about which You do not care.

But most astonishing of all, precious Savior, is that You are daily in the throne room, interceding for us who draw near to God through You. PRAISE YOU, Lord Jesus!

JULY

JULY 1

"...He went about...healing
all who were oppressed by the devil,
for God was with Him."
– Acts 10:38b

From Fern:

O my Lord, help me to define these unseen realities. The contrast is plain. You are good, and You want good for your created. You came that we might have abundant life, abundance in all things: health, wealth, friends, achievement. You desire unity within persons, within society, while the devil is divisive, scattering thoughts, confusing purposes, giving unclear signals.

But God, who and where is he? In the cosmos, outside myself, waging war with You for my soul? Or within me, as Your Spirit is within me, and the conflict is taking place there?

I know, God, who I want indwelling my life, but there *is* that other nature that inclines me to be less than You would have me be. I know this nature as "What About Me?" It dies hard!

Lord God, help me to decrease the Me in favor of Thee. Let me live in this awareness this day, giving You the praise, in the Spirit of Jesus.

JULY 2

"What do you have that you did not receive?"
— 1 Corinthians 4:7

From Fern:

O God, I am in awe to realize what has been done for me that I take for granted: my salvation, which cost Jesus His life; my Bible, preserved through centuries of tedious copying, through bloodshed and burnings at the stake of those who believed that I, a lay person, should have it; my church, whose founders suffered deliberate and sadistic persecution to bring it into being; my freedom, won through wars.

O Lord, I kneel in awe! How can I care so little when I remember those who cared so much? Help me this day to a new awareness of how precious is every aspect of my life! Help me to know how privileged I am, and then let me release that privilege to strive to bring it to lives of others.

Savior, my gratitude will move me to action. My gratitude to Jesus will prompt me to witness; to those who made the Bible available, to share it; to the founders of the church, to do my part to make it Christ's body in the world; to those who fought and died for my freedom, to see that it is extended to all. Help me so to do, I pray.

JULY 3

"Believe in the Lord Jesus, and you will be saved..."
– Acts 16:31

From Fern:

Jesus, help me take that step of faith into believing. It is not a mental exercise but a spiritual one that I cannot perform of my own volition. Try as I might, with my own mind I cannot force myself into the kind of believing of which You spoke when You said, "Whatever you ask in prayer, believe that you receive it and you will." The limitations of my mind tell me that I cannot believe into truth what seems untrue or into reality what seems unreal.

No, Jesus, I must enter the realm of "believing through Spirit," through my re-created spirit who gives me discernment of who You are. Your Holy Spirit, part and parcel of You, discerns for me Your true identity.

You are the Christ, dear Jesus. You are my Savior, Sovereign Lord. The Spirit of Truth tells me. I am convinced! I believe! I am saved! The words of John confirm it: "I write this to you who believe in the name of the Son of God, that you may know that you have eternal life." Thank You, Jesus!

JULY 4

"...all that Jesus began to do and teach..."
– Acts 1:1

From Fern:

O Divine Word, who speaks down through the ages, whose truth leaps off the pages in words that inspire, stimulate, and sometimes perplex us: Why did Dr. Luke choose the word "began"? Jesus *began* to do? He *began* to teach? What provision did You make to continue and complete what You began? Even as I ask, I know; because You said that You would empower your followers, and "*You* shall be my witnesses."

My Lord, and my God, how shall I read that "you"? Shall I take it to be a nebulous "you," meaning whoever reads these words down through the ages? May I take it to be a corporate "you" so that I can be lost in the masses? Or do you mean *you*, which is *me* – specifically, personally *me*?

Savior, I have given You my life. I have come to You individually and You have regarded me individually. You have equipped me individually, but if You truly mean *me*, I lean even more on You. I am so small and the need is so great, but I comply with what You ask as you give me the ability. Help me, Jesus, as I go in Your name.

JULY 5

"When fate hands you lemons, make lemonade."
– Elbert Hubbard (paraphrased)

From Cat:

I know. You've heard that a million times. But that doesn't make it any less inspiring when you see someone actually do it, or any less worthwhile as a reminder.

A few years ago I had a neighbor. I'll call her Lori, since that's her name. She was in her late sixties when we first met. She was just getting out of her car when I was walking by, and she looked like she was having a very bad day, so I stopped to introduce myself and ask if she was okay.

She wasn't. She'd just come back from her daily visit to her husband Jerry, who'd been in a variety of hospitals and care facilities for the past year. His already fragile health was continuing to decline, and the doctors had told Lori that day that they didn't expect him to live much longer. Jerry and Lori had been married for almost fifty years, they had no children, and they were best friends. I told her how sorry I was, gave her my phone number, and invited her to call if she needed anything, even if it was just to talk.

In the three months that followed, from our December introduction until the end of March, Lori lost her beloved seventeen-year-old cat, her beloved eighteen-year-old cat, and her husband and best friend, Jerry. A month after Jerry died Lori was hospitalized with pancreatitis. She'd fully recovered by the end of April, healing but understandably still grieving, and she'd done exactly what I asked her to do—called from time to time to keep me posted, and occasionally just to be sad, but she never leaned too hard or took advantage.

In May she called to say she was tired of thinking about and taking care of no one but herself and needed something happy to focus on...so could I help her find a kitten to rescue? Through my vet I quickly found not one, but two tiny abandoned kittens, a brother and sister. The one glitch: They wouldn't be able to come home with her for a couple of weeks because they were still being bottle-fed. No problem. She went to visit and play with them every day so they wouldn't be coming home with a total stranger. When she did bring them home, they were playful and silly and in need of cuddling, and they helped her heart heal without even trying.

I was a bit worried about her when Christmas came along, her favorite holiday and her first Christmas without Jerry in almost fifty years. I shouldn't have been. She bought herself a big beautiful tree and thoroughly enjoyed decorating it and her small living room, with the added delight of watching her kittens discover the joy of shiny ornaments.

And under the tree? My favorite part...

Without saying a word or making any fuss about it at all, at the beginning of the summer she'd started buying little items that caught her eye when she was out shopping—a cute sweater here, a fun plant pot there, a box of interesting looking tea bags, an inexpensive pair of pretty earrings. She brought each item home the day she bought it, promptly gift-wrapped it, and put it away in her closet until the day she decorated her Christmas tree, when she placed all her presents under the tree and had a great time opening them on Christmas morning. She'd forgotten what most of them were by then, and, as she pointed out to me, it was one way of making sure she'd love every gift she opened.

Today Lori is in her early seventies. She's in great health, as are her now full-grown cats, Oliver and Savannah, who continue to be as playful and affectionate (when they feel like it—they're cats, after all) as ever and delight her every day. She loves gardening and monthly lunches with a group of "girls" she's known since grade school, and once a year she travels by herself to the time-share condo she and Jerry bought in Jamaica decades ago. She misses Jerry every day, but it makes her smile much more often than it makes her cry.

Today I want you to focus on the lemons in your life, or in the life of someone you love, and whether you feel like it or not, find a way to make lemonade. It's healthy, it attracts more blessings than you could ever see coming, and it will inspire the people around you to do exactly the same thing.

❤ ❤ ❤

Dear God, I thank You for all those quiet,
anonymous heroes who live among us and,
if we'll take the time to notice, remind us
that we can't always choose what happens in our lives,
but we *can* always choose what we do about it. Amen.

JULY 6

"You did not receive the spirit of slavery to fall back
into fear, but you have received the spirit of sonship."
– Romans 8:15

From Fern:

Fear is defeating and inappropriate for my people. I did not give you a spirit of timidity but a spirit of power and love and self-control. There is no fear in love, but perfect love casts out fear.

Over and over I have told my people not to be afraid. These were the opening words of my messengers to Zechariah, to Mary, and to the shepherds. Do not fear the mystical breaking into the physical realm.

Do you fear what others will say if you are zealous for the Lord? Confidently affirm, "The Lord is my helper, I will not be afraid, what can man do to me?" Do you fear what I may call you to do? To Moses, to Gideon, to Jeremiah, and to all to whom I assign a task I gave assurance, "I will be with you. Fear competes with faith. Do not fear, only believe.

Do you fear loss of possessions? Even the wise die, the fool and stupid alike must perish, and leave their wealth to others. Do you fear loss of life? Do not fear those who can kill the body but cannot kill the soul; rather fear him who can destroy both soul and body in hell. Fear the Lord. This is the beginning of wisdom.

JULY 7

"And the Lord God made for Adam and his wife
garments of skin, and clothed them"
– Genesis 3:21

From Fern:

Dear God, You have always done it all, haven't You? Adam and Eve
attempted to cover their sin but their little aprons were inadequate.
You told them the consequences; then You sacrificed Your animals
and from their skins You made robes that covered Your beloved
completely.

Savior, You did it again in Jesus! You arranged the incarnation by
sending the angel Gabriel to Mary. You overshadowed her with Your
Spirit and *You* fathered the world's salvation.

How busy we get, dear Lord, in Your name! Help us to remember
that our activity is response to the love first shown to us, but does
not achieve salvation. That is already accomplished. Through this
awesome truth we discover that it is harder to receive than to give.
Our pride makes us to want to earn, to be worthy of, what we get.
We want to do something for it.

O God, help me know the meaning of Your having done it all. Help
me know that I cannot ever be worthy of heaven. Help me to accept
what Jesus has done and to be conscious of the cost.

JULY 8

"All authority in heaven and on earth has been given to me."
– Matthew 28:18

From Fern:

Jesus, I think of Your authority and how You did not allow it to corrupt You, or deter You from Your mission. You never used Your gifts for display. You knew that followers won that way would not be permanent or loyal.

Lord, I have little authority but wonder if I handle it well. I have authority over my own life—if not in every minute or activity, at least over my thoughts and responses. How I interpret life around me, the actions and words of others, is within the realm of my authority.

My Christ, help me examine the handling of my authority in the light of Yours. I also have some authority as influence over others. This, too, is a solemn responsibility. May I never use it to draw persons to me, but through me to You.

Authority is frightening. There is the powerful temptation to use it to glorify ourselves. But we remember Your example and Your caution that the humble will be exalted and the proud humbled. I pray for only as much authority as I can handle.

JULY 9

"...make ready for the Lord a people prepared."
– Luke 1:17b

From Fern:

Dear God, how much time and thought are invested in preparation for events! The house cleaned, food planned and made ready in the case of guests. Papers updated, figures examined, copies made available, in case of a meeting. Each aspect of appearance attended to in case of personal appointments.

But O my Lord, how casually I turn to You! How unprepared I come for these very important times reserved for us! I know You are a God of order. How dare I come with my mind cluttered and thoughts of past and future? I read of John the Baptist, the austerity of his living, and of Jesus whose single commitment characterized His life. And yet I dare to come with my life junked with possessions and a variety of unprioritized interests.

Jesus, divine Example, help me to rearrange and put my spiritual house in order. Help me to realize that no more than I would invite You to a filthy house in disarray, is it fitting for me to come to prayer time without preparation. Help me to "prepare the way of the Lord."

JULY 10

"I love the Lord..."
– Psalms 116:1

From Fern:

My Dear God, I affirm what the Psalmist said. I love You, I need
You, I want You in every minute, in every aspect of my life.
Rededicate my heart, I pray, that I may reaffirm this truth again and
again.

Lord, I pause to think of this phenomenon: How can I love You,
never having seen You? How can I love You simply because I have
been commanded to do so? Can I love You simply because I have
chosen to follow Jesus, who also said this is vital?

A startling revelation comes to me: I love You only because You
have given me the capacity! It is not a quality for which I can take
credit. It is nothing I can achieve. *You* have accomplished it! My love
is but a response to Your love!

Dear Jesus, You came to reveal this love, to demonstrate this love.
You came obedient to this love. And then You gave us the Holy
Spirit to indwell us in order that we can participate in this love!

Dear God, You have done it all! I am simply a channel. Help me to
be willing always so to be. Clear the debris from my life that the
channel may be clear.

JULY 11

"Let your light so shine before men
that they may see your good works and give glory
to your Father who is in heaven."
– Matthew 5:16

From Fern:

Lord, I have just read a question about the donkey on which Jesus
rode on Palm Sunday. Did he think the crowd was cheering for him?
This has touched the deeper levels of my soul. This question
challenges me to ask if there are times when I take to myself the glory
that belongs to You, and already I know the answer.

It holds before me the picture of my giving. Forgetting the Source, I
return a pittance—forgetting that through Your good earth, the sun,
the rain, the seasons, the seed, You have given food and drink for
sustenance. Forgetting that You have given the ability to think, to
plan, to remember, I envision myself as self-made—the donkey bows
and assumes the acclaim of the crowd.

Forgive me, Lord, and help me to move to a new level of awareness.
Redirect the intentions of my life that, as the donkey, I may carry
You on my shoulders; that my every goal will be to take You
wherever you desire to go.

JULY 12

"Nothing is more difficult, and therefore more precious,
than to be able to decide."
– Napoleon Bonaparte

From Cat:

Several years ago I was invited to work with a ministry outreach program, visiting women's prisons in Texas. The goal was to "bring the broken home," to help the inmates find the freedom on the inside that they'd forfeited on the outside, through an atmosphere of God's love, self-acceptance, self-forgiveness, and letting go of their "story" as a definition of who they are in the present moment.

I jumped at the opportunity, and it changed who I am. I've hoped ever since that those women received a fraction as much as I did from our time together. I had the amazing opportunity to offer spiritual nourishment to a group who needed it more than most, and it was nothing short of a privilege.

For those of you who are saying, "Catherine, the women in those prisons obviously earned their way there! I'm not shedding any tears over them!" as some of my friends said at the time—yes, they did earn their way there, and this ministry wasn't about shedding tears. It was about acting on my belief that God wouldn't withhold compassion from any of His children, no matter who or where they are, and as His steward, the very least I can do is assure offer that compassion on His behalf, whether they're ready to receive it or not.

The loneliness in a prison is more frightening than I'd ever imagined, and it turns out that female inmates have far fewer visitors than male inmates, despite the fact that they have families on the outside. Most of them are dropped off and forgotten, leaving them alone with the guilt of the crime that landed them there and the children they've let down. They're not aliens, or some other species, they're *us*, with horrible choices in their past, some carefully planned, some that happened in less than a minute, facing consequences they hadn't thought out. No excuses, no minimizing what they did, just a deep jolt of reality on my part that "there but for the grace of God go I"—none of us have the luxury of saying, "That would *never* happen to me." The extreme cases? Probably not. The woman who drank two glasses of wine at the office Christmas party, fell asleep behind the wheel on her way home and caused an accident that killed another driver? Never? Really?

Much of the despair those women were struggling so hard to overcome was their inability to stop defining themselves by nothing but their "story," the series of events that cost them their freedom. And it's an even harder struggle when all they have to do to be reminded of that "story" is look around and see where they are.

It haunted me for a long time afterwards, the way so many of us—and I absolutely include myself—let our past, our "story," keep us emotionally locked up as surely as if we were chained to it, the hurts, the mistakes, the situations we handled so badly, the times we were genuinely victimized, the times we turned our back on someone when they needed us, the foolish choices, all of it.

We either forget or can't accept the fact that while life doesn't give us do-overs, it gives us a limitless number of start-overs, opportunities to write new stories that won't erase the old ones but can most certainly outshine them. We can DECIDE today, with no steel bars in our way, that the darker parts of our past can *inform* us without *defining* us. We can DECIDE today to be "older but wiser," using past bad experiences as building blocks instead of stumbling blocks, toward a day when we'll have fulfilled so many of our dreams that we'll find ourselves thinking, with a smile on our faces, "If that's what it took to get me here, it was worth it."

The hope for those women in prison was self-forgiveness, new beginnings and the promise that while they may have turned their backs on God in their past, He never turned His back on them.

Isn't that really our hope too, especially when we know it's what He wants for us, through His pure, unconditional love?

Forget do-overs. START over.

Today. Now. Decide.

You can change your life.

Dear God, please help me hold on to the memories
that make me happy, let go of the ones that don't
but embrace their lessons, and, filled with Your all-forgiving love,
start writing a new story today that will make us both proud. Amen.

JULY 13

"The Lord shows no partiality,
but in every nation anyone who fears him
and does what is right is acceptable to him."
– Acts 10:34-35

From Fern:

Even though I have chosen certain persons, it is not for special privilege, but special responsibility; for all to be saved and to come to the knowledge of truth. Have I any pleasure in the death of the wicked, and not rather that he should turn from his way and live? I died for all.

Sin came into the world through one man and death through sin, and so death spread to all men because all men sinned. If many died through one man's trespass, much more have the grace of God and the free gift in the grace of that one man Jesus Christ abounded for many. Yes, God so loved the world that he gave his only Son, but this is not simply the world. He died for you. He so loved you! He desired that your soul be saved. Jesus' promise is to you and your children and to all that are far off, everyone whom the Lord your God calls to Him.

You are not simply one of billions. Two sparrows were sold for a penny and I assured you that you are of more value than many sparrows. Even the hairs of your head are numbered. Everyone who acknowledges me before men, I will acknowledge before my Father in heaven. You are my beloved.

JULY 14

"Do not believe every spirit, but test the spirits
to see whether they are of God."
— 1 John 4:1

From Fern:

Dear God, how quickly You show me that I do impede the authority
of Your Holy Spirit. I know well the spirit of pride and contention
that caused Eve to fall to the temptation to be like You; the spirit that
encouraged her to satisfy desires of the flesh rather than attending to
growth of the soul; the spirit of deceit that prompted Adam to be
evasive when You confronted him; even the spirit of jealousy and
anger that caused Cain to take his brother's life.

Father, forgive me for falling so soon and so often! Take from me
whatever contends with Your Divine Spirit within me. As Jesus
angrily drove out all that had no place in Your house, cleanse the
temple of my body of all that is inconsistent with Your Spirit.

But I recall, Lord, that exorcism is not enough. Matthew 12:43-45
tells me that a vacuum cannot exist. Therefore I pray not only for
cleansing but a refilling of truth, righteousness, peace, and faith
which Paul said quenches the flaming darts of the evil one. Thus I go
to meet the day equipped for whatever may arise.

JULY 15

"Whoever is of a generous heart, let him bring the Lord's offering."
— Exodus 35:5

From Fern:

Jesus, it was Your Spirit that prompted the formation of the church, but centuries earlier, in the days of Moses, the Spirit was also involved in constructing the tabernacle. How beautiful to read of the participation of those who were spirit-led to contribute to its beauty. Men and women brought gold and jewels, linens, skins, and wood. Those who had such ability spun the goat's hair, and wove the blue, purple, and scarlet cloth. Onyx and other stones were brought for the priests' garments, spices, oil for lamps, and fragrant incense. Then, God, You brought forth Bezalel whom You had filled with Your Spirit, gifting him with ability, intelligence, knowledge, and craftsmanship to design the gifts that had been brought. Another was inspired to teach.

Thank You, Lord, for this pattern! May our present congregations respond to the Spirit's nudge to put what we have at Your disposal, knowing that You will give us the ability, the design, the teaching by which the tabernacle may be made beautiful for You. Help me to take this personally, that the temple of my life may be well planned and beautiful for You.

JULY 16

"Do not grieve the Holy Spirit of God."
– Ephesians 4:30

From Fern:

Lord, as we move from babes in Christ toward maturity, we discover that the commandments You gave are not restrictive but guide us in how to live harmoniously with You and Your universe and Your people. Through Your laws and prophets, You told us specifically what to do and from what to refrain. You have gone further and told us the consequences for living in accord with or opposed to those commands. But throughout Biblical history Your chosen people disobeyed. They (we, I) did what was evil. They (we, I) served other gods. Consequently, they (we, I) lost the freedom You desired. Also throughout history, You have been the Rescuer. In Judges, Your Holy Spirit came upon Othniel and delivered Your people.

O God, You and I have chosen one another. You have made clear to me what is right in one word: love. Enemies of that state of living rule over me too often. I love too little to conquer my criticism, busyness, pride, a mistaken notion of where my security lies, and many others. Only by Your Spirit did Othniel, and can I, be victorious over this nature that would bind and imprison me.

JULY 17

"Do you love me more than these?"
– John 21:15

From Fern:

Jesus, You ask the same question of me than You did of Peter: Do I love You more than my friends, family, security, comforts, habits, routine, church, or other commitments? I want to say "yes," Lord. I want to be able to turn from any of these and rush as a bride to her beloved husband.

Do I love You more than these? Help me so to do. You said, "You will know the truth and the truth will set you free." You are Truth. Thus, when I know You, I will be set free from false values and priorities. I shall truly be free to walk away from all the baggage I am carrying, all that I will leave behind when I drop this body and my spirit returns to You.

Jesus, Your Spirit within me is the Spirit of love. To deny expression of love is to stifle or quench the Spirit. But when my love for You is greatest of all, then I am free to love in general, with all facets of life in proper order. Do I love You more than these? Enable me to say a resounding *YES* in every case.

JULY 18

"Yea, the Lord will give you what is good..."
– Psalms 85:12

From Fern:

Dear God, our definitions may often not be Your definitions. Our "good" may not be Your "good." You have not promised to fulfill our every desire, any more than a loving parent satisfies every whim of a growing child. A good parent considers the ultimate good.

My Lord, help me to see life from that perspective. Help me to ask for others and myself what is "good" by Your definition. You equip us for life in Your kingdom. For this we must be strong, courageous, living in a manner commendable in Your sight, not accommodating our lifestyle to what others may say or think.

Jesus, teach me what is "good," how to do "good," to give "good," according to what is best for the receiver. You have shown us that to *be* good is to live in the image of the One You said is the only true good, the Father. This was the image You chose for me.

This day help me be conscious of *good* in a way I have not known before, to see it in others and demonstrate it; for I want to live as You would have me live, the *good* life.

JULY 19

The Bible tells us that Jesus is the One who came to heal:
"Then Jesus said, 'Come to me, all of you who are weary
and carry heaven burdens, and I will give you rest.'"
– Matthew 11:28

From Cat:

I'm a Christian. That's as much a fact about me as my height,
weight, and eye color. But I have to admit, one thing I've never
understood about a lot of my fellow Christians is their resistance to
the ideas of extrasensory perception, or ESP, and channeling. Just for
starters, God is energy, right? Energy that He channels to us, every
minute of every day. We don't see Him, taste Him, hear Him, smell
Him, or touch Him—i.e., we don't perceive Him with any of our five
senses, which means our perception of Him is extrasensory. Excuse
me, but...uh...isn't that extrasensory perception?

Our feelings are energy as well, powerful and perceivable as
they're *channeled* from a source to a receiver. Anger, happiness,
compassion, healing, LOVE—all extrasensory, all real and
enormously powerful, and all would be useless if we and the people
around us couldn't experience them through—hello!—channeling.
You know how it feels to be on the receiving end of someone's love,
someone's anger, and someone's compassion. You also know how it
feels to be in the presence of negative energy, that discomfort and
uneasiness and often physical illness, even if the source of that
negative energy seems to be just sitting there minding their own
business. Prolonged exposure to negative energy can be debilitating
to the point of losing your clarity, your joy and your self-esteem, as
some of us sadly learn the hard way.

A girl with two young children approached me one night after
my stage hypnosis show and asked if hypnosis can heal depression. I
rhetorically asked if she was the one who was depressed (as if I
couldn't tell), and she answered, "Yes."

Hypnotherapy has its place, but in many cases, depression is
situational, so I asked her what was going on in her life. It seems
she'd been in an extreme physically and emotionally abusive

relationship for the past two years, and just a few days earlier she'd managed to escape.

It didn't take an expert to feel the fear in her energy, and the destroyed sense of self-worth. Being in an abusive relationship can absolutely alter a person's brain chemistry, and this girl, only a few days "liberated," was still suffering more from two-year negative spiritual warfare than she was from depression, with no positive energy left of her own to fight back. Luckily, I had enough of that for both of us.

I asked if she truly understood the amount of courage it took for her to leave, and the incredible personal power she'd demonstrated by refusing to subject her children and herself to one more moment of dark, Godless pain. Escaping an abuser isn't just hard, it's often the most dangerous point in an already dangerous relationship. I urged her to get help from her family, friends, and one of the many life-and-soul-saving domestic violence organizations online to keep her and her children protected, and also to keep her from being drawn back into a horrible situation just because it was familiar.

And then, I took her hands and we prayed—that God would fill her heart and give her the answers she needed to move forward in a positive and healthy direction...that He would help her restore the self-esteem she desperately needed to become the woman, the provider, and the mother her innocent children deserve...that despite a two-year habit, she'd start focusing on herself and her babies rather than on her abuser...and most of all, that she'd receive every bit of the healing, loving energy God will be channeling to her to affirm that she'll never, ever be alone.

I felt her calming as she took in that prayer. I felt the light in her beginning to flicker back to life, reignited by Him, through me and into her spirit, and a whole new hopeful energy was radiating from her as she walked away, that bore no resemblance to the frightened, beaten-down energy of the woman who'd approached me just a few minutes earlier. Her healing had already started.

Another day, another Christian extrasensory channeling transaction.

I'll keep her in my prayers, and not waste a moment's thought on her abuser. God will take care of him too, in ways that are just plain none of my business.

If someone you care about is in trouble or some kind of despair today, sit with them and give them all the positive energy you've got—not just words, but *energy*. It will make a difference to them, and to you, too. It's a funny thing about positive energy. Like everything else in God's universe, the more you give, the more you get back.

Dear God, the most powerful Energy of all,
please help us be mindful of the energy we transmit
to the world around us,
so that everyone we come in contact with
feels better, feels safe and feels Your presence
through us, Your beloved children. Amen.

JULY 20

"You will know the truth."
– John 8:32

From Fern:

I met a man from India who talked to me about life from his perspective of reincarnation. His piercing brown eyes looked through me as he spoke, he said, to my angel. They talked about my purpose for being and he told me that it was important that I write. "Write about the cross..." and as he elaborated he suddenly stopped, looked at me, and said, "Why am I saying this to you? ...Oh, you were there!" What was he saying? I was one of Jesus' followers? "Oh, no, you were too busy for that. You were a housewife in Jerusalem. In another period you were a philosopher studying in Egypt. Later, a member of the Albigenses who went into France to purify the church. You were persecuted there..."

Truth? I don't know. If it is, it answers some questions: It explains why my interests are different from persons around me; why, in Israel, I had a sense of at-homeness and simply fell in love with the Arab people; why, in a museum in Cairo, Egypt the statue of a scribe communicated to me so personally that I would return just to see it; and why the latter gospel accounts are so horrible to me that I can hardly bear to read them. Reincarnation intrigued me for some years. I read everything I could find that supported and denied it. Now I trust God's arrangement of life, and accept whatever it is.

JULY 21

"Who are you to pass judgment
on the servant of another?"
– Romans 14:4

From Fern:

It seems reasonable that the purpose of life may be to learn to love; for the Creator who gave us life *is* love. Jesus left only one commandment, to love, and the example, for He told us to love *as* He had loved. Never since the beginning of time has there been such opportunity to broaden our love for persons of other races, cultures, beliefs, sexual preferences, and mindsets. Within my lifetime, persons and situations have been "brought out of closets." God may be saying, "Will you love this creation of mine? Will you give thanks in this circumstance? Will you all be one?"

The development of technology can be regarded as God's revelations toward this end. All the facets necessary for air flight have been available from the beginning. In the twentieth century it was made possible, and now there are no limitations to where we can go in this world, even into space. The same can be said of radio and television and the Internet, which likewise expose us to events and customs on a world scale. Acquaintance with other peoples reduces fear and brings understanding. Knowledge of how Christianity developed, why groups broke from the mainstream and became denominations, increases respect and promotes ecumenicity. All this is happening now! What a great time to be alive!

JULY 22

"You know him for he dwells with you, and will be in you."
– John 14:17

From Fern:

Lord God, Giver of every good and perfect gift, thank You for the greatest gift of all—that of Your divine Self; for You have made yourself known as Creator God, as Jesus the Son, and as Holy Spirit. Had we known You only as Creator You would have been remote, so divine that we could have known *about* You, but could not have known You. Had You added only the humanity of Your Self as You came to earth in Jesus, we could have known *of* You historically; but greatest of all, You have come as Spirit, individually and presently! Through Your Spirit we can know You as Father, understand You as Jesus, experience You as indweller of our lives.

O God, Your Spirit is like a golden thread that ties together the pages of Your book, from before time began, when Your Spirit moved over the face of the waters in the promise when time shall be no more, "The Spirit and the Bride say 'Come.'" The very Spirit in whom I live and move and have my being has ever been and ever shall be. Dear Lord, increase my awareness of this truth.

JULY 23

"The word is very near you."
– Deuteronomy 30:14

From Fern:

Dear Lord, You have said that what You command is neither hard nor distant. It is not in heaven that someone must ascend and bring it to us. It is not beyond the sea that someone must go fetch it. It is very near.

In Moses' day, You gave the commandments on tablets of stone. Jeremiah prophesied that You would bring Your word even closer. You would write it on our hearts. John wrote that in his day, You had come in Jesus, Your Word made flesh. Those alive in that day saw You with their eyes and touched You with their hands.

Thank You, Father, that You also provided for Your ongoing Presence. Jesus said, "It is to your advantage that I go away for...if I go I will send the Counselor to you." The Counselor is Your Holy Spirit, the third revelation of Your Divine Self. You made the printed word come alive. The promised Spirit of truth dwells with me and is living in me! This reality, God, has changed my life from defeat to victory, from futility to hope, from insecurity to confidence! Thanks be to God!

JULY 24

"The spirit of God has made me,
and the breath of the Almighty gives me life."
– Job 33:4

From Fern:

Lord God, You have said, "My thoughts are not your thoughts,
neither are your ways my ways; for as the heavens are higher than the
earth, so are my ways higher than your ways and my thoughts than
your thoughts."

And although I do not understand how, You took the lump of clay
that is my body, blew into it the breath of life, and I became a living
being. It is Your breath, Your Spirit, that gives me life! This earthen
vessel contains this remarkable treasure!

Dear God, Your breath, the source of my being, is holy and therefore
my nature is holy if I do not impede it. I am not "only human,"
inescapably doomed to err and return to dust. You have made me in
Your image! Your Spirit dwells in me, and as in creation, when Your
Spirit moved over the waters, out of the darkness of my life You
have brought light; out of formlessness, You have given purpose; out
of void, You have given meaning.

O God, let me do nothing this or any day that prevents Your Spirit's
holy activity in my life.

JULY 25

"When a needy person stands at your door,
God himself stands at his side."
– Hebrew proverb

From Cat:

I'm not Superwoman, but I've learned enough to set my stuff aside when I'm face to face with strangers who just might need a gentle moment in their day...and who among us doesn't? And on those rare occasions when I could use a reminder...

It was a few years ago. Mid-morning. I was getting ready to move. I was stressed out, crabby, and in need of breakfast, but—o, the misery! —everything in my kitchen was packed up in boxes! Since Fate had left me no alternative (back of hand to forehead), I threw on some clothes and headed up the street to a coffee shop in search of eggs, coffee, and a break from cardboard and packing tape.

The hostess led Snarky, Party Of One through the busy coffee shop to a small table where I could eat and sulk in peace. I hadn't been there long when I overheard a man at the table behind me order breakfast and then add offhandedly, "And if it's not too much trouble, see that soldier over there? I'd like to pick up his tab, too. Just don't tell him who paid for it, okay?"

I looked around for the first time since I'd arrived and saw a soldier sitting several tables away, dressed in Army issue fatigues, eating breakfast by himself, as the waitress replied to the man behind me, "Of course it's not too much trouble! What a nice thing to do! You just made my whole day!"

This small, quiet transaction instantly pulled me out of my own dark cloud of a head, and I turned around and said, "For the record, you just made my whole day too."

The man gave me a little smile and a shrug and said, "Hey, the guy deserves a 'thank you,' don't you think?" and he went right back to reading his morning paper.

I kept my eye on the soldier, and I wish you could have seen his face when he finished his oatmeal, reached for his wallet and was told by the waitress that his breakfast had already been covered. He was touched, he was blown away, he looked around and saw no familiar faces beaming back at him for credit, then stood and gave a salute to the diners in general before he headed for the exit.

Even though I'd been nothing but a witness to this whole thing, I was walking on air for the rest of the day. I'm sure the soldier and the waitress were too, and probably most of all that generous, anonymous man who, for maybe nine dollars plus tip, had bought himself and at least three strangers a reminder that there's amazing transformative power in a simple random act of kindness.

I unapologetically admit it, I'm a heat-seeking missile now for any chance to transform a stranger's day. No luck so far in spotting an obvious soldier in a restaurant whose meal I'd be honored to buy, but every server, store clerk, busboy, cab driver, cashier, and you-name-it gets a big smile from me and a genuine, "How's your day going?" no matter how I'm feeling or what mood I'm in. My hat's off to anyone who puts in an honest week's work, especially in a job that can't be easy. And if they're rude to me? All the more reason to be pleasant to them and become part of the solution rather than part of the problem.

We really can change this abrupt, troubled, busy world, one act of kindness at a time. Oh yes we can! We're that powerful, each and every one of us, so imagine what we can do if we join forces!

Go change someone's day today, and then tweet and tell me about it.

Dear God, thank You from the bottom of our hearts
for the power You give us every single day
to make a difference with a kind, simple gesture and a smile
that takes no more time and energy than a frown
and, as an added bonus, causes few wrinkles. Amen.

JULY 26

"Wait for the Lord; be strong, and let your heart take courage."
— Psalms 27:14

"Guard the truth that has been entrusted to you
by the Holy Spirit who dwells within you."
— 2 Timothy 1:14

From Fern:

Truth is not something told but lived. Jesus said, "I am the way, the truth, and the life." The Christ Spirit is the Spirit of truth and those who submit to the infilling, the prompting, the directing of the Spirit of truth live and emit truth everywhere in all circumstances. Truth is reliable. It does not need written contracts or other signs of pledge. Let what you say be simply yes or no.

Truth is forthright. There is no guile in true relationship, for pure love and truth are aspects of the same Holy Spirit. Owe no one anything except to love one another; for he who loves his neighbor has fulfilled the law. Truth is courageous. It is not the way of or understood by the world. If the world hates you, know that it hated me before it hated you. You pose a threat to those who are false, but with the Lord on your side you need not fear. What can man do to you?

Truth is victorious. Nothing is covered that will not be revealed or hidden that will not be known. You have chosen the winning way.

JULY 27

"Be silent, all flesh, before the Lord;
for He has roused Himself from His holy dwelling."
– Zephaniah 2:13

From Fern:

Father, let me compare this time to coming to my earthly parent, or meeting with my friend. What is prayer but that meeting—to say the things that are on my heart—the funny and the sad, the serious and the flippant, the confusing and the logical?

And sometimes, dear God, to say nothing at all—just to be completely still, to quiet every aspect of my being and enjoy the privilege of fellowship with You.

In reality, Lord, there is nothing to say, for You know—You know all that is in my life and You know beyond what I know, for You understand what I do not. You know cause and effect. You who made this being realize all the facets of this life. And so we sit in silence, in love, in the warmth of being together, enjoying the closeness and the time. And I shall arise, strengthened for the day. Thank You, blessed Lord.

JULY 28

"If anyone says, 'I love God' and hates his brother,
he is a liar; for he who does not love his brother
whom he has seen cannot love God whom he has not seen."
– 1 John 4:20

From Fern:

Creator God, when You designed the world and chose to be Love, did you foreknow how love could ache? Did you know how vulnerable love could make us? Those who followed and still follow closely in your steps have experienced the hurt so deeply—in rejection, in ridicule, in love taken advantage of.

> All this happened to You
> and *is* happening to You,
> and Your love goes on.

And we who are called by Your name, O Christ, know that we have missed the mark of what You have called us to do and to be. In stilled services, in humorless rituals, that show so little love, we call it worship. In a few dollars here and there in service *for* but not *to* the needy, we call it charity.

In obvious disapproval of those we label "sinners," we say we are following the Christ. But where is our love?

O help us, Jesus, to live more truly in Your name and Spirit!

JULY 29

"And I saw the dead, great and small, standing before the throne, and books were opened...(also) the book of life."
– Revelations 20:12

From Fern:

Dear Lord, I wonder what it would be like to see the book of life— Your book of *my* life. How would yesterday appear? What You record might be totally different from what I recorded. What You saw as important may have passed me unnoticed, and what seemed significant to me may have been as nothing in Your sight.

Was something begun that will come to fruition later—a seed planted that will grow and flourish—something of which I may not be aware until it is visible and full-blown? Was there anything I stifled— someone's enthusiasm or hope, someone's offer of friendship or trust?

O God, I desire to be positive, helpful, progressive. Help me, dear Jesus, through Your Holy Spirit. I know there shall come a day when that book will be opened. Will there be pages blank that should have been filled? Will there be pages I cannot bear to have read? Only as You help me, guide and fill me, can I accomplish what You would have me do, go where You would have me go, and be what You would have me be.

This day, Father, help me be conscious of the book, that a record is being kept which Your divine eyes see. Help it be good!

JULY 30

"I am thy servant."
— Psalms 143:12b

From Fern:

As one who serves I go out this day, but let my service, Lord, be for the proper Master. Let me not go as a "man-pleaser," responding to the voices of those who could but simply do not want to bother to do what needs to be done. Let me respond only to that inner voice of direction—the still, small voice that sometimes is not so quiet that I fail to hear it for the other noise.

Your voice, Dear God, is so different from the others—not demanding but pleading; not urging but patiently waiting; always giving choice to the ones who will hear.

And so I pray, Lord, that You will allow me to serve You. Into what fields will You have me go this day? To what persons will You have me speak? What tools (my gifts from You) will I employ? Let me use them all to Your glory and for the building of Your kingdom. I need not serve in a visible place where I shall get publicity or appreciation. Just let me have the Spirit of my Lord and Savior who, though God's Son, chose to serve as one of the least.

Give me this Spirit so to live and so to be. I ask it in Jesus' precious name.

JULY 31

"And after six days Jesus took with Him
Peter and James and John his brother,
and led them up on a high mountain…"
— Matthew 17:1

From Fern:

To Thee, O God, do I lift up my soul. As Jesus took Peter, James, and John, His disciples on earth—and very earthy men they were—to the mountain top, so may I bring the earthiness of my life into Your radiant presence. Bless these aspects of my life, dear Lord, and purify them. Fill them with Your precious love. From the inner to the outer, let Your light shine that I may return from that experience to face the tasks below. For Jesus and His men came down from the mountain and found other disciples who could not handle the challenge they had been given. They found a situation beyond the capacity of humankind to cure and Jesus said, "Only by prayer."

Eternal God, only by prayer can my earthiness be cured. Only as I ascend the holy hill with my Savior and Lord can I hope to catch a vision of Christ. He was man, but it was given to those who went with Him the privilege to see the shining glow of His divinity and to hear the voice from heaven. So may it be today, dear God.

O, may I walk and talk with You and catch a glimpse of holiness in You, and in me as You live within my life.

AUGUST

AUGUST 1

"I always advise people never to give advice."
– P.G. Wodehouse

From Cat:

(...she said, about to do the very same thing, just so you know I get the irony...)

Have you ever noticed that when you're going through a serious decision-making process or life change, there always seems to be someone who insists on telling you exactly how to handle it and what you should do? I call them "armchair therapists," although to be fair, a good therapist doesn't tell you what to do; they simply guide you through your struggle so that you can arrive at the solution yourself.

I once had a dear, cherished friend cross that boundary and aggressively tell me what I should be doing about a certain situation, and I found myself growing more resentful by the minute. I hadn't asked for their opinion, let alone their advice, about the subject I was suddenly getting lectured on. I understood that they were genuinely trying to help, but I also understood my resentment—I felt disrespected, as if they were implying I was incapable of coming up with a solution myself at a pace that worked for me. I'm sorry to say it created an unspoken distance between us that's never quite disappeared, because I simply stopped confiding in them to prevent another unsolicited dissertation on their truth for my life. I'll live my own truth, thanks, and learn from the mistakes I'm bound to make along the way. And when I really do get stuck and need help, I'll gladly ask for advice from someone whose opinion I trust, and who's advising me agenda- and judgment-free.

More often than not, when we sit down with someone close to us to talk through a dilemma, what most of us (particularly us women) want and need is just to be heard by a patient, loving, compassionate *listener*. LISTENING, and REALLY HEARING— two of the most priceless gifts genuine friends and partners can give each other.

276

We've all been on both ends of that situation, that's for sure, and after a lot of trial and error, mind study, and observing people who are really gifted at this kind of thing, I've finally found a way to handle each of them with ease and a complete lack of resentment:

If you're on the listening end, *listen, really hear them.* Be compassionate, be patient, be attentive, be honest but not judgmental with your feedback as they go along, and assume from the beginning that they're not building to a request that you "fix" the situation. When they've finished telling you what's going on, simply ask, "Can I help?" It gives them permission to ask for your advice if they want it, confirms that you care, and nine out of ten times leads to the response, "You already have."

If you're on the venting end and they begin peppering you with solutions you neither asked for nor want, interrupt with a calm, genuine, "Thanks for your love and concern, I appreciate it so much, but I really just needed to talk this out." Again, nine times out of ten, that works beautifully, and they'll appreciate your clarity. As for that tenth time, just end the conversation and make a mental note to yourself to go elsewhere next time.

Another lesson in teaching people how to treat us, and I hope it helps you as much as it's helped me:

Dear God, please help me remember that sometimes
the most helpful, loving thing I can do is just *listen.* Amen.

AUGUST 2

"What God has cleansed you must not call common."
— Acts 10:15

From Fern:

What a surprising revelation this was to Peter who had lived by the Jewish rule of not associating with or visiting anyone of another nation. But I am always doing a new thing. I always call you to go from where you are to a place that I will show you—a new way of thinking and living and being. In that way, you shall see that through the cross I cleansed all people. I bore the griefs of all humankind. I carried your sorrows. It was for your transgressions that I was wounded and for your iniquities I was bruised. I accepted the chastisement that made you whole. By my stripes you were healed.

I made of myself a sacrificial offering, not taking the blood of animals but shedding my own blood for you, to cover your sins, that your conscience might be purified. I cleansed you. You need only to realize your cleanliness and your relationship to me as child to Parent.

And not only you but I died for all. All had gone astray. Everyone turned to his own way. My sacrifice covered the iniquity of all. Therefore you must not think of anyone as common. There is a God-implanted uniqueness in every person. Learn to see them this way.

AUGUST 3

"Glory to God in the highest, and on earth
peace among men with whom He is pleased."
– Luke 2:14

From Fern:

Today is a blank sheet of paper. What shall I write? It is an empty canvas. What shall I paint? What colors will I use? What mood will I depict? You have given me this gift and the choice of what to do with it.

O, my Lord, help me to portray something beautiful for You. Let me fill it with love! Let the words that proceed on paper or the colors that flow from the brush be acceptable in Your sight. Let them proceed from joy and give joy, from peace to give peace, from forgiveness to forgiveness.

Dear God, help my colors be bright and energizing—colors that reflect growth and new birth—greens of grass, reds of tulips, yellows of daffodils, blue of the clear sky.

Let the song in my heart match the picture that I paint—not to hug it to myself, but to paint it to Your glory, to bring joy to Your people.

And I will give You the glory, in Jesus' name.

AUGUST 4

"Be still, and know that I am God."
– Psalms 46:10

From Fern:

To listen, dear God, help me: to so still myself—my racing thought, my nervous energy that leaps inside, eager to bound into the day— that I may hear Your directions, that I may sense Your presence, ready to go with me.

Help me to that state of perfect quietness for preparation. I do not know what the day holds, but I know this: I shall need You with me, Your fortifying strength within and around me, Your lamp of truth and wisdom as light for my path.

May Your words undergird me: "Be still and know that I am God." "You shall know the truth, and the truth shall set you free." "Be not a man-pleaser but as a servant of Christ doing the will of God from the heart." "Come to me, all who labor and are heavy laden, and I will give you rest."

My child, let these words of calm, of freedom, of priorities and assurance give you strength for the day. "Lo, I am with you always."

AUGUST 5

"And they were bringing children to Him, that He might touch them."
— Mark 10:13

From Fern:

My God, I am thinking today of "touch" and how much it means to
have the touch of a friend: hand shaking hand...a pat on the
shoulder...the warmth of a hug. O Lord, how much is communicated
by a touch! How we long for the touch of acceptance and
reassurance! These are the physical touches that convey messages to
our souls, but we are touched as well emotionally. We are touched by
a sad report and moved to sympathy. Our souls are touched as we are
encouraged by an expression of love and understanding.

Thank You, God, for the gift of touch! Thank You for the capacity
to reach out to touch another life as well as the capacity to respond
to touch.

How interwoven in all of life is the rhythm of reaching out and
responding, giving and receiving; the oceans' tide, the earth's
receiving seed and giving fruit, the female egg receiving sperm,
producing life.

Creator God, open our eyes continually that we may perceive the
unity of all life and our need and opportunity to participate by such a
small gesture as giving and receiving a touch.

AUGUST 6

"Thy word is a lamp to my feet and a light to my path."
— Psalms 119:105

From Fern:

Thy word, a lamp unto my feet. A lamp! A light for my way.

Oh, Father, how blessed we are by light. As the sun rises in the morning it sends rays to dispel the darkness and we SEE!

We see the way ahead. We see our surroundings. We see those whom we encounter.

In the beginning You said, "Let there be light," and the light shone. And now You say, "Let there be light," and the light shines literally and symbolically. For Your Holy Spirit lights the lives of those who seek, dispelling the negatives: the fear and distrust, the suspicions and anxieties, the hatreds, resentments, and prejudices.

And we see! We see those whom we have avoided. We "see" by understanding those whom we have not understood. We perceive the differences between us and grow to love and appreciate the individuality You have placed within us. Dear God, thank You for that light!

AUGUST 7

From Fern:

"Come into my presence with singing
and into my courts with praise, says the Lord.
For I am with you! With the Lord on your side,
what is there to fear?
It is the Father's good pleasure
to give you the kingdom."
– Psalms 100:2, 4; 56:11; Luke 12:32

"I have promised to care for you. I have assured you
that no problem too weighty shall confront you.
I do not send you out alone to face life.
I shall be with you, always!"
– 1 Peter 5:7; 1 Corinthians 10:13, Matthew 28:20

"What can man do to you, for all that is human
is for the moment, but in me is eternal life.
You have my book—these are the words of life.
See, I have given you the world,
and in your segment of the world I have made you king,
with complete freedom of will. You have dominion."
– Psalms 118:6; John 3:16, 20:30-31; Genesis 1:26

"Fear not! Go forth in confidence!
You are my beloved child!" – John 3:1

AUGUST 8

Settle into your sacred space, light your candle,
a long inhale of peace...a long exhale
and feel the stress leave your body...
...and start this day with a prayer from your heart to God's.

From Cat:

Heavenly Father, thank You for another day of life.

I thank You for opening doors that no man can close. I rest in the comfort of knowing Your immense love for all of Your children, of which I am one, and I feel Your love for me everywhere I go. I love You back.

I thank You that I don't have to worry about any injustices that have been done to me, because I know You see everything and I trust that You will take care, so I don't ever have to busy my mind with thoughts or actions that hurt myself or others. I know You see my heart, and what my heart's desires are, and I have faith that You will help me rise up to have them.

Give me strength to face my fears and turn them into an energy that propels me, never immobilizes me.

Let me see the good in everyone; and if there is something else that I need to see, let me feel Your gentle tap on my shoulder, which I know is the gift of intuition showing me when it is time to walk either toward or away from it. I understand the importance of blessing another and sending them on their way and to wish no one ill, no matter what, as it is truly the key to letting go.

Please illuminate my path and guide my earthly journey by giving me signs, and Lord, make them unmistakable. Let me be in tune with You and so connected to You that I feel calm and peaceful no matter what is going on around me.

Thank You for Your favor on my life, my day, on my every hour.

Father God, please heal the burdens of my heart. You know all I have been through, and it is bigger than I can carry on my own anymore. I ask You to take this hurt and anger from me so I can feel all that is good in my life and experience the joy You meant for me to live.

That having been said, if what I have been through is to teach me how to be closer to You, or to know You better, then it will have been worth all of it, and more.

I need You and I believe You are there for me, always. I believe.

I feel You there. I am ready now, to go out in the world and do great things, no matter how small. Let Your light shine bright through me so that I radiate Your Love and Grace to every person I meet, and in doing so, I delight in and honor You.

Amen.

AUGUST 9

"If we are faithless, he remains faithful."
– 2 Timothy 2:13

From Fern:

I created humankind in my image but the first man and wife contended with me for my position. Defying the image of love, their son killed his brother. By the time of Noah, humanity had grieved me to the heart, but I saved Noah who found favor in my sight. Later, in Sodom and Gomorrah and surrounding cities, I could not find even ten good men.

I heard the cries of my people in Egypt and rescued them with many miracles, but when their leader Moses was on the mountain, they gathered gold and built a calf to worship. For the sake of my promise to their forefathers, I did not destroy them then and there, but of those who started out, only Joshua and Caleb lived to enter the Promised Land.

Still my people resisted. They were always unfaithful, both priests and people, following the abomination of nations, even to polluting my house. Throughout the centuries I sent my servants, the prophets, to speak to them, but they beat and killed them. Then I reasoned, "I will send my Son. Surely they will respect Him." Even him they put to death.

O faithless people, how long? You who hear my voice, give ear to my teaching. Be my holy nation, my own people.

AUGUST 10

"For everything there is a season,
and a time for every matter under heaven."
– Ecclesiastes 3:1

From Fern:

Lord God, into Your hands I commit this day. It is full of tasks that I feel must be done, and yet, were this the last day of my life, and I knew that to be true, how important would they be?

Dear Lord, give me a sense of priorities; help me to sort and exclude from my life that which is trivial. I realize that I also must examine "trivial," for You are able to take what seems to me to be trivial— unimportant tasks or persons, minutes squandered in leisure—and transform them to great relevance.

I need Your guidance, Lord, in every moment and every decision. I need to be able to see from Your divine point of view an overview that encompasses the past, present, and consequences, all one.

I need to see beyond time, beyond this immediate day and what I think are its demands, and look to how it will affect the future.

Oh my God, thank You for going with me into the day and throughout its hours. I need You! Amen.

AUGUST 11

"So we do not lose heart. Though our outer nature is wasting away,
our inner nature is being renewed every day."
– 2 Corinthians 4:16

From Fern:

Dear Lord, Creator of all—that which is visible and that which is
invisible, the body as well as the soul—thank You that not ALL is
temporary. Thank You that while the mirror reveals a deterioration
of the outer self, there is confidence that the inner self is growing.
Forgetfulness may be frightening and frustrating but wisdom is
available—wisdom which does not have to be remembered but rises
to the need—wisdom which has come with the years in the trial and
error experience.

And while names of persons may slip the mind, love is there—that
steadfast love which has learned to overlook many things that
formerly frustrated. We become less judgmental. We develop more
patience because You have shown that many situations are worth the
waiting, many must evolve over a period of time; and some things
which we thought we could not live without, we did, and were the
better for it.

Yes, dear God, our inner selves *are* growing even though the outer
husk dies away. Thank You, for this realization is the promise and
assurance of eternal life!

AUGUST 12

"Let the words of my mouth and the meditation of my heart
be acceptable in thy sight, O Lord, my rock and my redeemer."
– Psalms 19:14

From Fern:

Lord, speak to me that I may speak the living echoes of what You
impart to me. Let the words of my mouth, springing from the
meditations of my heart, reflect the love, joy, truth, and kindness that
You have given me as fruits of Your Holy Spirit.

O my God! How hungry is our world for all of this! How lacking are
Your attributes of purity and goodness, justice and righteousness,
because we have neglected the first requirement—obedience. You
gave us the formula for right living, but we thought we knew better.
We have neglected our duty of dominion over the good earth and
have trespassed the laws that would have given peace and prosperity
for all.

I cannot change the world, dear God. I cannot even change me, but
by the transforming power of the Holy Spirit, my yielded spirit can be
made right.

And so, again, I submit my life to You. Recreate my heart that I may
resemble You. My corner of the world will thereby improve, and I
may see life with new courage and hope.

AUGUST 13

"We love because He first loved us."
– John 4:19

From Fern:

I love You, Eternal God, with the love You first gave to me. I do not remember when we first met. It seems to me that all my life I have known You, and I remember Jeremiah speaking thus about the covenant which You would write upon our hearts." (Jeremiah 31:33)

And yet it was many years before we walked together—years of going my own way, rebellious and stubborn. How patiently You waited! But when I turned I found You there beside me! I did not have to go looking. I had only to reach out, and I found Your hand and Your love reaching to me! And we began our walk together with my awareness of our relationship.

I still had to grow. I still had the consequences of my own ignorance, but You have never left me; and my love for You, my gratitude to You, has increased continually.

What shall today bring, dear Lord? Who will You bring into my life that I may share some of this love? What evidence will You give me of your presence? I can hardly wait! Lord God, let the day begin!

AUGUST 14

"We look not to the things that are seen
but to the things that are unseen;
for the things that are seen are transient,
but the things that are unseen are eternal."
— 2 Corinthians 4:18

From Fern:

O Lord my God, unto You I look for all the necessities of life—the true life. Not the shallow, narrow box of existence, but life of wisdom and beauty, of joy and adventure, the permanent life of faith and love.

Dear God, everything that has happened to me has had meaning when I can discern it. All has been beneficial when You teach me to evaluate it properly. All in the right time—like the construction of a dwelling, stone upon stone, structure upon foundation.

Continue to guide me as You have in the past. Help me to use the past as I face the unknown future, in confidence that there is meaning and purpose, in faith that I walk neither alone nor in uncharted lands. And I will give You the praise. I will tell others the interpretation of life that You give to me. I will sing of Your faithfulness that has existed in all time and is now alive and active in me.

Glory be to the Father, and to the Son who lived in history, and to the Holy Spirit who is always present tense.

AUGUST 15

"Everything you *have to have* actually owns you."
– Dr. Wayne Dyer

From Cat:

Oh, look! It's another inventory day! Yay!

Today's focus: your closet. (If that word puts a knot in your stomach, all the more reason for you not to skip over it and rush on to tomorrow instead.)

I have a feeling you might relate to this: When my closet is a cluttered mess, it's usually a tip-off that my mind and/or life is a cluttered mess too, filled with so much "stuff" that I can barely find the quality buried under all that quantity, let alone appreciate it. And running around accumulating new "stuff" only means bringing it home and cramming it in with all the other "stuff" so that in no time at all, it's exactly as unsatisfying as everything I already had.

It's no way to keep a closet and definitely no way to live a life. Time to get rid of the quantity to make sure there's plenty of room for the quality that will make a lasting difference.

Make *absolutely* no mistake about this: By "quality," I don't mean designer clothing any more than I mean "friends" who pretend to love you because they think you might be of use to them someday. I'm talking about clothes you feel and look good in and actually wear, no matter what label is sewn into them. I'm talking about real friends who are there for you through the best and worst times of your life, who let you just BE and who make you feel great about yourself, no matter what designer you're wearing, what kind of car you're driving, and what size flat-panel TV is wall-mounted in your living room.

I'm not a fan of the term "retail therapy," or any of the cutesy sayings that encourage people to overspend, get lured into the insanity of conspicuous consumption, and/or become addicted to the temporary distraction of shopping and then head home with the same problems they already had, and the added bonus of a maxed-out credit card. Legitimate therapy with the right therapist can

292

improve your life for the rest of your life. Retail therapy is a brief rush that won't even last until the next morning.

To keep from getting overwhelmed, look at your closet one item at a time with a focus on quality, not quantity, and the goal in mind to get it organized, uncluttered, and uncramped. Have a friend come help you who's good at this kind of thing if you want to actually make it fun. Don't even glance at the labels or give a thought to what you paid for them—if they're hanging there doing nothing but adding to the clutter, they're now worth officially $0.

Here's the yardstick: Keep what you truly enjoy and what makes you feel confident and comfortable when you're wearing it. Anything that falls under the following categories is OUT OF THERE, off to eBay or your favorite charity (and by the way, if you've never shopped at Goodwill, you don't know what you're missing):

"love the color, hate the way it fits"

"should work on me but doesn't"

"not sure what mood I was in when I bought this"

"looked great in the store/catalog"

"adorable purse, goes with absolutely nothing I own"

"these shoes are fabulous, as long as I don't have to actually walk in them"

"keep meaning to have this repaired/altered"

"might want to wear this someday"

"thought it would fit but didn't have time to try it on"

"hate it, but it was on sale, and/or I got a free tote bag with it"

And last, but not least...

"I have *how* many pairs of jeans?!"

Now, get those piles of clutter out of there ASAP and thank yourself for demanding the luxury (not too strong a word) of *simplifying* both your closet and your mind. And here's a great rule to keep it that way where your closet is concerned: For every new dress/purse/pair of shoes/whatever you buy, you have to come straight home and get rid of, by donating or selling on eBay, a dress/purse/pair of shoes/whatever that you already own. If that makes you think twice about buying it, so much the better.

Whether we're talking about closets or the infinitely more important subject of our emotional and spiritual health, *learning to want what we have*, once we've weeded out the debris, is one of the most fulfilling, most lasting gifts we can give ourselves.

Dear God, I'm excited today
to get rid of the useless clutter in my life,
to make room for the true quality
You intended for me from the beginning,
and I thank You for clarity I need to do it
and do it *right*. Amen.

AUGUST 16

"In the beginning was the Word,
and the Word was with God,
and the Word was God."
– John 1:1

From Fern:

Jesus came as Word, expression, revelation. Words have power. I spoke the earth into being. I spoke and plagues occurred in Egypt. I healed; I commanded nature by my word.

Your words also have power. Learn to use them wisely and appropriately. Avoid the godless chatter and contradictions of what is falsely called knowledge, for by professing it some have missed the mark as regards the faith. Let no evil talk come out of your mouth, but only such as is good for edifying, as fits the occasion, that it may impart grace to all who hear.

Your words reveal how well or poorly you have bridled your tongue. You put bits into mouths of horses that they may obey. Thus you guide their whole bodies. The tongue is a small member in the body and must likewise be bridled. No human being can tame the tongue. Consider the good it can do or the hurt it can cause.

Your words reveal what is in your heart. Therefore, keep your heart pure. Pray as the Psalmist prayed: "Create in me a clean heart, O God, and put a new and right spirit within me. Take not thy holy Spirit from me."

AUGUST 17

"He pours contempt upon princes...
but He raises the needy out of affliction."
– Psalms 107:40-41

From Fern:

Dear Lord, how gracious You are, how sensitive to our needs. "Princes" are those in power, in control, whose self-sufficiency renders them ignorant of their need of You.

Throughout the Bible are illustrations of "My grace is sufficient...my power is made perfect in weakness."

Now, God, I suddenly know that the self-sufficient prince and the afflicted needy are not two persons or even two classes, but my own self. Your word has rightly described the times in my life when all is well, and I become vain, confident of my adequacy to meet life.

Then something happens to remind me of my limitations, my mortality. I become "needy" and rush to You.

Thank You, God, that You meet me there! Never has impatience been Your answer. Never have You refused me in my need. As I grow and mature, help me constantly to be aware of that need. Help me to learn from recurrent experiences that my own sufficiency is temporary, that I must never go far from the position of need. In Jesus' spirit, help me live.

AUGUST 18

"As they were going along the road, a man said to Him,
'I will follow you wherever you go.'
And Jesus said to him, 'Foxes have holes,
and birds of the air have nests;
but the Son of man has nowhere to lay his head.'"
– Luke 9:57-58

From Fern:

Compassionate Christ, it is hard to watch the struggles of those dear to me! It is perhaps like watching birth as new life struggles into this realm. But You have also made known in the hatching of an egg that to help the new chick is to weaken it and bring it unprepared into life.

Help me, Savior, to apply this as well to spiritual rebirth and life. I tend to want to help, to give those I love the easy way but You are bringing to me anew the realization that was not Jesus' way. Your way works. Your way brings fulfillment and right relationships. It offers no false illusions.

Bless those for whom I care, dear God. Watch over them in their foolishness as You watch over me in mine. Help them and me to reevaluate priorities, to clarify that when we make a decision for You, we automatically make many decisions. What we have regarded as Your "hard sayings" become easy when we have specified one goal.

My life is Yours, Lord. I reaffirm it, but I need Your help to apply that to every instance.

AUGUST 19

"...Walking and leaping and praising God."
– Acts 3:8

From Fern:

Dear Lord, today I met a man who could not walk and I thought of the one whom Peter and John had healed. Today I talked with one whose hearing was impaired and I thought of Your restoring hearing. Today I read for one who was blind and I thought of Your bringing sight.

But I also thought of these gifts in my own life and how unmindful I am of their wonder. The man healed by Peter and John expressed his joy by walking and leaping and praising God, rightly discerning that his gift was from You.

Dear Jesus, help me to know that this is not a history lesson. Help me to see that this happens every day: I walk! I speak! I hear and see!

I should not be less appreciative, but more, so that I have not lost and must regain these gifts! I should leap and praise God with every step. My whole life should be—and shall this day—be one of thankfulness. Help me, God, not to hold these blessings to myself but to use them in service of the Giver. This is an expression of praise.

AUGUST 20

"They cried to the Lord, and He answered them."
— Psalms 99:6b

From Fern:

Dear Jesus, each day I bring to You these persons on my prayer list. I do not have specific requests of what I want for them. They are my loved ones, my special people, and I want for them what is best. I want love in their lives, and joy and success in their ventures—but day by day, I see little happening by way of change. In fact, I have sometimes wondered if they would do better not on my list.

My child, do you remember those years ago when you first gave me your life? What person came to your mind? One you had not thought of for years; one who faithfully prayed for you beginning as long ago as your high school days, decades before.

Do not be impatient—submit to the timing of God and God's eternal plan. Do not abandon your people, for by your prayers great good is done. Your prayers to me, my thoughts to those for whom you pray—a triangle of love. Your thoughts to me, mine planted in them, become as their own thoughts and through their thoughts, change begins. Be steadfast, watch, and wait.

AUGUST 21

"She did not know it was I who gave..."
— Hosea 2:8

From Fern:

O God, You are our Source! From You comes light and food and drink. From You comes all that we need to sustain life and from You comes very life itself.

Help me, dear God, to know this with a deeper and deeper knowledge. Help me to see that behind every situation in life or death is Your loving hand. It sometimes brings joy; help me to attribute it to You. If someone brings pain, help me to adopt the attitude of David that it may hold a lesson You would have me learn.

Keep me looking steadily to Your light, Jesus—the light of Your wisdom and counsel. Neither textbooks nor professionals shall be the source of my knowledge unless they be guided by Your Spirit. Neither banks nor investments shall be the source of my security, for I shall see all provisions as having come from You.

You have promised peace. You have promised to meet all my needs, be they material or spiritual.

Help me grow in this awareness, dear Lord, I pray.

AUGUST 22

"You have the ability to choose your reactions."
– Steve Maraboli

From Cat:

On any given day, life hands us countless opportunities to choose how to deal with circumstances we can't control. And yes, hard as it is to believe sometimes, it really is a choice. We can blow them up into crises that eat up hours of our day and everyone else's, hours we'll never get back, or we can shrug and keep moving and put no more energy into those non-events than they deserve.

I know. There are some psychological disorders that make it impossible to "not sweat the small stuff." If you suffer from one or more of them, I genuinely wish you a great therapist to give you the help you need, and God bless you.

But for the rest of us, how about a little perspective, a sense of proportion? It's a guarantee that life is going to hand all of us more than enough genuine crises, so why on earth go out of our way to create them out of what really boils down to nothing in the bigger picture? Are we really that desperate for attention? Do we really have nothing more worthwhile to focus on? Wouldn't it cause us and the people around us a whole lot less stress if we *chose* to de-escalate situations in which the stakes are so relatively low, and put a higher premium on living calm, peaceful lives we can truly enjoy?

We all know people who seem to look for things to explode over or get indignant about. Have you ever envied them? Me neither. Instead, haven't you found yourself rolling your eyes and wishing they'd stop trying to involve you in their drama? That's not the reaction I'm striving for in people—how about you?

So, several years ago, when I decided I needed a quick, easy reminder to not let trivia dictate my life and to save my energy for real crises, I developed the habit of jumping straight to what have become three of my favorite words in the English language:

"AND SO WHAT?"

Here are a few examples:

Someone cuts you off in traffic. AND SO WHAT? (If they keep this up, and they will, let someone else deal with them, and they will.)

There's a long line at the grocery store. AND SO WHAT? (No one, including the cashier, is probably any happier about it than you are, and it's costing you, what, an extra three minutes? Sorry, it doesn't really rise to the "nightmare" level.)

Someone you thought was a friend betrayed you in some way. AND SO WHAT? (In fact, thanks for the information. If you'd known that's who they were, you wouldn't have become friends with them in the first place. Good riddance.)

Someone insults you to your face. AND SO WHAT? (Their opinion of you matters because...why, exactly?)

Someone you're attracted to doesn't ask you out as you'd hoped. AND SO WHAT? (Who wants someone who's not as interested in you as you are in them? That sounds like a fun relationship, doesn't it?)

You didn't get a job you wanted. AND SO WHAT? (Disappointing, sure, but you can't lose something you never had to begin with. Next!)

You get the idea. Those three words work in your favor all over the place. I can't even count the number of times they fill my "thought bubble" in the course of a day, or calculate the amount of stress they save me and all the people around me who just plain don't want to hear about it, nor should they.

Try "AND SO WHAT?" starting today, in situations that currently have the potential to send you into a worthless snit, and keep right on using it for however long it takes to make *choosing* stress-free reactions to everyday annoyances your new, healthier habit.

Dear God, please help me today
to keep the events in my life in perspective
and, as best I can, to live by Your words:
"Give thanks in all circumstances." Amen.

AUGUST 23

"You shall not take the name of the Lord in vain..."
— Exodus 20:7

"...for the name of the Lord is Holy."
— Isaiah 57:15

From Fern:

So sacred was my name to the Israelites that they did not speak it. "Holy and terrible is his name!" When Moses asked my name, I answered, "I AM WHO I AM." Not I WAS or I WILL BE. I am the God of Abraham, the God of Isaac, and the God of Jacob—and I am your God. I AM depicts the nature as well as the identification. Thus Jacob's name was changed after he had wrestled through the night with an angel. He had been Jacob, Supplanter, and became Israel, "God rules."

Hearing your name arouses you to respond. The speaker has honored you to call you by name. It is therefore a serious transgression to use the Lord's name lightly, particularly in prayer. Jesus promised, "Whatever you ask in my name, I will do it." That is, whatever you ask that accords with Jesus' nature, which is to do the will of the Father, will be honored. When you lift a name to me in prayer, I know of whom you speak. The Lord knows who are His. I am the good shepherd. I know my own and my own know me. Your name is written in the book of life which will be opened. At that time many who sleep shall awake—some of everlasting life, some to shame and everlasting contempt, being repaid according to what they have done in this life on earth.

AUGUST 24

"When we cry 'Abba! Father!' it is the spirit Himself
bearing witness with our spirit that we are children of God..."
– Romans 8:15b-16

From Fern:

O Lord, I think of the little boy who wanted nothing from his daddy but to be with him. Abba (the equivalent of Daddy), may I so come to You today—nothing to say, no want to express, all my thoughts already known to You. Simply let me bask in the sense of Your presence.

LOVE fills the air. It pervades my spirit. It reaches to my very depths and cleanses and purifies me. I shall be an expression of this love all the day long.

GOODNESS surrounds me. It, too, pervades my spirit and I am changed by its presence. I shall be influenced all day as I mingle with people, as I observe their actions and hear their words. My interpretation of them will be affected by this time of exposure to the goodness of God.

PEACE fills my heart, a peace beyond what the world can give; peace as an assurance that God has the ultimate answers, and love and good will have the final word! Thank You, Father.

AUGUST 25

"Behold, I send you out as sheep in the midst of wolves;
so be wise as serpents and innocent as doves."
– Matthew 10:16

From Fern:

Dear God, I am praying today for discernment—the ability to penetrate the curtains that surround me, to discern first of all Your will for my life—not only in total but in every day, every minute and every decision.

I realize, dear Lord, the constancy of change, that with every choice I make of what to do with what I have been given—time, talent, money, thought, energy, skills—I move either toward or away from the idea You had of my purpose when You created me. And so I ask for the ability to discern what that is.

I also ask, God, for discernment in regard to other persons. I am easily deceived. A little flattery will get them anywhere with me.

I do not know how others perceive me. I am willing to trust them, but I pray that it may be deliberate, knowing acceptance, instead of blind trust.

Help me to see as You see—into hearts, rather than relying only on outward appearance and spoken words.

AUGUST 26

"Praise God from whom all blessings flow!"
– The Doxology

From Fern:

God, help me to interpret "blessings." Help me to see them in the broader view, to know that not only what seem to me to be blessings of health, prosperity, and good fortune are rightly so classified; but that everything in life is a blessing—even pain, disappointment, and loss.

It requires a vision beyond the immediate to know that, dear Lord. It requires a faith in the loving nature of a Parent who has a plan, in a God who can bring good from all situations.

It requires the kind of love that permits discipline in order to turn the confused and the lost onto the right course.

O, dear God, give me: that vision, that faith, that love, along with the patience that knows that in Your sight a day is as a thousand years and a thousand years as a day. Guide me, Lord, I pray.

AUGUST 27

"It is better to take refuge in the Lord
than to put confidence in man."
— Psalms 118:8

From Fern:

Jesus, Lord and Savior, thank You for Your presence, Your nearness
in the Holy Spirit. Thank You for making me aware of angels who go
before me, preparing the way, and then shielding me as I go through
it.

Thank You for the directions, the relations, the understandings that
come in the night. Even as my body takes its rest my mind, relaxed, is
more receptive and You speak to me of things I need to know.

You who neither slumber nor sleep, You who are never preoccupied
or distant, You who know my total self—past, present, future—and
accept me as I am! Of what person could any of this be true!

Yes, I shall put my trust in You who have never failed me, who have
stood beside me through every experience; we go forth into this day
and every day, together. Thank You, Jesus!

AUGUST 28

"Do everything in the name of the Lord Jesus."
– Colossians 3:17

From Fern:

Lord Jesus, once again You give us help in knowing how to live abundant, joy-filled lives. In answer to what shall I do, how shall I feel toward this person, dare I retaliate for this wrong, You reply, "Do everything in the name of Jesus."

> Can I get even, in the name of Jesus?
> Can I be prejudiced in the name of Jesus?
> Can I do anything less than loving, in the name of Jesus?
> NO! He is my norm.
> He is my way.
> By His nature I may test my motivations.
> Whatever is inconsistent with His divine nature cannot be done in His name.

So I perceive, dear Lord, that this is not only a directive through which to have a proper attitude. It is a personal test that I may apply, and subtly it is an acknowledgement of Whose I am, and from whence comes my ability. Thank you, dear Lord!

AUGUST 29

"Listen to your being.
It is continuously giving you hints; it is a still, small voice."
– Osho

From Cat:

It was December of 2006. I was in Florida, visiting my mom and my sister, loving them, loving the sun, loving that I had a week more of this mindless luxury to look forward to before I flew back to the cold, relentless busyness of winter in New York.

So when that still, small voice in the back of my head starting whispering something about getting on a plane to New York that day, a week early—in fact, ASAP—I did everything but put on ear muffs trying to block it out. No way was I leaving, and whatever/whoever this voice was could just go bug someone who didn't need a vacation as much as I did.

But that voice wasn't about to be ignored. It kept getting less and less still and small and more and more insistent, until finally, downright angry about it, I went through the motions of calling the airlines, counting on them to laugh in my face at the suggestion that I could catch a last-minute flight during the holidays.

Well, they didn't laugh. I was in luck. They had one seat available on the next flight out. One seat. The words "I'll take it" were out of my mouth before I could stop them, and I was still convinced I'd lost my mind when the plane touched down in New York.

And because of that voice I listened to in spite of myself, I had the honor of spending my dog Chica's last hours on this earth with her before she suddenly and peacefully passed away after a very long, exquisite life. I'll treasure those hours as long as I live, and thank God for the voice that said, "Go home. You're needed there."

The late spiritual teacher and psychic Sylvia Browne, in her bestselling book *The Other Side and Back*, wrote about her belief that before we come here from our real Home to start a new lifetime, we write a detailed blueprint, or chart, to help us fulfill our specific plans for this particular incarnation. According to her, that "voice" and the "coincidences" it helps to create are our spirits, remembering the chart they wrote and urging us toward the big and small goals we designed for ourselves, because they all matter. I love the thought that Chica and I charted each other and that when it counted, I remembered my promise to be with her when her time here ended.

There was one aspect of my chart that Sylvia especially got a kick out of. As most of you know, a very long time ago, I was married to David Hasselhoff, who, during our marriage, starred in the series *Knight Rider*, playing a character named Michael Knight. After our divorce I moved to New York, where I married an actor named...Michael Knight. As Sylvia said, "You forgot to remind yourself when you wrote your chart to be sure to wait for the right Michael Knight!"

Another philosophy of Sylvia's that I love deals with the issue of fulfilling the purpose we came here to accomplish. That gets confusing for all of us, I know, but according to her, when you cut through the details and get down to basics, we're here to simply learn to overcome and defeat negativity.

Wouldn't it be great if we could all just accomplish no more than that? Negativity gains us nothing, earns us nothing, and gets us nowhere. It fills space with darkness where light belongs; and every moment we spend indulging in a negative thought, or word, or act is a moment spent betraying the reason we're here.

That life's purpose we worry about and fret over and endlessly search for? In the end, Sylvia said, it's no more complicated than a formula I think we should all be required to memorize and follow every day of our lives:

Do good,
love God,
then shut up and go Home.

AUGUST 30

"We piped to you, and you did not dance;
we wailed and you did not mourn."
– Matthew 11:17

From Fern:

When I was on earth, people tried to box me in by their expectations. But I could not be contained within their box. They were like children calling to their playmates, "We piped to you, and you did not dance; we wailed, and you did not mourn." John was an ascetic, neither eating nor drinking, and they said, "He was a demon." I came eating and drinking and gained the reputation of being a drunkard and a glutton, a friend of tax collectors and sinners. Some would not believe I was the Christ because I came from Galilee, and they said that I should have come from my ancestor David's city of Bethlehem. Some indicated that their belief could be influenced by my doing signs and miracles, but I was not a magician. I had long before met the temptation to gain followers by doing the spectacular, by quoting from the scriptures, "You shall not tempt the Lord God."

No, I burst the man-made boxes as new wine bursts old skins. I could not be confined by the expectations of humans but I fit perfectly into those of God. For centuries, God had given the prophets very specific details of my life, and I came to fulfill that prophecy. I declared that not one iota, not a dot, would pass from the law or prophets until all was accomplished. It was all accomplished in me.

AUGUST 31

"Speaking the truth in love,
we are to grow up in every way
into him who is the head, into Christ."
– Ephesians 4:15

From Fern:

Christ in heaven and in my heart, Paul has held before us a challenge that only expands upon Jesus' own, that we be perfect as our heavenly Father is perfect. Moses called the people of his day to be holy and his words came from You.

We know, dear Lord, that you would not call Your children to impossibility. There is a way by which this can be done, and You have provided the way: being filled with <u>You</u>. Being *filled* with You— not simply guided by or reaching toward but, filled with Your very Spirit, we will become more and more You as we become less and less our selves.

Savior, help me to know this in a greater way than ever before, to get my*self* out of the way and submit to the holiness and perfection within me. Help me to grow into Christ as He grows in my life. Let His Spirit guide and rule me until all my expressions reflect Him. For you are my Lord, my light, my life. From You comes my wisdom and my strength. Spirit of truth, guide me this day.

SEPTEMBER

SEPTEMBER 1

"Having gifts that differ
according to the grace given to us,
let us use them."
– Romans 12:6

From Fern:

Father, these words remind me that You do not call equipped persons.

> You equip those whom You call.
> This I know to be true! I do not go into this day alone.
> I do not face the challenges or opportunities alone.
> That to which You call me, for that You will equip me.

Tune my sensitivity, Lord, that I may be alert for Your training and receptive to Your equipping.

Gear up my courage and confidence so that when I am asked to do a great task, far beyond my own capacity, I will not back away with excuses but boldly accept and give You the glory when You enable me to accomplish it.

Spirit, help me to realize Your divine law that supersedes the physical law, that takes me into a new realm of life—life without limitations while yet aware of the need to attend to what You assign me here.

SEPTEMBER 2

"And all who believed were together."
– Acts 2:44

From Fern:

Savior, I thank You today for my friends, for those whom You have brought into my life, sharing my convictions and commitment.

We become a chain of love and service that extends throughout the world. Sometimes our efforts seem unproductive and we need the encouragement of one another. Occasionally we have a victory for You, and it is enriched as we share it with others.

You knew that would be true, for in the beginning You said, "It is not good that man should be alone." You inspired the Hebrews' writer to say, "Let us consider how to stir up one another to love and good works, not neglecting to meet together, but encouraging one another."

Dear Lord, let me not be one who only receives encouragement; let me give it as well. Increase my sensitivity to know when a fellow worker needs encouragement. Bind us together in the oneness for which Jesus prayed, and we shall give You the praise in His holy name.

SEPTEMBER 3

"He is not far from each one of us."
– Acts 17:27b

From Fern:

O God, You are not beyond my reach. Though beyond my sight, You are not beyond knowing! You care for me! You know what is happening in my life and You are with me to help me through it!

Blessed Lord, Master, Savior, earthly relatives and friends may fail. They, like myself, are sometimes less than they choose to be. They are not always available when my needs are great.

But You, dear God, are dependable! Your guidance is always ready to be used. It comes through the words, inspired by You, in the Bible. It came as your Word, in Jesus. It comes in visions, thoughts, and nudges, day and night. Thank You! I am not alone! When life seems overwhelming, You are here. When there is joy too great to be contained, You are here; and as I bring it to You, it increases.

Lord God, life is too heavy for me to bear alone. The swings from burden to joy are too wide for me to handle. Thank You for going with me through it all. I love You, dear Lord.

SEPTEMBER 4

"...Choose life..."
– Deuteronomy 30:19

From Fern:

My child, the choice is yours. I have laid a banquet before you and pray that you will feast upon that which nourishes the body, mind, and soul; for there is also garbage—the food that leads to deterioration—physically, mentally, and morally. The change is not immediate. It is a process that corrupts steadily and subtly. But as a loving parent desires the best for the child, so I pray that you desire the good. Garbage kills, but my food brings life that is victorious over death.

O that my beloved would choose life! O that you had a mind to fear me and keep my commandments that it might go well with you; for the consequences of disobedience produce sorrow for you and for me. I have longed to gather you to me as a hen gathers her brood under her wings.

Beloved, choose life. Walk with me in paths of righteousness— rightly using the life you have been given. I love you and desire the best for you.

Choose life that you may truly live.

SEPTEMBER 5

"If you don't ask, the answer will always be no."
– Nora Roberts

From Cat:

My friend Lindsay and I were sitting with a lovely group of women we didn't know at a reception following a preview of Debbie Reynolds' second Hollywood Memorabilia Auction. I happened to be wearing a treasured, beautiful eagle feather I'd attached to an earring, and one of the women complimented me on it. The conversation went exactly like this:

Woman: "Oh, I love your feather!"
Me: "Thank you."
Woman (without missing a beat): "Can I have it?"

It wasn't the follow up I was expecting to my thank you, and there was a long silence, during which I turned to Lindsay with a look on my face she still laughs about to this day. Finally, I turned back to the woman and simply said, "Uh...no."

While I recommend against asking total strangers to give you their accessories, and against any other silly requests that are pretty much guaranteed to fail—dropping out of high school and applying for a teaching position at Harvard, for example, or auditioning for the Los Angeles Philharmonic when you don't play an instrument—I've been inspired by and followed the advice "If you don't ask, the answer will always be no" since the first time I heard it years ago.

Believe me, I know the drill of trying to work up the nerve to ask the right person for help with a career move or dream, or even just for a personal favor. I remember the hours of anxiety I used to waste having imaginary conversations with the person I wanted a "yes" from, trying to anticipate how I would word the request, how they might respond, how I might respond to their response, and, and, and. And when I say "waste," I mean *"waste"*! Have you ever known anyone who succeeded at anything as a result of an imaginary conversation with themselves? Me neither.

If what you're asking for is reasonable, and you can be counted on to come through like a champion if you do get a "yes," don't just sit there—go for it!

If what you're asking is a personal favor, the rule of thumb is, "Would I do the same for them if the situation were reversed?" If you would, ask away. If you wouldn't, frankly, no fair asking in the first place. In fact, I won't even accept a favor from someone I know I'd never repay in kind. It's like taking on a debt I have no intention of paying, and where's the honesty and integrity in that?

In the end, look at it this way: If you ask and the answer is no, the worst that can happen, other than a few minutes of disappointment (and keep that brief!), is that you're in exactly the same position you were before you asked, so you've really lost nothing at all.

"If you don't ask, the answer will always be no," simple and obvious as it is, has provided me with more wonderful experiences than I can begin to count, not to mention saving me a ridiculous amount of self-inflicted anxiety. Whatever big or small dilemma you've been struggling with, trying to work up the nerve to ask for something you're confident you've earned and you'll make good on, today's the day! Either a yes or a no is a whole lot better than not knowing, don't you think?

Dear God, I could use some extra courage today as I ask
for something that's important to me.
Please help me ask with grace and clarity,
respond to "yes" with gratitude,
and accept "no" as a positive sign that I can now
put that question mark behind me and move on. Amen.

SEPTEMBER 6

"The foolishness of God is wiser than men
and the weakness of God is stronger than men."
– 1 Corinthians 1:20, 25

From Fern:

Be aware of the difference between worldly and spiritual wisdom. In the beginning, God created the heavens and the earth. No human being in all the ages, with all the advanced technology, has ever exhausted what is to be explored. The natural laws remain stable, the basis of all discovery. The wise person recognizes this. In the beginning, God gave the laws by which humankind can live harmoniously with God, with fellow beings and self. These were written for your instruction, that by steadfastness and by the encouragement of scriptures you may have hope. They have never been changed. They are still reliable guides for wholeness. The wise person lives by them.

In the beginning, God was active in Spirit through whom is transmitted God's wisdom. The unspiritual person does not receive the gifts of the Spirit for they are folly to him, and he is not able to understand them because they are spiritually discerned. Where earthly wisdom reigns there is disorder; God's wisdom is pure, peaceable, gentle, open to reason, full of mercy and good fruits, without uncertainty or insincerity.

SEPTEMBER 7

"...He is a chosen instrument of mine..."
– Acts 9:15

From Fern:

Dear Lord, You have always chosen the least likely: the weak Gideon through whom to show Your strength; the elderly Abraham and Sarah through whom to show that procreation is according to Your timing, not that of humankind; the common and uneducated disciples to bring good news to the world. Into the mouth of Moses, a stutterer, You provided a tongue for leadership; into the mind of Jeremiah, a babe in the womb, You injected Your message for the world.

Divine Wisdom, Your choices would not be ours because we look at what is and not what can be. We look at the outside and judge from a worldly point of view. We do not see what can happen to a life yielded to Your re-creation and empowerment.

You, dear God, have chosen me. To what You call me, I cannot guess. But these examples remind me that to whatever task You assign me, You will equip me. I do not go in my strength, for You will give me Yours. I do not rely on my abilities, for You will provide. What an adventure as You lead the way!

SEPTEMBER 8

"The Spirit of God was moving..."
— Genesis 1:2

From Fern:

O God, with what anticipation do I begin this day; for the scriptures have reminded me that Your Spirit was not only moving at the time of creation, but is moving now! Results were apparent as Your Spirit of love and truth moved over the face of the waters. How marvelous to know that these qualities are built into the framework of creation!

Holy Spirit, You were moving throughout the Old Testament, creating new from old, stirring the prophets to hear and speak the message of God for the world. You became human in Jesus that we might hear and see Your word, that Your nature might be revealed.

Then, dear Jesus, You left Your Spirit who is *now* moving among us! We sense the presence. We see the results of re-creation power as a new person appears where the old had been. New life! New zest! Whole groups, whole congregations, come alive as You sweep through their midst. It is NOW! It is happening! We do not know where to expect You next. Keep me alert that I may not miss Your coming.

SEPTEMBER 9

"Be strong, and let your heart take courage,
all you who wait for the Lord."
— Psalms 31:24

From Fern:

Dear God, "wait(ing) for the Lord," or "upon the Lord," are familiar phrases in Your word. How hard it is to wait! How hard to have patience and to trust that behind the scenes, beyond sight, things are happening!

Slow me down, Lord. Help me to know that life moves on as days and weeks flow into another progressively. Events and situations evolve. Preparations must be made and I need not be aware of each aspect.

So I lift my prayers in confidence, because You are more knowledgeable and even more concerned than I, because I know Your power to bring changes, and in some mysterious way to bring all things to a good conclusion.

Increase my faith, God. "I believe, help my unbelief." Help me know that my prayers *are* effective, that blessings *are* coming into lives, changes *are* occurring even though at this time I see no evidence. I must accept on faith.

Praise You for hearing, caring, and responding!

SEPTEMBER 10

"I have prayed for you
that your strength may not fail..."
– Luke 22:32

From Fern:

Jesus, *You* are praying for *me*! You are interceding for me! You are my Advocate in the court of justice. Beyond where I can go, You are there!

O my Lord, how comforting that is, for life is not easy. Decisions become less and less clear. The gray expands where black and white, wrong and right, seemed once so well defined.

Thank You for the strength You give me! Thank You for life that has shown me the invariable truth of Your promise that good does come from all things for those who love the Lord and are called according to His purpose.

Knowing all of this, Jesus, I can relax. I can trust. I can rest in the knowledge that I do not have the last word—that my judgment which is often flawed is not final; for Love and Truth are always present.

These, at the foundation of creation remain central to the operation of the universe. It was thus before I came into the world. It shall be thus after I leave. I pass through, sustained by Your prayers, guided by Your wisdom. Thank You, Jesus!

SEPTEMBER 11

"We are His workmanship,
created in Christ Jesus for good works..."
– Ephesians 2:10

From Fern:

Dear Lord, I, too, ask, "What must we do to be doing the works of God?" There are many voices begging for my time, my energy, my dedication. There is a sharp contrast between my hurried dash from project to project, concern to concern, and the steady pace of Jesus. He always had time to *see* persons of low and high degree and the impact of His words on them. He withdrew for long periods of prayer.

God, teach me so to live. You have given the answer to the question: "This is the work of God, that you believe in Him whom He has sent." Believing manifests in action, but help me to have every action spring from that source. Help me to rely on the Spirit within, for the Spirit is focused and prioritized.

Give me calmness for the day, and the ability to concentrate fully on its demands. You have clarified for me that I can neither project ahead nor change what has gone before. You have given me one minute at a time. Help me to live it fully, focused on the One in whose name the good works are done.

SEPTEMBER 12

"I will no longer allow anyone to manipulate my mind
and control my life in the name of love."
– Don Miguel Ruiz

From Cat:

Years ago the Olay company came up with a great slogan for their face creams and body lotions: "Love The Skin You're In." At first, it just made me want to buy their products. The more I thought about it, the more I realized it's a pretty foolproof philosophy in general.

I'll tell you the truth (always) as the founder of Cat Cosmetics: skin care and beauty products are wonderful, and no one loves them more than I do. But even the most renowned beauties in the world will back me up on the fact that falling in love with the *real* skin you're in works from the inside out. There's nothing you can buy at your favorite department store or send away for with "three easy payments" that's going to make a lasting difference in the kind of self-confidence it takes to say to yourself and everyone around you, "I love who I am even more today than I did yesterday and almost as much as I will tomorrow, because I am a work of art in progress." No product exists or ever will that gives you the substance it takes to live up to your full, beautiful, God-given potential.

One of several books that made a lasting impression on me in my never-ending effort to love the skin I'm in was *The Four Agreements: A Practical Guide to Personal Freedom* by Don Miguel Ruiz.

I was still making my living as an actress when I read it, and take it from someone who's been there, all the hair, make-up, wardrobe and breast implants on earth can't get you through the often brutal rejection you face when you're going through one audition after another. "Too tall"; "too short"; "too fat"; "too skinny"; "too flat-chested"; "too busty"; "too blonde"; "not blonde enough"; "not good enough/just plain wrong"; "unprepared"; "over-prepared"; "too sexy"; "not sexy enough"—you name it, you hear it all in the course of an acting career. But I'm grateful in so many ways for all that career gave me, including the best lesson of all: Without building a strong internal identity to fall back on, in any career, in *life*, you're just faking it and hoping no one will notice.

The Four Agreements helped reinforce that fact for me at a time when I really needed reminding. I highly recommend it, but in the meantime, with apologies to Mr. Ruiz for over-simplifying it, those four agreements basically boil down to:

1) Never make assumptions. (You really have no idea what others are thinking unless you ask, and the truth is, your mind hardly ever jumps to the right assumptions. You can only operate effectively by *knowing* what is, not by guessing.)

2) Always do your best. (Putting yourself in a constant position of wondering how much better something might have gone if you'd really thrown your shoulder into it leads to nothing but perpetual disappointment in yourself.)

3) Never take anything personally. (A hard one, I know, because so much of what goes on around us feels *very* personal. But as *The Four Agreements* wisely points out, nothing others do is ever because of you. What others say and do is a projection of their own reality and really has nothing to do with you at all.)

4) Be impeccable with your word. (Squandering your credibility on the nonsense of lies and broken promises is like squandering an essential part of your soul, and that's a higher price to pay than any of us can afford.)

Today I want you to take a step toward falling in love with the skin you're in...without spending a dime or looking in the mirror.

> Dear God, help me to never be neglectful or insulting
> to You, my Creator, by being neglectful or insulting
> to the beautiful spirit You gave me,
> where my true beauty resides
> and where You live in me. Amen.

SEPTEMBER 13

"He who does not take up his cross and follow me
is not worthy of me."
– Matthew 10:38

From Fern:

There is a cost to discipleship and only those willing to bear the cost will remain. To Ananias I said, "Go to the house of Judas and find a man of Tarsus named Saul. He is a chosen instrument of mine; I will show you how much he must suffer for the sake of my name." Do not think I have come to bring peace but a sword. Allegiance to me will cause division, but he who does not take up his cross and follow me is not worthy of me.

To those who declared impulsively, "I will follow you wherever you go," I had to remind them of hardships. To those who were attracted but procrastinated, I said, "Leave your former life and go proclaim the kingdom." To those who came reluctantly, I had to say that they were not ready for the kingdom of God.

Spreading my word is like the sowing of seeds. Some fall on packed earth and take no root, some on rocky soil and take root, but there is no depth. Some fall among thorns that, like the cares and delights of the world, choke them. But some fall on good soil and bring forth grain! I offer life and he who loses his life for my sake will find it.

SEPTEMBER 14

"A new commandment I give to you,
that you love one another,
as I have loved you..."
– John 13:34

From Fern:

Dear Jesus, Master, Lord of my life, *one* commandment You have given, *one* requirement only, to replace and encompass all that have gone before. It is new, in the sense that love for God and one another has new application and new depth of meaning; for You injected into the command the powerful two letter word "as."

As You loved, so You bid me, Your disciple, to love. You gave command, example, ability, because You bestowed upon me Your Spirit of love.

Help me, Jesus, to read of Your love more personally than I have until now. Help me to note its constancy, particularly extended to those whom society has labeled unlovable. Reach into my life to remove any shred of separation from others, in prejudice or resentment, in placing them in a lower or higher regard than myself. Remind me of Your compassionate forgiveness, "They know not what they do."

My Father, this very day I will have opportunity to practice all of this. Help me, I pray.

SEPTEMBER 15

"He...rebuked the wind and the raging waters;
the storm subsided, and all was calm."
– Luke 8:24

From Fern:

Lord Jesus, You who still storms and command demons, yet bid little children to come; You who have the greatest of powers and the gentlest of natures, be with me as I seek Your guidance for this day. Walk with me through it. Furnish my mind with thoughts consistent with Your purity. Give my hands work that promotes Your kingdom on earth as it is in heaven. My Lord, it is so easy for my feet to slip off the path; for my mouth to utter the unkind, impatient remarks. "I need Thee every hour."

Do You know what I want? I want this very day to have the opportunity to speak to others about my relationship to You, about the important role You play in my life. Do I know how it will happen? Yes, by my being intentional. By determining that I *will* do this and then listening for the opportunities You give me to witness to Your love and nearness in my life. By fixing my mind upon You and the way in which You lived, with Your priorities in their proper order. God, the Father, always came first; Your purpose of telling about and bringing persons into the kingdom was Your underlying motive for all that You did and all that You were. Help me so to live, I pray.

SEPTEMBER 16

"...The things that are seen are transient
but the things that are unseen are eternal."
– 2 Corinthians 4:18

From Fern:

My child, I have bid you to come to me to share your life, your whole life. Do not ignore or disdain the body, for I created it. When Jesus came to earth as the ultimate revelation, he came in a body. He used human form to relate to people, to express lessons of the meaning of life.

You have been given a body. Use it as Jesus did, to relate to people, to witness. Do not give undue attention to it. Do not allow it to be your dictator. You have been given time which is a material, not a spiritual, reality. Use it, make it your tool. Do not allow it to be your dictator. You have been given material possessions. Use them. Make them your tools. Do not allow them to be your dictator. There is no security in them.

All that you see with physical eyes, hear with physical ears, taste, smell, or touch, is temporary. It was all made from earth and exists by rules of the earth. It will all return to dust.

But there is the permanent, the eternal. There is that which has everlasting value. Concentrate on it. Use the temporal as the gift God has given, but see it for what it is, "here today, gone tomorrow."

SEPTEMBER 17

"...Jesus Christ is Lord,
to the glory of God the Father."
– Philippians 2:11

From Fern:

Jesus Christ, my Savior and my Lord, I take pen in hand to write You a letter, to tell You how much You mean to me. I have received Your letter which is so full of love that it excites me every time I read it. Thank You for all your admonitions. I am more convinced, the older I grow, that they are all valid—that every warning I heed saves me from errors that are costly to mind, body, and soul.

And how can I express my gratitude for Your promises? That You care for me...You know that is happening to me...You experience everything with me in spirit; how precious is that realization!

And best of all, of course, is that one day we shall be together, and that will be eternally true. Yes, I understand that we are together now, but more fully then. You will not change, but I will be changed. Your servant Paul said "in the twinkling of an eye."

But in the meantime, dear Jesus, I want to live for You, sensing Your nearness and guidance. I want to demonstrate that You are at the center of my life, my highest priority. I want to do everything in Your name and to the glory of God our Father. I love You, You know. Sincerely Yours...

SEPTEMBER 18

"While the earth remains, seedtime and harvests,
cold and heat, summer and winter, day and night,
shall not cease."
– Genesis 8:22

From Fern:

O Lord, my God, I thank You for the night. I praise You for life's rhythms of activity and rest: planting and harvesting, investing and reaping. It is the earth's pulse, the inner heartbeat of man responding to outer pulsation.

The tide goes out and comes in; the land responds to planted seed, stable, certain, sure. Day and night do not cease. The planted seed yields according to its kind.

And as I, one individual in the universe, lay hold of this law, life responds to me: what I invest is returned in kind. What I worship, I become. What thoughts pervade my days pervade my nights.

O Lord, I praise You for this truth. I praise You for revealing it to me. Help me to apply it to every facet of life, to invest it totally to Your glory, and I will give You the praise. In Jesus' name, Amen.

SEPTEMBER 19

"A person who never made a mistake
never tried anything new."
– Albert Einstein

From Cat:

Since we all know that nobody's perfect—nobody ever has been and nobody ever will be—isn't it about time we start embracing the inevitable mistakes we're all going to make, owning up to them, and learning from them? Personally, professionally, and spiritually, even the very best we can do is guaranteed to include some mistakes, big and small. It's how we handle them that makes the difference between success and failure, between growing and staying stuck exactly where we are, between freedom and holding ourselves hostage.

We've all seen it, done it, or both—a careless slip-up at work over something that matters; giving in to a sneaky, snoopy, or dishonest impulse in a relationship; a betrayed confidence or thoughtless moment of disloyalty in a friendship; and next thing you know, if we give in to our short-sighted, fearful, "don't-want-to-get-in-trouble" instincts, we're throwing all our efforts into trying to cover our tracks and hoping against hope we'll somehow get away with it. Of course, sooner or later, the truth comes out, as it always does, and we have no one to blame but ourselves for the added stress we've taken on—not to mention the fact that the cover-up turned out to be much more offensive than the misstep/mistake we made in the first place.

Here's an easy way to look at it: Do you like finding out that someone's lied to you or kept something from you that you had a right to know? Me neither. So where on earth would we get the idea that anyone else likes it one bit better than we do?

Waiting for the other shoe to drop over something we've done really is a form of creating our own hostage situation—it puts us completely at the mercy of the person or situation that's holding the shoe, and all we can do is brace ourselves and wait for it to happen.

Which is why I'm a strong believer in the opposite approach: Instead of waiting for the other shoe to drop, grab that shoe and throw it down yourself. Get it over with. If it results in an explosion, at least you chose the time and place. And that explosion is bound to be easier to deal with than the one you can count on if you're stuck trying to come up with an explanation for the fact that the truth came from someone other than you.

Like most people, I actually admire those who own right up and admit, "I made a mistake," or "I was wrong," or "I did something I shouldn't have done." Even if I'm not pleased with what comes next, I appreciate the honesty and just *knowing*, which is the only real starting point toward doing something about it.

If some mistake you've made is holding you hostage, wouldn't this be a great day to step up, own it, and deal with the consequences, so you can finally lift that weight off your mind and heart and feel good about yourself again?

And speaking of self-created hostage situations, the fear of making mistakes in general practically guarantees them. Einstein was right (there's a surprise): The minute we become such unrealistic overachievers that we can't accept the thought of missteps along the way, we actually become *under*achievers who cling to situations we've already mastered rather than take a chance on something new and unfamiliar and challenging. In a way, it's like being so determined in school to ace every test we take that we refuse to move on from first grade, taking and acing the same elementary tests over and over again, never giving ourselves a glimpse of the limitless knowledge and skills and experiences that are waiting out there for us to learn about, explore, and conquer.

Next time you're in your sacred space, having a quiet talk with your Wise One, I want you to think of one thing, just one, you'd love to try that you've been putting off because you're afraid you'll be less than perfect at it. You will be. AND SO WHAT? Promise yourself that you'll try it anyway, because you want to, because you might love it, because it's a new challenge that excites you, and most of all because you're not defined by your mistakes and limitations—you're defined by what you do about them.

❤ ❤ ❤

Dear God, I thank You today
for creating me as an imperfect spirit,
so that I can spend my lifetime on this earth
learning from and overcoming my mistakes
rather than simply marking time
until You bring me Home. Amen.

SEPTEMBER 20

"The Spirit and the Bride say, 'Come.' And let him
who is thirsty come; let him who desires take
the water of life without price."
– Revelations 22:17

From Fern:

*One day the disciples and I were returning to Galilee from Jerusalem by way of
Samaria. I stopped to rest at Jacob's well and a woman came to draw water for
the daily needs. We had a conversation about water. Her mind was on water that
cleanses and satisfies immediate thirst. I know this need. I who formed the body,
do I not know its needs? I supplied my people in the wilderness with water when
they feared they would die for its lack. But my words in this case had deeper
meaning. I offer water for the quenching of the thirst of the soul. I was issuing an
invitation. If anyone thirsts let him come and drink. Even in the wilderness, I
was the Rock from whence water came.*

*Water that quenches the thirst of the body was part of my creation; but that
satisfaction is temporary. Thirst will come again. Water of baptism signifying
repentance and forgiveness has profound meaning, but I offer even more.*

*The invitation is for you to drink of the spring that wells up to eternal life. He
who believes in me, out of his heart shall flow rivers of living water, even my Spirit.*

SEPTEMBER 21

"Then God said, 'Let us make man in our image,
after our likeness, and let him have dominion...'
Then the Lord God formed man of dust from the ground,
and breathed into his nostrils the breath of life;
and man became a living being."
– Genesis 1:26, 27

From Fern:

Dear God in whom we live and move and have our being, You have given us life and light. You have given us purpose and place, and here we are, Your ambassadors on earth.

We represent You. As Your body we would continue the work You have begun.

But life has become increasingly difficult. Problems are complex. Answers are seldom clear, or neatly defined. You are the Rock who never changes. Your everlasting arms are waiting to bear our weight.

I come to you, Lord God, Master of the master plan, Creator of all; still in command, still in control. I bow before You in supplication and servitude. Be my Guide this very day as I seek to have dominion as You planned from the beginning.

SEPTEMBER 22

"He did not know that
what was done by the angel was real..."
– Acts 12:9

From Fern:

O God, when has an angel rescued me? From what prison has an angel brought me forth unchained? In such natural ways, by such natural intervention do these things happen that even Peter did not know it was an angel. So it was then and now.

For you, O Lord, do intervene in life. In the midst of my days and nights, directions come, nudges guide me as to what to say or do. And following this leading opens upon adventure that gives life to existence and leads me to the High Way and not the Low.

Thank You, God! But acceptance and gratitude are not enough. I desire to share, and I seem to do so little of that.

Lord, help me. If I am using the gifts I have in ways pleasing to You, it is enough for me. But if there is another field ripe for the harvest, in which You would have me labor, I pray for the angels to liberate me from the present, cast off the chains that bind me to the usual and the comfortable, and send me forth to serve in Jesus' name and spirit. Amen.

SEPTEMBER 23

"...Conduct yourselves with fear
during the time of your exile."
— Peter 1:17

From Fern:

Dear God, my home is in heaven. That is my promised land, as surely
as You designated a geographic area and promised it to Abraham,
provided he had faith enough to set upon the journey to reach it.

You have set me upon earth at a particular time and for a particular
purpose. I am in exile from my *real* home as from time to time the
Israelites were living in exile, away from their home. But they never
forgot to Whom they belonged. They never forgot where they
belonged, and in due time the Lord returned them there.

Lord Jesus, help me in this time on earth, this time of living in exile,
to do the same. Help me remember where and to Whom I belong.
This is my temporary home. I am living here, but I am not confined
here.

Help me, therefore, to be influenced every moment by that
knowledge. The awareness will direct my decisions and my values.
May those from my homeland walk with me this day as I set about
the duties You have assigned me here on earth.

SEPTEMBER 24

"The Lord hears the prayers of the righteous."
– Proverbs 15:29

From Fern:

Jesus, I bow before You this morning...before Your love, which gave itself for me...before Your perfection. For although you came in the image of humankind, You revealed to us God, our divine Lord. You became man who opened the way for us to be filled with the Spirit of God. You became like us in order that we may become like You.

I bow before Your attention to purpose so that I could say, "I have accomplished the work which Thou gavest me to do." I bow before your humility, which prompted You to say that You came not to be served but to serve.

Jesus, in this, your Spirit, let me live *this* day. How can my love be manifest in giving myself—my time, my talent, my energy—for others? How can I reflect to those around me the perfect Spirit within me?

Help me to be purposeful, accountable, responsible in the spirit of service, in Your precious name.

SEPTEMBER 25

"Who knows whether you have not come
to the kingdom for such a time as this?"
– Esther 4:14

From Fern:

Lord, You are showing me that every moment has its significance
and every situation its importance when we have put ourselves in
Your hands.

You made no provision for waste. Every aspect of creation
contributed to the whole, as every part of our lives prepares us for
the next.

Gracious God, help me to be alert to every moment.

Help me to see the potential in every act, every word, every person I
meet.

Help me to live on tiptoe, expectant and aware, applying all that You
have shown me.

Be my Guide, Blessed Lord. I have given You my life.

Help me accept whatever you choose to do with it and I will give
You the praise, in Jesus' name. Amen.

SEPTEMBER 26

"The greatest good you can do for another
is not just share your riches,
but reveal to them their own."
— Benjamin Disraeli

From Cat:

Isn't that a beautiful thought, and so true?

Can you think of a more perfect definition of friendship than "those people we choose to let deep into our lives who believe in and inspire our greatest potential"?

Rather than focus today on how many people in your life that definition describes, I want us to focus on how many people would use that definition to describe you.

I hear from a lot of women throughout the year who sadly tell me that they would love to have closer, more satisfying friendships. Most of them have lots of acquaintances who drift in when there's something they need and disappear again at their convenience, who make all the right loving noises without the behavior to back it up, who make them feel diminished rather than valued. They're lonely, and they don't know what to do about it.

As I always remind them, because the universe works on the basis of reaping what we sow, and getting back what we give, the key to having great friends is to BE ONE, just as the key to receiving all blessings is to BE a blessing. It all starts with us and the simple gestures and heartfelt loving words we can offer that make the difference between acquaintances and genuine friends.

Is there someone in your life you need to make amends with? Do you owe a debt of some kind that you never acknowledge? Is there someone who's hurting because you underestimated how much words matter? Is there someone who could use an ear, a strong shoulder, or just a long, warm hug from you? Is there someone who could use a few heartfelt words of encouragement right now, or a round of jealousy-free applause? Is there someone you need to thank

343

who may be feeling taken for granted? Is there someone who could really use hearing the words "I love you" from the seat of your soul?

Open your eyes wide today to look past your own life to the lives of those who might need your friendship as much as you need theirs, and tell them how important they are to you. Let them know that you really see them, hear them, understand them whether you agree with them or not, and appreciate them. Tell them out loud that they're special, they count, and they matter.

Remember, just because we *think* the words doesn't mean others feel them. Say them. Speak love. Think love. BE love, and watch as true, quality friends begin finding their way to you and loving you back.

Dear God, I value friendships so much.
Please help me express that out loud,
with my words and my actions,
and become the kind of friend I'm yearning for. Amen.

SEPTEMBER 27

"How good and pleasant it is
when brothers dwell in unity."
– Psalms 133:1

From Fern:

The early converts to what would become the Christian church were caught up in the spirit of unity in Christ. Instinctively they became one body, of one heart and soul, devoting themselves to the apostles' teaching and fellowship, to the breaking of bread and prayers. Yielding to the Spirit of the Lord, which is the spirit of generosity, they held all things in common. They sold their possessions and goods and distributed them to all, as any had need. There was not a needy person among them, for as many as were possessors of lands or houses sold them. They brought the proceeds of what was sold and laid it at the apostles' feet for distribution.

Such is my desire for all my people. Those whom I have empowered to gain wealth have a responsibility to share it. I do not mean that some should be eased and others burdened, but that there be equality. I was rich and became poor for your sake, that by my poverty you might become rich.

Wealth separates and I desire that all be one. I prayed to the Father, "All mine are yours, and yours are mine. Keep them in your name, which you have given me, that they may be one even as we are one."

SEPTEMBER 28

"...The new wine will burst the (old) skins..."
– Luke 5:37

From Fern:

Jesus, thank You for bringing the "new wine," good news of such dimensions that it cannot be contained in rigid concepts or old ways. Thank You that You continually call us to change, to be adaptable to mind-expanding concepts. Thank You that each time we open the scriptures You reveal new truth, applicable in our lives every day. Through Isaiah You told us that You are always doing new things. Thank You for revealing them to us.

Lord of my life, help me to adopt this flexibility increasingly, while still retaining standards of truth and justice and love. Increase in me Your Holy Spirit who, like the God of whom the Spirit is one facet, does not change.

Thus I can attain a balance that does not revere the past as the only right way, nor blindly accept what is new because it is new. Your wisdom will achieve this—Your wisdom, available through Your blessed Spirit.

Thank You, Jesus, that You promised to send the Spirit to me. Open my life increasingly to this magnificent Comforter.

SEPTEMBER 29

From Fern:

God of timelessness, You who are past present, future, all one, whose truth never changes, Your word speaks to me, for it is my inclination to philosophize about what happens.

I arrive at reasons why and project the outcome of situations. How You must smile at these attempts by one who does not know what will happen one minute from now! Peter reversed himself completely when he realized the significance of what You were about to do.

How often would I do that if I knew what the future would reveal? This, Father, is my prayer: that You increase my patience and my trust. Save me from anxiety and pessimism. You have shown me again and again that in everything You work for good.

My mind is limited to a time-space world. I expect things to happen more quickly than they do. Yet I know that your promises are never nullified by time. Looking back over the years, I can see that there have been good results from all situations. Help me, Lord, to accept and live by Your words to Peter, "afterwards you will understand."

SEPTEMBER 30

"And Paul was consenting to his death."
– Acts 8:1

From Fern:

Dear Lord, You show us many times that death is not an end, but
that what we have begun lingers on. The contemporaries who
opposed Him thought to put an end to Jesus' influence by taking His
life, but His Spirit lived on, enabling His followers to do even greater
things than He had done.

Father, You have given us the account of Stephen who was full of
faith and of the Spirit. His hearers could not bear the truth he spoke
and they intended to rid themselves of him, also, by taking his life.
But standing in the crowd, holding the coats of those who
participated in the stoning, was one of the enemies of the early
church. He watched. He heard Stephen's description of the opened
heavens, and his asking forgiveness for those whose stones were
pelting his body. Was that preparation for his meeting Jesus on the
Damascus Road, and being turned from zealous opponent to avid
follower?

Father, help me to witness, not looking for results. Instill in me the
Mother Theresa spirit that calls us not necessarily to be successful,
but always to be faithful.

OCTOBER

OCTOBER 1

"...By no human hand..."
– Daniel 8:25

From Fern:

God, Father of all humankind, what impact is in those words! How many times history has shown power broken by no human hand. It is so wonderful to have that evidence! In it lies hope.

By human hands, Jesus was put to death. By no human hand, He was raised. By human rationalization, nations go to war. By the quiet, steady power of Your hand, peace eventually is restored. By human devices, evil reigns. I do not know what to do to combat it. It is too strong.

But You, O Lord, are goodness and light. You are present, working quietly and steadily; and Your goodness will overpower evil, and Your light will dispel the darkness. This is why I pray and for what I pray: that I may be attuned to the assurance of Your triumph over evil, injustice, and darkness in all its forms; that I may position myself to know any way in which my human hands may be of use to Your almighty power.

Thank You, Jesus, for Your example. Thank You for the unwavering rule that, appearances to the contrary, right is always more powerful than wrong. Help me hold steadily to that conviction and operate always with that principle in view.

OCTOBER 2

"...It is fitting for us to fulfill all righteousness."
– Matthew 3:15

From Fern:

My Lord and my God, perfectly pure and perfectly good: You have made me in Your image, and therefore I have an obligation and the potential for purity and goodness. I am not "only human." I am not bound to the limitations of the earth and its senses. You have placed in my spirit a longing to transcend all of this and incorporate into my daily living the ways of Your Spirit.

Thus equipped, Father, I set forth this day to fulfill all righteousness. That is, I am inspired by Jesus' words to put to right-use-ness all that has been given to me. I will put to right use my choices, the thought process, "May the words of my mouth and the meditations of my heart be acceptable in Thy sight" throughout this day.

I will put to right use the time You have given, the opportunities and obligations; for You put me here with a purpose for my life. With Your divine help, I shall fulfill it today.

I will put to right use my relationships. I shall regard them as sacred trusts because they have been given to me by You. This day I will look upon them from this perspective—with Your divine help.

OCTOBER 3

"When one door of happiness closes, another opens.
But often we look so long at the closed door
that we don't see the one that has been opened for us."
– Helen Keller

From Cat:

It's just a fact that change is the one constant we can count on in our lives, which is one of many reasons why I find that quote so reassuring, especially since it was written by a woman who was left blind and deaf from an illness during her infancy. (Helen Keller went on to become a brilliant author, humanitarian, and activist, which does make me look around sometimes at the rest of us and our mountains-out-of-molehill problems and think, "Wow, what's *our* excuse?")

We've talked about how resistant most of us are to the whole idea of that one constant in our lives, and how often we reach the other side of change and discover that we were actually resisting an outcome far better than we ever imagined.

It's true, and it's been proven time and time and time again, but I know it can be cold comfort at the moment for those of you who've lost jobs, homes, marriages, or anything else that poses a serious threat to your security.

So today is a reminder to keep your eye out for the door that's being opened for you right this minute. Look forward, look up, look down, look around, so that you won't miss it. Just don't look back— you're not going that way.

And while you're being vigilant, if only to keep your mind off your loss and get your bearings again, *get busy*!

In the face of change, do good and expect a miracle. Find a safe place to put your heart while it heals—a rescue mission, an animal shelter, Project Angel Food, Habitat For Humanity, a children's hospital, a nursing home, the Special Olympics organization—any one of countless places where you can make an even bigger difference for yourself than for the people and animals whose lives will be changed your kindness. Or start a charity of your own, like two friends of mine who started a discretionary fund at their veterinarians' office to help animals whose owners and rescue groups can't afford their essential medical care (www.williecoppeefund.org).

Wear yourself out opening your heart and your arms, and count on it that one day you'll wake up to see an open door right in front of you that you almost forgot you were looking for.

Heavenly Father, please take today's worries and losses
and help me turn them into tomorrow's triumphs and blessings.
Inspire me to give love where it's needed
and be of service where I'm able to contribute,
knowing that sometimes the most important thing I can give
is the very thing I need the most.
I'm ready to receive a miracle by being one.
Please show me the signs, and make them unmistakable. Amen.

OCTOBER 4

"My ways are not your ways."
– Isaiah 55:8

From Fern:

Would you have brought a beautiful—sometimes fluorescent—multi-colored butterfly from a caterpillar? Would it have been your way to bring a living plant from what appears to be a lifeless seed? And would you have extended that truth so that it applies to deeds as well as seeds? Whatever you sow, that will you also reap.

My thoughts are not your thoughts, but I attempt to convey them to you in order to reveal the great truths. You have my promise that while the earth remains, seedtime and harvest, cold and heat, summer and winter, day and night, shall not cease. Do you not see in that the promise of resurrection? Do you not perceive that the seed does not come to life unless it dies? As the heavens are higher than the earth, so are my ways higher than your ways. I continually surprise you, choosing not only the most unlikely way but the most unlikely person—the unwilling, the weak, the common, uneducated, the enemy—for the great work I have for them to do. Through my Spirit I recreate them and empower them.

Never underestimate my ability to surprise you. Always be aware and expectant of miracles, for my ways are quiet, my teachings subtle. They surround you. You need only to be alert.

OCTOBER 5

"Greater love has no man than this,
that he lay down his life for his friends."
— John 15:13

From Fern:

Lord Jesus, what love You have for us that caused You to take our form and come to dwell among us. From a throne in glory You chose to don earth's clothes, with all the limitations.

Not only that, but You put yourself at the mercy of those who did not know who You were, did not understand the lessons You tried to teach, which, if learned and practiced, would have given abundant life.

Jesus, my love pales in contrast to Yours. I love those with whom I can relate, those who are like myself. But You, perfect and sinless, loved the sinner enough to go to the cross "for the least of these." You shed your blood that we might be washed clean. My Lord and my Christ, help me grow in love! Help me to look at every person I meet today and see them as Your beloved, worth Your dying for their salvation. Then, with the empowering of Your Holy Spirit, increase my love for them. Help me to forfeit self-centeredness on their behalf, to give of me, in Your name, for their sakes.

OCTOBER 6

"Let everyone who names the name of the Lord
depart from iniquity."
− 2 Timothy 2:19

From Fern:

Jesus, the church is on my heart today. I know where we have come
from. I see the reasons we have evolved as we have. I recognize that
in no period in history has it been a perfect institution. There is much
humanness in the body of Christ.

But, Lord, help us from where we are to what You would have us be.
We have become a church where the poor and disreputable feel
unwelcome. Doing has gained more importance than being. Some
laity and clergy are thereby burned out. Some have lost their early
love. We have become comfortable with formalities and hearts are
untouched. Our budgets weigh heavily on the side of maintaining
poverty. My God! This is iniquity. It is the very antithesis of the life
of the One in whose name and for whose sake we exist. We are
polluting the very body of the Holy Son of God! Help us, I pray!
Instill in us the commitment of Jesus, to serve the Father. Center us
that we may reach through all the extraneous and go to the heart of
our reason for being. Help us who claim Your name to walk in Your
footsteps, and begin with me.

OCTOBER 7

"This stone shall be a witness...for it has heard..."
— Joshua 24:27

From Fern:

Creator God, I have much to learn about the one-ness in Your world. Jesus said that if the crowds did not shout His acclaim, the very stones would cry out. When Cain killed his brother, God said that Abel's blood cried to Him from the ground. Isaiah wrote of the trees clapping their hands in joy.

Lord, we think of these as inanimate, but You brought them into being. Your word, Your divine touch linked them to You and to us. It is not surprising that there is a unity. Now, a way has opened whereby humankind could destroy it all. Your latest creation, to whom You gave dominion of all else, can now demolish it.

Father, help us! Only You can save us from ourselves. You told us how—by loving. It is lack of love that would result in destruction. All these unloving vibrations affect Your universe, and I sense it crying out in pain. You will heal our land if we humble ourselves, pray, seek Your face, and turn from our wicked ways (2 Chronicles 7:14). I am a part of Your universe, affecting the whole. I cannot do everything but I can do something.

Help me to live accountably, I pray.

OCTOBER 8

"So we are ambassadors for Christ,
God making His appeal through us."
– 2 Corinthians 5:20

From Fern:

Unto Thee, O Lord, do I lift up my soul. Unto Thee do I dedicate each activity of the day. Thank You for giving me a place to be and persons to relate to, with whom I exchange an influence. For we are one. Their lives intertwine with mine and as we know one another as Your own, we know that our relationship is infinitely richer centered in You.

O, the dear friends I have because of You, dear God! The doors You have opened to me are a blessing! When I know persons of like priorities, we are bound by cords invisible and powerful. God, unite us in Your ministry to make it alive, effective, dynamic! Protect us from the busyness that gives the illusion of accomplishment but only has us rushing around in a circle, going nowhere.

Your world is not what You intended it to be, is it? Your church is not a continuation of what Jesus did when He walked among us. We who call ourselves Your people are more of the world than of You. O God, enliven us with Your Spirit. Clarify our purpose and send us anew to be Your ambassadors in a world alien to Your will, I pray in Jesus' name.

OCTOBER 9

"He who enters by the door is the shepherd of the sheep.
To him the gatekeeper opens; the sheep hear his voice
and he calls his own sheep by name and leads them out."
– John 10:2-3

From Fern:

"I am the good shepherd," You have said, dear Jesus; and I recall the hills of Israel and the shepherd boys with the family's flocks. I have been told that each shepherd has his own special call, recognized by his flock and when the sheep hear, they respond.

O Jesus, there are so many voices in our world bidding us to come, follow: "Join our group. We have the answers you need." "Buy our product. It will give you popularity." "Invest in what we sell. It will make you successful."

Dear Lord, from where comes Your patience to wait for us to try this or that, finding no satisfaction until we finally turn to You? Finally, amid all the clamor, we hear *Your* voice and recognize it as the personal call from our own shepherd. The *Lord* is *my* Shepherd. I shall want for nothing, for suddenly I discern that what the world offers is tarnishable and perishable. Only what the Shepherd offers is eternal, gaining in beauty and worth every day. My Shepherd stands between me and the wolves of the world. I shall follow Him in perfect assurance all the days of my life, confident of broad meadows and still waters ahead.

OCTOBER 10

"If it's working, keep doing it.
If it's not working, stop doing it.
If you don't know what to do, don't do anything."
– Dr. Melvin Konner

From Cat:

I love any quote that reminds us of one of the most easily forgotten basics of a well-lived life: SIMPLIFY!

Between work, significant others, family, friends, pets, and our own upkeep, it's easy to get so overwhelmed with busy-ness that rather than enjoying the gift of each new day, we wake up feeling as if we've got nothing to look forward to but the endless, relentless chore of trying to stay on top of an avalanche. And what's even more frustrating is that very often we don't even realize that we're bringing a whole lot of it on ourselves.

Been there, done that, bought the bumper sticker. Sometimes I don't even realize I'm doing it until I'm advising an overwhelmed client about how to simplify *their* life. The words "physician (or, in this case, Cat), heal thyself" leap to mind. But it's also a good reminder that if we can't find a way to step outside of ourselves and take an objective look at what's going on with us, another pair of smart, trusted, caring eyes can be very helpful.

Of course, there are a few people who are brilliant at time management and thrive on being perpetually busy, and to them I say, "God bless you!"

Then there are those who stay compulsively busy because it keeps them from having a spare moment for thinking, self-examining, and just plain feeling, which inevitably catches up with them in the form of high blood pressure, ulcers, and any number of other chronic illnesses.

I've also known my share of those who start every conversation, and I mean *every* conversation, with an exasperated description of how swamped they are, how they don't have a single moment to breathe and how they don't know what to do about it. When invited, you make suggestions, every one of which they respond to with an impatient, "Yeah, but..." Believe me, two or three "yeah, buts" in a row is a tip-off that they'd rather complain about the problem than solve it, and that they believe there's more attention and sympathy to be gained from "swamped" and "don't have a moment to breathe" than there is from, "Busy as usual, but everything's good, how about you?" I tend to end those conversations very quickly, thanks to the excuse they've handed me: "Oh, well, if you're swamped, I won't keep you."

There are those whose lives get clogged with countless obligations because they haven't learned yet that sometimes it's really okay to say no.

And last but not least, there are those who simply don't know or haven't thought of an easier way to do things—who'll run around to four different stores in search of a specific hard-to-find light bulb they need, for example, or a special brand of dog food, when in ten minutes or so they could find it and order it online (thank you, Amazon.com!) and have it on their doorstep in a couple of days.

The quickest, easiest way I've found to simplify my life when it seems to be galloping away from me is my answer to so many other things as well: Write it down. It's obvious, and best of all, it's SIMPLE. A to-do list and diligently maintained calendar really can make a huge difference in pulling the rat's nest of errands, obligations, and commitments out of your head and onto paper or your laptop screen where it belongs. Once you're looking at all those items rather than just thinking about them, you can start organizing them, consolidating them, rescheduling or eliminating some of them, finding some you can take care of with a few clicks of your touchpad or a few quick phone calls, and—my favorite part—checking them off one by one as you accomplish them.

Again, if simplifying isn't something that comes easily to you—remembering that complicating the process of simplifying is exactly what we're *not* doing today—share your list with a smart, trusted friend, co-worker, family member, et al. you have reason to believe is good at this kind of thing, and ask for their help until you get the hang of it. As soon as you tell them that you have a specific goal in mind—to SIMPLIFY—chances are they'll be only too happy to help, because it's a goal every one of us can relate to.

Make simplifying a habit, and mark my words, one morning you'll wake up and realize that you're in charge of your life again, rather than your life being in charge of you.

Beloved Father,
I know the life You've given me is precious,
and that I tend to overcomplicate it and overpopulate it
when I'm not paying attention.
Please give me the clarity to simplify it wherever I can,
so that I can truly appreciate Your gift to me
as You intended. Amen.

OCTOBER 11

"I send you out with eyes wide open, as sheep
in the midst of wolves; so be as wise as serpents
and innocent as doves."
– Matthew 10:16

From Fern:

I call you to live by faith but not blind faith. I commend the one who desires to build, who first sits down to count the cost. Otherwise when he has laid a foundation and is not able to finish it, all who see it will mock him. Or the government leader, going to encounter another in war, who first sits down to take counsel whether he is able with 10,000 to meet him who comes against him with 20,000. If he does not, he must soon send a delegation to ask the terms of peace.

I gave you a mind and bid you to reason with it. I call you in discipleship but there is a cost to be considered. It requires bearing your cross and following after me. I offer new life and equip you with my Spirit, but if your commitment is shallow and your mind is weak, you cannot endure. In that case you are a city divided against itself, and no city or house divided against itself can stand. Lot's wife looked back and was caught in destruction. Let that be a caution, for anyone who puts his hand to the plow and looks back is not fit for the kingdom.

Have faith. Believe. But come with eyes open to know that I do not call you to a privileged life, but one worthy of your commitment.

OCTOBER 12

"If then you have been raised with Christ,
seek the things that are above, where Christ is,
seated at the right hand of God. Set your mind on things
that are above, not on things that are on earth."
– Colossians 3:1-2

From Fern:

Lamb of God, Jesus, who came to reveal the Father, who made the ultimate sacrifice to take away the sins of the world: be with me, I pray. Cleanse my thoughts and the heart from which they spring in order that no malice may remain in my life—no garbage, no pleasure from that which would be offensive to You. Purify me, dear God, and then may I rise from this place knowing I am pure. May I arise *knowing* I am a new person, ready to live a new life. The old is behind me; behold, the new has come!

A new person, ready to meet a new day! A new approach built upon new attitudes! Memory shall serve as a teacher, positive and constructive! It shall be creative; a springboard to the future, not an anchor to the past.

Thank You, Lord Jesus, for the life You lived and the death You suffered—for me! Thank You for becoming part of me and of my life. Thank You for recreating me this very day and for going with me now into the future.

OCTOBER 13

"Never overestimate yourself
or be wise in your own conceits."
– Romans 12:16b (Amplified Bible)

From Fern:

Precious Lord, how sadly You must smile to see us taking pride in what we think we know. How sure we are in early years that we have all the answers when we are not even asking the right questions. How less sure we become as we mature, and how we really know nothing on any subject until we begin to perceive how much we don't know. How far we consider our technology has advanced until we face the truth that we have not even learned the basics of how to live together in harmony and love.

O Lord, we observe that those of greatest maturity speak the truth in the simplest ways, as did Jesus. He revealed the way to love. He commanded it and He lived it. He promised peace—that deep inner peace without which there cannot be outer peace. He told of a simpler way to live, with singleness of heart and mind and the assurance of abundant life.

Dear God, help me turn more and more from worldly wisdom to the simple faith of a little child, faith centered in You, loving as You loved, living as You lived.

OCTOBER 14

"The Holy Spirit will come upon you
and the power of the Most High will overshadow you;
therefore the child to be born
will be called holy, the Son of God."
– Luke 1:35

From Fern:

O my God, I stand in awe! There is a sense in which what happened to Mary can happen to all who are open to receive! This which was brought about when You chose to become visible to the world in Jesus, can ever after come true for his followers!

We saw it become true as reported in Acts, and those who received the Spirit received power and the very nature of Jesus in order to carry on his work.

Lord God, where have we gone wrong? Why has Your Holy Spirit, the enlivening, empowering Spirit, been diluted, resulting in the dullness, dryness, deadness, and powerlessness we have now?

We gather in your church if it is convenient. We give a paltry portion to its support but we feel no zeal about it. We give money or time but not ourselves. O God, give us rebirth! Choose more Marys in whom Your Son can be reborn! Recreate Your church, Your body, to go again into the world to heal and teach and mend. We need you, dear Jesus!

OCTOBER 15

"Aim at righteousness, faith, love, and peace...
Have nothing to do with
stupid, senseless controversies."
— 2 Timothy 2:22-23

From Fern:

Dear God, what a complex system we have developed. With justification and sanctification, reconciliation and retribution, we have surrounded You with words that challenge us and are unintelligible to those outside the faith.

Loving God, You would not have had it so! When You had a word to impart to humankind, You sent Jesus—Word become flesh. And Jesus talked in simple terms that did not require education or an intellectual genius to comprehend. He talked about birds of the air and lilies of the field. His parables were about loving fathers, roving and resentful sons, about a housewife who lost a coin, and a shepherd who had lost a sheep. He did not reveal a heavenly Figure aloof and unapproachable, but a Parent who reaches out in love to welcome children and bring them home.

Thank you, God, that we do not need to comprehend but simply to believe. You are not the possession of the intellectually superior—the little child can know You. We stray from that position as we get into studying and discussion. Help us back to the time of simply knowing and accepting Your love.

OCTOBER 16

"Did you not know that I must be about my Father's business?"
– Luke 2:49b

"Safely through another week
Thou has brought us..."

From Fern:

So begins the hymn, but what does it mean, dear Lord? What has this week added to the total? Have I been a dog chasing its tail, or have I contributed to some total good?

Dear God, I want to be counted on. I want to be a factor for good. There is so much evil. The purveyors of pornography and drugs, those who would destroy personalities and homes, are about their business every day. Am I equally industrious for good?

Lord, You want for us better than we have. These persons deal in death and You want for us life. They are into destruction while You are intent upon building your kingdom. I want to be on Your side, dear Jesus. I want to participate in that building program. How can I help? What would You have me do? The problem is so large and I so small. But the Holy Spirit + I = a power beyond myself.

Precious Lord, team me with You, I pray in Jesus' name and Spirit.

OCTOBER 17

"It's all about paying attention. Attention is vitality.
It connects you with others. It makes you eager. Stay eager."
– Susan Sontag

From Cat:

A connection happens when two points of energy are on the same wavelength, which is why like attracts like. We attract what, and whom, we choose to direct our thoughts toward, so it's important at any given moment to connect with *ourselves* and examine what we're thinking.

What are your thoughts about yourself right this second?

What kind of energy are you attracting with those thoughts?

Stop reading. Take a few minutes to really explore your answers to those two questions. Write them down.

Next, what did you wake up thinking about this morning? Were you thinking about how much you had to do today and how hard it would all be? How there aren't enough hours in a day? Did you wake up worrying, or angry and resentful?

Or, did you wake up with joyful thoughts? Thoughts about how excited you were to have another day of life? Thoughts about how, for your sake and everyone else's, you could make your corner of the world a better place by day's end? Did you have thoughts about your dreams and goals and how you can be proactive toward making them a reality?

Stop reading. Think back to your first waking moments today and your thoughts when your eyes first opened.

Write them down.

Whatever your answers to those questions, good for you—as you thought and wrote, you were connecting to yourself and recognizing that you get to choose what kind of day you're going to bring yourself, no matter what the rest of the world seems to have in mind. We're connecting, plugging in to that world every moment of every day, with our thoughts as the magnet that draws to us whatever we put out.

Negativity? Meanness? Controlling behavior? (Remember, by the way, we're in control of no one but ourselves and our own reality.) Revenge? Resentment? Hidden agendas? Selfishness? If that's what's filling your head, that's the energy you're attracting, so prepare to duck, and good luck with that.

Make it your business today to do random spot-checks on your thoughts. Plug in. Connect. Write it down. The better you get at thinking and therefore plugging in to positive energy and *staying there*, the more you'll distance yourself from years of plugging in to all the negativity out there (old behavior patterns).

Yes, you can. Starting right this second. Literally imagine yourself unplugging from an old dirty wall outlet with burn marks all around it and plugging into the spotless, freshly painted outlet you'd never noticed before instead.

See it.

Smile.

Pantomime it if it will make it more real.

What kind of day are you going to have tomorrow?

Which outlet are you going to plug in to and connect with?

The choice is yours.

And isn't that a beautiful, powerful fact?

Dear God, I'm so grateful that You've given me the ability
to connect with myself and those around me
through the power of my own thoughts.
Please help me make it a habit to check in with those thoughts
several times throughout the day
and make sure they're worthy of a child of Yours. Amen.

OCTOBER 18

"To each is given a manifestation of the Spirit
for the common good."
– 1 Corinthians 12:7

From Fern:

The gifts are for equipping the saints for the work of ministry, for building up my body, the church, until all attain to the unity of the faith and of the knowledge of the Son of God, to mature manhood, to the measure of the stature of the fullness of Christ.

What is maturity? It is attaining the mystery which is Christ in you, the hope of glory. It is responding to the Spirit within you, the Holy Spirit, the Spirit of your Lord. It is daring to be peculiar, to accept the command to be perfect as your heavenly Father is perfect. It is taking Jesus as your example.

Then your purpose becomes not that of doing your own will but the will of him who sent you. It is seeing life in the broader context, knowing where you have come from and where you are going. It is having life in its proper perspective. What do you have that you did not receive? You brought nothing into the world and you cannot take anything out of the world. If you have food and clothing, be content. You will discover, as Jesus said, that when you seek first his kingdom and righteousness, all these things will be yours as well.

OCTOBER 19

"The kingdom of God
is like a grain of mustard seed, the smallest of all seeds,
but when it has grown it is the greatest of shrubs
and becomes a tree."
– Matthew 13:31-32

From Fern:

Lord Jesus, I want to live in Your kingdom. I long to live where love, peace, and trust reign—trust of the King to such a degree that I take all my orders from the King. Whatever I am called to do, I will do. Wherever I am called to go, I will go, knowing there is reason and purpose behind the call.

Trust of one another, knowing that he or she is overseen by the loving King; and while I may not understand, I can trust. While I may not clearly interpret words or situations, I can trust.

King of my life, I suddenly perceive that I can live in that kingdom now! It can become *this* kingdom! Love, peace, and trust can encompass me. Your Holy Spirit can enable me, and as I move into this new realm, it will begin to grow like a planted seed. It needs nourishment—the food of Your word. It needs tending—communion with You in prayer. But You provide the growth. It is up to me to keep out the weeds of immorality, of disobedience; for such chokes off the free flow that produces life.

Help me so to live, dear Lord, I pray.

OCTOBER 20

"What shall I render to the Lord
for all His bounty to me?
I will lift up the cup of salvation and call on the name
of the Lord."
— Psalms 116:12-13

From Fern:

Dear Lord, on my journey of faith I will stop to gather the manna You provide—the manna of the wilderness which later became the body of our Lord Jesus, and remains to us available in the Eucharist.

I will pause to drink from the rock that Moses tapped to quench the thirst of the wilderness people, which became the living water provided by Jesus, which is available now as it symbolizes the blood He shed for us on the cross. His blood—his life—poured out for me! My salvation cost Him that much!

O Jesus, I take the bread and the cup and accept it into my own life's blood. When James and John asked to share Your glory, You asked, "Are you able?" Am I able to endure the cup You have for me? Not in my own strength. Not in attempting to project what that might be. But You offer Your strength and light enough for each step of the way just as You did for Your wilderness people. Help me to see the relevance of their experience in my own journey.

OCTOBER 21

"You also must be ready; for the Son of man
is coming at an hour you do not expect."
– Luke 12:40

From Fern:

Jesus, You said You would return, and whether or not You will do this as humankind envisions, You will come for each of us individually and we do not know when. You caution us to be ready—perhaps like a pregnant lady whose bags are packed, awaiting those distinct indications.

How do I become ready? I will leave behind all that belongs to this earth, so it is my spirit, my soul, which must be ready. First, I think I must be ready in attitude. I am not going into the unknown unescorted. My closest Friend is coming for me! I have many friends who have gone before who will be greeting me! It will be a time of great fellowship!

Second, I want to be able to say, "It is finished." You have appointed me to a certain role that will remain undone unless I do it. I do not know in total what that is, but I know what to do today, and as I am faithful daily to Your direction, the total will begin to unfold, and I shall be ready. Thank You, Jesus, for the warning.

OCTOBER 22

"Create in me a clean heart, O God..."
– Psalms 51:10

From Fern:

Divine Word, this is my prayer today. I am conscious of what goes into my body—the calorie intake, the balance of foods. But Jesus said it is not what goes into the body that defiles it, but what comes out of the mouth; for what comes out of the mouth proceeds from the heart.

Dear Lord, I am often ashamed of what comes out of my mouth. I am appalled to hear myself uttering words of division, discontent, lack of forgiveness and of love.

FORGIVE ME, I PRAY!

Cleanse me of all that is opposed to Your divine nature. Create in me a clean heart.

Thank You, Holy Spirit, for new beginnings. Thank You that forgiveness is possible and that repentance means change. Thank You for filling our lives and creating a new person in place of the old.

To you, O God, I lift my soul as a cup to be filled. Pour into me the portion of love, peace, and faith that will fit me for this day, whatever comes.

OCTOBER 23

"Suffering produces endurance,
and endurance produces character."
– Romans 5:3-4a

From Fern:

Suffering Servant, John Wesley's covenant prayer includes "put me to suffering." It requires maturity to realize that suffering is preparation for kingdom life.

How different from world concepts, where suffering is avoided at all cost. We pamper our children that they may not have to suffer any want that we can avoid. We consider it a goal to be attained if we can achieve a position of no suffering, discomfort, or loss.

But, dear Lord, You have shown us that preparation for kingdom living requires different values. You have demonstrated in our lives that sensitivity to others comes best from experiencing what they experience. We have watched the pampered become weak and the sufferers become strong, if they use that situation to come closer to you.

O, Divine Love, You suffered intensely! You open the relationship between us by allowing us to walk the same path. Help me to thank You for my suffering and rejoice that You are thereby making me strong.

OCTOBER 24

"Finish each day and be done with it.
You have done what you could,
some blunders and absurdities have crept in,
forget them as soon as you can.
Tomorrow is a new day, and you shall begin it serenely,
and with too high a spirit to be encumbered
with your old nonsense."
– Ralph Waldo Emerson

From Cat:

Are you struggling with a decision—small, or huge, or as simple as deciding what you're going to do today?

Whenever you're facing a fork in the road and trying to figure out which one will take you where you want to go, stop. Breathe. Get quiet. Throw out your emotions, and tell your ego to take a hike while you're at it. Listen to what your instincts have to say.

Promise yourself, out loud or on paper, that any decision you make will include the words, "I will never harm myself in any way." That means that you'll think through every angle, but any outcome that involves sacrificing your peace and well-being to please someone else is "off the table." Not for anyone or anything will you give away the last bit of you, because, in the end, no one is more responsible for taking care of you than you are.

Don't procrastinate, don't overthink it to death, but don't allow yourself to be pushed into being impulsive, either. Someone wants your answer NOW? Ask, "Where's the fire?" From time to time, there are people who genuinely need your decision sooner rather than later. More often than not, though, there are people who are hoping that by rushing you, they'll keep you from doing your homework, getting good advice, or carefully reading a contract. They want a decision, but certainly not an informed one, and they're counting on you to be impulsive, because it's to their advantage, not yours.

Be calm. Be still. Be responsible. Just BE.
BELIEVE.

Believe that the decision you make will be the right one, because you'll see to it. You have that power. Whatever you decide, it can be a success or a disaster, depending on how you handle it. Make the most of it or make the worst of it. Your power, your choice. It's up to you, and isn't that great to know?

Believe that when a decision gets made for you that's not the one you were hoping for, it's the right one too, even if you can't see the good in it today. You can struggle and rage and scream against it all you want, but it won't change the outcome. All you'll be left with is struggle, rage, and a sore throat.

Choose the alternative: the belief that the universe has a better plan for you than you had for yourself, and this unwanted decision is part of that plan.

BELIEVE! TRUST that the day will come when you look back on it, realize that it got you exactly where you're supposed to be exactly when you were supposed to be there, and you'll be saying, "Ohhhh, I get it now!"

Loosen that grip on the way you think things are supposed to go. Have faith that if your intentions are pure and you're doing the absolute best and most you can, you can safely hand over the controls to Someone who's able to see the bigger picture and collaborated with you on designing it.

Proceed with faith and confidence. You're not in this alone.

Dearest Father, I thank You
for Your perfect guidance, and for Your patience
when I forget that no matter what,
You're always in charge and always, always
so much wiser than I. Amen.

OCTOBER 25

"Father, forgive them,
for they know not what they do."
– Luke 22:34

From Fern:

These were the words of one who came to live among you, of one divinely conceived, yet born as all humans are born—the man Jesus. He grew as humans grow, in wisdom and in stature. He was tempted in every respect as you have been, yet without sinning. He knew what it was to be fully human.

But he was also God. In him all the fullness of God was pleased to dwell, and his purpose was to reconcile all things to himself, whether in heaven or on earth. Separation between God and humankind had existed from the time that Adam and Eve fell victims to the serpent's temptation to become like God, and they were expelled from the Lord's presence.

It is the nature of children to resemble their parents. You have borne the image of the first Adam, the man of dust. But that is not the end, for Jesus came to heal the breach, to pay the ransom for your soul. He came to be the last Adam, a life-giving spirit. You are no longer confined to the limitations of dust. As you have borne the image of the man of dust, bear now the image of the man of heaven. Inherit the imperishable kingdom.

OCTOBER 26

"Prayer is a happening."
– M. Basil Pennington

From Fern:

Master, I pray this day that what I know in my head will reach into my heart.

With my head I know that You are with me, loving me, knowing me better than I know myself, knowing all that is happening in my life, and caring.

Send that knowing from my head to my heart, I pray.

With my head I know that the Biblical promises are true—they have been proven true in the lives of those I know and in my own life, again and again.

Send that knowing from head to heart in order that it will create faith that it will always be.

With my head I know that I want to do Your will. I want to yield my life to You, wholly and completely.

Send that conviction to my heart in order that my desire may be truly carried out and become my way of life this very day. Amen.

OCTOBER 27

"I called on they name, O Lord,
from the depths of the pit;
thou didst hear my plea..."
– Lamentations 3:55-56

From Fern:

Precious Lord, wipe out of my mind all ugly thoughts. Help me to know that You are God, You are in Your heavens and all is right.

I may not see the right because it is hidden in the future, outside the range of my vision. Help me to know that it is *there*, that You have designed it all, and it is *good!*

I thank You, God, for the opportunities You have given me. They are challenges far beyond my capacity to perform; but You strengthen and inspire me. You surprise me all along the way.

I praise You, Holy Lord, for Your mercy; but I praise You, too, that You permit us to suffer the consequences of our errors. You discipline us that we may know the permanence of Your law and of your love.

Heavenly One, take my hand and lead me through this day. May I go forth, as I pray, in Your holy name.

OCTOBER 28

"For we know that if the earthly tent we live in
is destroyed, we have a building from God,
a house not made with hands,
eternal in the heavens."
– 2 Corinthians 5:1

From Fern:

Eternal God, this earthly tent is weary. It shows the ravages of time
and wear. Thank You for preparing another into which I may slip, a
house not made with hands, which Jesus has gone to prepare.

Help me, Lord, neither to spend my days in anticipation of that time,
nor clinging too firmly to this. Help me in this life, this very day, to
fulfill its purpose for me, thus helping to build that heavenly house
toward which I go.

I cannot walk alone. I need to feel the everlasting arms. I need the
reminders that You plan and lead and guide me through the plan.

I know the destination to which You are calling me. My citizenship is
in heaven. Help me to approach it progressively each day. I dare not
waste Your precious gift of time.

OCTOBER 29

"I know my own and my own know me,
as the Father knows me and I know the Father,
and I lay down my life for the sheep."
– John 10:14-15

From Fern:

O Jesus, shepherd me.

Help me to recognize Your voice among the many and follow in
perfect confidence that You will lead me beside the still water, to the
living water...

...that You will keep me safe from the wolves that seek to devour
me...

...that You will lead me to green pastures, where I may feed on
satisfying food that will equip me for this day and for life.

O Shepherd of my soul as well as body, You gave Your very life that
ageless life may be mine eternally.

Can I do less for You? In exchange for Your *all*, help me to give *my*
all—NOW, this moment, for the sake of all those whom You have
assigned to me, who are influenced by my life and my witness.

Amen and amen.

OCTOBER 30

"Rejoice always, pray constantly,
give thanks in all circumstances;
this is the will of God in Christ Jesus for you."
– 1 Thessalonians 5:16-18

From Fern:

Dear God, give thanks in *all* circumstances? In my concern for my loved ones? When, to all appearances, there is tragedy involved and happiness is eluding those for whom I care? Give thanks when I cannot see ahead?

Precisely then, for in giving thanks you acknowledge faith and trust. You acknowledge that I AM in charge. Place your confidence in the assurance that I AM working still toward the goal "that all be saved and come to the knowledge of truth." You know my all-encompassing love and that all *creation was and is purposeful.*

Recall Ephesians 3:20: "Now to Him who by the power at work within us is able to do far more abundantly than all we ask or think,"

God's power is at work in your life, in the lives of others, and in all the created world—a power that is itself creative, making a difference, able to do far more abundantly than all you could ask or think! If you believe this go forth rejoicing, claiming the promise.

OCTOBER 31

"Those who don't believe in magic will never find it."
– Roald Dahl

From Cat:

It was ten years ago. I was walking down the street in New York, headed home after a really challenging day on *One Life to Live*, when an adorable little boy came running up to me.

"Are you an actor?" he asked.

I said yes, to which he replied, "Me too!" and proudly handed me a card advertising a play he was in.

Now, I'd worked with a lot of child actors in my career, and I've always worried that they miss out on their childhoods, working so hard, preparing for countless auditions, and facing rejection they shouldn't be exposed to so early in their lives. So I asked him if he loved acting, watching closely for any sign of "not really, but my parents have their hearts set on my being famous."

Not a chance—this boy answered, "Yes!!!" with such conviction and passion that I didn't doubt it for a second.

I still felt a little protective of him, though, so I held up my hands, my palms facing him, and asked him to put his hands against mine, palm-to-palm. "That way we can transfer our special magic to each other for success in our hopes and dreams."

He did it immediately, loving it with the delight of a child. While our hands were still touching, I made him promise me one thing or the magic wouldn't work: neither of us would EVER pin our self-worth on what anyone else said about us, or on whether or not we got a part.

We promised each other, and I believed him. Eight years old, and he totally got it. Sadly, I misplaced that card and don't know his name. He was a little knockout, and I'm willing to bet that he's either enjoying a great acting career right now or he lost interest and is a huge success at something else he's passionate about.

Ten years later I still think of him every time I even start to get my feelings hurt by something cruel someone says about me. I made a promise to that little boy, and I'm keeping it—I don't want the magic to stop working!

I meant it then and I mean it now: Giving away our power by letting another person dictate our value is simply out of the question. No. Just no. Each and every one of us is a child of God, a God who adores us, and we're going to let anyone on this earth overrule Him? Why would we do that?

We're incredible, we're enough, we're beautiful works in progress, all of us, not because of who we are but because of *whose* we are. Now, *that*'s power!

I saw in his eyes that an eight-year-old boy wasn't about to give his power away. He thought he'd had a special moment with me that day. The special moment was all mine, as is the magic of that promise a decade later.

Starting today, no one but you and your Creator have a vote in your self-worth. Remember it, believe it and keep the magic going.

My Father, my promise to You today
is simply to never again give a second thought to anyone
who thoughtlessly dishonors You by dishonoring me,
Your child. Amen.

NOVEMBER

NOVEMBER 1

"Fear not, I will be with you."
– Exodus 3:12

From Fern:

There is a Gethsemane moment familiar to many, a moment of praying, "Father, if thou are willing, take this cup from me." Those of greater faith and courage proceed, "Nevertheless not my will, but thine be done."

Esther was a beautiful Jewish girl who became Queen of Persia. Her cousin, Mordecai, saw her as the one who might have been called to save the Jewish race from extinction in that land. She could have lost her life but replied, "I will go to the king, though it is against the law; and if I perish, I perish."...Three young Jews defied the order to worship the golden image of the Babylonian king, knowing the decree that whoever did not do so would be cast into the fiery furnace. They answered, "Our God is able to deliver us, and He will. But if not, we will not serve your gods or worship the golden image which you have set up."...Ruth, a Moabite, chose to accompany her Hebrew mother-in-law to a land where her reception would be uncertain, to a people who had been enemies of her people for centuries. "Where you go, I will go. Your people will be my people, your God my God."...Mary risked her reputation when she gold Gabriel, "Let it be to me according to your word."

Why do you hesitate when I call? Fear not, I will be with you.

NOVEMBER 2

"And Gideon said, 'How can I?...
My clan is the weakest...and I am the least...'
And the Lord said to him, 'But I will be with you.'"
– Judges 6:15-16

From Fern:

Be sure, be confident in life. Grasp it. Do not let it grasp you. Through my Spirit within you I am with you, as I promised. You shall not falter or fall. You shall prosper and grow, for you have put yourself in my hands. I will not leave you hopeless. I will not leave you without guidance and direction.

Only one step at a time. It is all you can *take. It is all you have light to take. Take it, therefore, in confidence. Fear not, for I AM with you. I will not forsake you or leave you desolate.*

One step at a time. The future looms unknown, but I AM in it as I AM in the present.

Be sure. Be confident of yourself and of me. Together we meet the day which is part of the future. Lo, I am with you always—to the end of the age.

NOVEMBER 3

"We have this treasure in earthen vessels."
– 1 Corinthians 4:7

From Fern:

God, like the notes of the scale You allow me the range of emotions. They are not all in the treble clef, which I would like. Sometimes they are bass—negative—and I wallow in self-centeredness.

Is it in order that I may experience all that my Lord experienced and overcame? Is it to give me the full and rounded life in order that I may relate to and understand all persons and emotions? Is it to keep me humble, to realize how far I am from totally yielding my self to You?

This I know: You have gone before me and are walking with me now. You became Man in Jesus. You were limited in the flesh, submitting Yourself to the whims of humankind, accepting jibes and insults, emotional and physical torment. When I thus hurt, You know—not only that I hurt, but how it feels to be hurt.

Help me, dear Jesus, to keep Your life before me, to see the victory and accept it. Help me become less in order that You will become more, in me.

NOVEMBER 4

"Now to Him who by the power at work within us
is able to do far more abundantly
than all we ask or think."
– Ephesians 3:20

From Fern:

Here we are, Lord Jesus, in the midst of a miracle. It is a continuous state of being, for life is a process and creation goes on.

Did not Jesus say, "My Father is working still and I am working"? (John 5:17)

Did not Isaiah speak God's word, "Behold I am doing a new thing; note it springs forth, do you not perceive it?" (Isaiah 43:19)

Thank You, Lord, for not abandoning the earth but, indeed, for being present among us, continuing the creation that You pronounced good.

Help us to know that. Help *me* to be convinced of Your leading. May my life be a part of Your project and me a contributor. Let me not be fruitless and unproductive. Let me not get lost in busyness, but may each of my days be counted for good.

This day be with me in every activity. Help me, in Your image, to likewise be creative of good.

NOVEMBER 5

"Prayer is as essential to a successful life
as air is essential for breath.
Prayer is the breath of faith."
– Paul Yonggi Cho (paraphrased)

From Fern:

To Thee, O Lord, do I lift up my soul. O, my God, I trust in Thee. As he who said, "I believe, help my unbelief," I pray for the ability to trust, to lay aside my own strength and be reliant on strength from You.

Give me the courage to face life aware of my inadequacy, and lean only on my trust in Your promises.

Give me the awareness that trust conveys confidence, appearances to the contrary, or situations that do not seem in accord with the goodness You desire. Help me to know that You are in control. Your hand has not been shortened. Your presence has not been denied. Your power has not been exhausted.

From all of this Your blessings flow, recreating, refreshing, renewing. Help me to stand receptive to the flow. Pour over me, around me, and in me the cleansing water of renewal as I go forth this day.

NOVEMBER 6

"You have one Master, the Christ."
– Matthew 23:10

"O, Jesus, Lord and Savior,
I give myself to Thee,
For Thou, in Thy atonement
Didst give Thyself for me.
I own *no other* Master..."
– *Living for Jesus*

From Fern:

Dear God, allow no other power in my life. Let fear have no place in me, or distrust, or suspicion. Put within me a right spirit, one that shall be pleasing in Your sight.

Help me through this day, Lord; give me the ability to thank You *sincerely* for all the circumstances involved in it.

I do not ask for ease but for assurance that I am not alone, and for sensitivity to Your direction.

Thank You for guidance in the past; and for all the evidence in my life that You have been with me, leading and protecting. Thank You! You have brought me to this moment for Your own divine purpose. May I live it fully to Your honor and glory. Amen.

NOVEMBER 7

"In the middle of every difficulty lies an opportunity."
– Albert Einstein

From Cat:

New York City. Many years ago. One of my best friends and I were having lunch. He'd gone through a horrendous time of struggle and sadness, but a book he'd stumbled across had helped him through it, a book called *The Four Agreements* by Don Miguel Ruiz. He was so excited about *The Four Agreements* that he bought me a copy that very day.

My life happened to be in a great place at the time, so while I loved my friend for the gesture, I wasn't feeling the need for a self-help book. I took it home and put it on a shelf with hundreds of other cherished books I kept there, waiting to be read someday. And then I went right on with my smooth, happy life and didn't give it another thought.

A few years later, things weren't going nearly so well for me. I found myself darting around looking for answers in all the wrong places and feeling worse by the minute. Instead of stopping to learn something valuable about myself that might give me some traction on a path back to normal, I was distracting myself with every shiny object I could find, anyone or anything that could waste my time and keep me too busy to think. Sure enough, nothing felt better. In fact, before long it all began to feel unmanageable.

One morning, after another agitated night of too little sleep, I was sitting on the floor rooting around for something when a heavy object fell on my head. It hit me so hard that I saw stars. When the birdies finally stopped chirping I looked around to see what had clocked me, and found the book my friend had given me three years earlier lying there beside me.

There was no logical reason for that book—let alone *only* that book—to come tumbling off that tall, heavy shelf where it had been tightly wedged since the day I brought it home. I immediately thought, "Apparently I *do* have to be hit over the head," picked up the book, headed to my room, curled up in bed, lit a candle...and read that book cover to cover.

The principles in *The Four Agreements* woke me up, jerked me off that hamster wheel I'd been using to pretend I was doing something, and sent me down a path I'd been yearning for, where my soul could be nourished rather than ignored. I read it four or five times, and I still reach for it when my "batteries" run low. It inspired me to study everything I could get my hands on that would fill my heart, mind, and spirit, and learned to reconnect with myself.

I was so on fire that I wanted to pay it forward. I wanted to give other people the same life-changing wake-up call I'd found in the pages of a book, and that's how I came to write *The 30-Day Heartbreak Cure*.

To this day, I look back on that morning when I was sitting so sad and empty on the floor and wonder how long I would have gone on like that if I'd just picked up that book, put it back on the shelf, and climbed back into my hamster wheel.

I also wonder how many other "life rafts" I must have missed along the way to so thoroughly exasperate the universe that it had to whack me in the head to snap me out of it.

If you're running on empty like I was, I guarantee there are answers being put in your path out there. Help is on the way, and you're being divinely guided toward it. Don't ever get too "busy" or wrapped up in your own head to miss it. Stay vigilant and have faith that you're closer to it today than you were yesterday. Whether it comes in the form of a book, or a person, or a situation, or a bumper sticker, or a church service, or a walk down the street, *help is on the way* in all sorts of seemingly ordinary disguises. And when it arrives, follow your God-given instincts. Don't bury it back on a shelf and ignore it. Light a candle, embrace it and, when you've come out of the darkness again, remember and smile.

♥ ♥ ♥

Heavenly Father, I thank You with all my heart
for that wake-up call (and the aspirin to go with it),
and for the truth that Your Hand is always there
to pull me up from my knees
if I'll just pay attention and trust my soul to find it
and reach for it. Amen.

NOVEMBER 8

"Even the hairs of your head are all numbered."
– Matthew 10:30

Jesus, we are to love ourselves.
How do we properly do that?

From Fern:

_____ (your name), *in relationship. In relationship to me, for I formed you as a potter forms a vessel. I breathed into you my own breath and you became a living being, unique in all creation. After you were formed, I broke the mold. There is not another like you.*

As you love me, you will love yourself as one of my designs. You were an idea in my mind before you had being. If you have misused the vessel, or used it for purposes other than I intended, that does not demean it. It can be cleansed and recommitted to proper use.

Love yourself because I love you. If there had been only you, I would have laid down my life for your soul. Love yourself in relation to others. There is a false interpretation of self-love, which can be thought to elevate the self above others. Love of self does not call you apart from but into community. True love desires the best for the beloved, and one who truly loves his/her self, desires the highest and best for all who are touched by that love. The love I call you to express is my love, prompted by my Spirit, extending to all, including yourself.

NOVEMBER 9

"Truly, unless you eat the flesh
of the Son of man and drink His blood,
you have no life in you."
– John 6:53

From Fern:

My child, you come to me with emptiness asking that you be filled in order that you may serve. Thank you for being my disciple with that quality of willingness. For this is as I came to the Father in prayer; and as he sent me, so I send you.

Everyone who so comes has a unique ministry as specifically his or hers as that individual is unique. Every one who comes receives the equipment he or she will need for that assignment, gifts of the Spirit to be used to produce desired results. And it is both daily and long term equipping.

And just as the future is veiled from you, so the immediate purpose of your life remains hidden. "Sufficient for the day is the day's own troubles." And just so, the opportunities of the day are sufficient for your knowledge.

Eat of my flesh for your strengthening. Drink of my blood, my life, for quenching your spiritual thirst. In these ways you take me into your life, and your day. Your resources, then, are superior to your own. These elements are nourishment to the Spirit within you. Take power.

NOVEMBER 10

"In the morning sow your seed,
and at evening withhold not your hand;
for you do not know which will prosper, this or that,
or whether both alike will be good."
– Ecclesiastes 11:6

From Fern:

My Child, one day you will know how insignificant is time! One day you will stand above time and look on eternal vistas, seeing one continuing thread—no past, no present, no future, but all one whole. What prompted the past fashions the present and creates the future.

All life is one with incidents marking the division. One incident is birth, another is death, but it is all part of the whole, the purpose of which is the soul's development. The events of life seeming so crucial now appear only as cracks or bumps in the total view. Only the outcome affects soul growth and it is significant.

So do not trip over these events. Do not linger over them in regret for what is past or spend time in anticipation or dread for what is future. Do not attach to them undue importance but add them to your file of experiences and move on.

Life moves forward. Go with it. And my love goes with you.

NOVEMBER 11

"Love is patient and kind."
– 1 Corinthians 13:4

From Fern:

My child, you are disappointed in someone today, but do you not realize the cause?

In your mind you created an expectation of how that person would respond. Do you not know that he is presently incapable of that response? Can you accept him as he is and not as you wish him to be? Can you love him with his weaknesses as well as his strengths?

This is true love: to acknowledge the personhood without pretense, without closing the eyes to what you wish were not there. True love accepts the blemishes as well as the beauty. True love acknowledges growth and waits patiently and lovingly for maturity.

If you are hurting because of disappointment, it is all within your own self. It is an indication of your failure to understand, to accept, and to love.

You taught your children to walk. You were not blindly expectant of immediate success. You were not disappointed in them when they fell, but rejoiced with every step they accomplished. Apply the same attitude and patience in this situation.

NOVEMBER 12

"He was praying...and when he ceased, one of his disciples said,
'Lord, teach us to pray as John taught his disciples.'"
– Luke 11:1

Jesus, as you taught the disciples, will you teach me to pray?
Will you help me to be intent upon my prayers without distraction?

From Fern:

_____ (your name), *in a manner of speaking, prayer cannot be taught. You should know that from the number of books you have read on the subject. Words of prayer can be learned, formulas can be followed; but true prayer issues from the heart, motivated by love, directed to God. Your mind is distracted because it is full of many things. I came with a single purpose, to do the will of the Father who sent me. My directive was clear while you, in your desire to live a life of service, hear so many voices that you are confused. You care what others think of you and give that more attention than what your Lord thinks.*

Clear away the clutter. Clarify between you and God what your priorities are to be. Listen to God. *What does He seek for you? What role does He have in mind for you to fill? He will equip you for it, and walk with you in it.*

Do not listen to the clamor of the world, but to that still, small voice within. The more you listen, the more clearly you will hear. My own, know my voice, the voice of the Good Shepherd.

NOVEMBER 13

"He is not far from each one of us."
– Acts 27:17b

From Fern:

_____ (your name), *this is my covenant with you: If you will apply yourself to my teachings, if you will ask of me, if you will seek to know and do my will, I shall be near you and direct your ways and make you a productive servant. You do not know the effect of your words or your testimony as you go about the duties of your days. You do not know because you cannot read the minds and hearts of those with whom you come in contact. How often you return home following an encounter and berate yourself for having said too much, or too little, or spoken inappropriately. You seldom consider the possibility that I put those words in your thoughts, to accomplish what I know needed to be done in the life of a hearer.*

Be not concerned for what another thinks. Care that you responded to the leading of the Spirit. Do not wonder about hearts and minds of others. It is not your prerogative to know. This is why each is given individuality, as each has been given freedom to choose. You are free to choose, but this is the covenant I offer: You desire that your life bear fruit. This is the way.

NOVEMBER 14

"Life by its nature cannot have guarantees,
or its whole purpose is thwarted."
– Neale Walsch,
Conversations with God: An Uncommon Dialogue

From Cat:

It's another inventory day, and the assignment is both simple
and challenging: I want you to think about everyone in your life who
really matters to you.

Now I want you to think about the last conversation you had
with each of them.

And now, I want you to ask yourself this question:

"If I got a call five minutes from now telling me that that person
who matters to me has died, would I be at peace with our last
conversation really being our *last*?"

If the answer is "no" about anyone you care about, today's the
day to make it right. This isn't to be morbid or negative in any way;
it's just a reminder that there really are no guarantees, no matter what
age we are, that we'll be given another opportunity to say "I love you"
or "I apologize" or "Let me help you" or "I'd like to make amends
about the last time we talked." It's up to us, for our own peace of
mind and the satisfaction of doing what's *right*, to keep everything
current with the people we've chosen to draw closely into our lives.

E-mails and texts are off-limits for this particular assignment.
You owe it to yourself and anyone with whom you have unfinished
business to have an actual conversation, on the phone or in person.
Say what's on your mind and in your heart, and hear them out as well.
But most important of all, no matter how the rest of it goes, end your
time together as if this will be the *last* time and make sure they know
beyond all doubt that, even if the most you've accomplished is to
agree to disagree, they hold a unique, special place in your life.

And from this day forward, apply this rule to every conversation:
*No unfinished business ever, nothing left unsaid between you and those you cherish,
because none of us can afford the luxury of taking anything for granted!*

They'll thank you for it, whether they say it out loud or not...almost as much as you'll thank yourself.

Take it from someone who's grateful every single day that my final words to my precious mother before she went Home were "I love you," four times in a row. I wouldn't trade that for all the money in the world.

Lord God, please help me remember
that there's no promise of tomorrow in this earthly life,
and no greater gift I can give myself
than to live every day
and end every conversation with those I love
as if they'll be my last. Amen.

NOVEMBER 15

"No one has ever seen God;
the only Son has made him known."
– John 1:18

Blessed and only Sovereign, King of kings, Lord of lords,
how dare I approach You? Those who perceived Your glory
could not stand but fell before You.

From Fern:

_____ (your name), *for this I came, to reveal the Father.*
Who the gospels report that I was, God is. What the gospels tell that I did, God
does. How the gospels recite my response to people is God's response. Note
particularly the latter. Compassionate God desires justice for all. Loving God
wants all to be saved. Caring God longs for your companionship, to walk and
talk with you, to give you life abundant with blessings.

This is impossible for those who are blinded by the fascination of this world's
values, whose time is filled with this world's demands. Such appetites are never
satisfied. Those who desire to be rich fall into temptation, into many senseless and
hurtful desires that plunge men into ruin and destruction.

The Father would not have it so. The promise stands, seek first the kingdom and
all of these will be yours as well. As wise parents seek lasting happiness for their
children, God wants eternal life for you.

NOVEMBER 16

"There are no failures. We're either succeeding,
or we're learning something."
– Unknown

From Cat:

We're here to learn.

We all know that, and if we really think about it, we wouldn't have it any other way.

But really, how can we know what we want, or what works and what doesn't, if we don't end up exactly where we don't want to be once in awhile? As Sylvia Browne used to ask, rhetorically, "What have you learned when times were good?"

Sometimes circumstances put us where we don't belong, and other times we insist on finding our way there with no help at all, usually because we made choices without bothering to consider all the facts before we leapt in. I've known people, and so have you, who invest more time and research into buying a car than they do into starting (or ending) a job or a relationship. I mean, seriously...?

I've come to believe that one of the most important ingredients for living a life that really works is becoming a fact-gathering, fact-checking machine. Life decisions deserve the respect of our due diligence, which includes the emotional intelligence we've gained from past failures. Once we've taken responsibility for them and stopped blaming everyone else for our choices, we can turn those experiences into valuable lessons, rather than a trail of regrets to beat ourselves up about.

Imagine the trouble we could save ourselves, and the scammers and catfishers we could put out of business, if we refused to take our feet off the brakes until we thoroughly, responsibly educated ourselves what we're getting ourselves into.

We are, indeed, here to learn. Now let's get in the habit of making it a point to learn before rather than after as often as we possibly can!

❤ ❤ ❤

Dear God, I thank You with all my heart
for the mind you gave me, with its limitless potential
and its ability to learn.
I ask for Your guidance in helping me
make better use of it with every passing day
and every experience, both good and bad. Amen.

NOVEMBER 17

"...perfect love casts out fear."
— 1 John 4:18

Jesus, You healed a demoniac and the people asked You to depart,
for they were in great fear.

From Fern:

_____ (your name), *hear a message from that account: The people had become accustomed to a mad man roaming among the tombs. They did not know him as a person. If some had felt compassion for him, it had long since gone. Now there was only fear and a desire to avoid him. This is the profile of prejudice.*

Then I came. He was healed, but the townspeople did not rejoice. Fear remained, now transferred to me. So how this speaks of fear of one another and of change. In ever so many cases, situations are not good, but there is no trust. The result is that people would rather live with what they know than to trust the unknown. I was in a strange country. I was unknown. The townspeople did not know what I might do next. The man I healed, now clothed and in his right mind, was unknown. What might he do next?

Examine your attitude toward change. Know that I can bring change for the better but need to exorcise what has been in order to clothe you and give you a right mind for the future. Fear not, for I have plans for you, for welfare, not for evil.

NOVEMBER 18

"Truly, I say to you, it will be hard
for a rich man to enter the kingdom of heaven"
– Matthew 19:23

From Fern:

_____ (your name), *I had so little time to impart my message and live on earth my love for God, for all the created, and for myself. Yes, I did love myself; for my kind of love desires the best for the beloved; and what I allowed to happen to me fulfilled the purpose for which I came. Recall that I wasted no time on trivial matters. What I talked about was of utmost importance and a key subject was money. You have observed and felt its power to bind, to enclose its talons around a life more and more tightly until the victim is paralyzed. What begins as storing a little for a rainy day becomes an obsession, and the unknown needs of the rainy day demand more and more. Meanwhile, thousands of my children perish in want. Not that money will save them, but the situation exposes the ungenerous heart of the hoarder who is first concerned with his/her own needs. That kind of life was not my example or command.*

Be open to my leading in this regard. Love more and be thankful. This will create an openness in every aspect of your life and free you from the clutches of this world's values and demands.

NOVEMBER 19

"I give thanks for the goodness of the Lord,
for steadfast love."
– Psalms 107:1

From Fern:

_____ (your name), *I designed the world to be good. Oh, how much I desired that my created would choose to obey me and thereby be blessed! How I longed, even in their most determined rebellion, to gather them in my protective embrace. Instead they have seen my rules as restrictive, my commands as limitations. From the beginning they wanted to compete with me instead of loving me.*

_____, *you know the feeling, for you were there. You lived in that mindset for many years until you finally came home, and the angels rejoiced, as is always the case. You kicked against the goads for a long time and then you turned! Hallelujah! You are ready to receive the good which is the kingdom. You do not receive it all at once, but progressively as a light that begins to shine under the door, then around the sides, and more and brighter as the door opens. The light shines into the dark areas of your life, exposing them, acknowledging them, then cleansing them. Evil cannot tolerate the light of goodness. It is by my design and demonstration that good always overcomes evil.*

NOVEMBER 20

"My thoughts are not your thoughts,
neither are your ways my ways, says the Lord."
– Isaiah 55:8

From Fern:

_____ (your name), *do not try to comprehend or anticipate
what I will do. It is beyond what your eye can see or ear hear or heart imagine. I
have so arranged the world that you can live but one day at a time. Do not be
anxious about tomorrow, for tomorrow will be anxious for itself. Live today. Live
it fully, in awareness of what it offers. Appreciate your faculties and what they
behold, for God has created a world of beauty. Be conscious of the colors. Savor
the tastes and smells. Realize those abilities as gifts provided for your pleasure and,
in some cases, your safety. Relish the interaction with family and friends.
Appreciate the uniqueness of each one and realize this has not been happenstance.
It is by your heavenly Father's design.*

*Treasure your relationship to God. This is a particular gift, provided because it is
the Father's nature to love. God is always near, always available, hearing prayers,
knowing your needs, desiring for you abundant life. Why do you ponder the what-
ifs that you cannot know, when today overflows with more than you can absorb?
Live now. Live fully now!*

NOVEMBER 21

"Of that day or hour no one knows,
not even the angels in heaven, or the Son,
but only the Father."
– Mark 13:32

Dear Lord, there are things happening in our world
which are startling. Is this the end time?

From Fern:

_____ (your name), *it is not for you to know the times or seasons. Believe. I came as truth. Time and again I prefaced my remarks by saying, "Truly I say to you." If what I said was not true, would I not have told you? I said that I would come again. The angels said that I would come again. The God-inspired prophets told that there would be an end time, a day of the Lord. You can believe that it is true. It will be.*

The significant aspect is not when but who will be prepared. When the Son of man comes again, will he find faith on earth? Live every day in the awareness that I have already come in the sense of being present, alive, active in your life. Be open to direction. But live also in the awareness that another event is going to take place, a cataclysmic happening. Be watchful for it. As in the fullness of time I came once, so preparations are being made for me to come again. Do not be preoccupied with it, but be ready.

NOVEMBER 22

"I am the resurrection and the life."
— John 11:25-26

From Fern:

_____ (your name), *there was a time when I restored a dead man to live. Do not be preoccupied with that instance, for the truth is that I have power to raise all from the dead. I demonstrated that death has no finality. I conquered death, which has deeper than literal meaning. Paul, who received new life and direction, expressed the thought by saying that he had been crucified with me, that it was not he who lived, but I who lived in him. He perceived baptism as going under the water and leaving there all the uncleanness of the old life, coming up out of the water clean and new.*

I am the resurrection and the life. He who believes in me, though he die, yet shall he live, and whoever lives and believes in me shall never die. I am life. I have the power to give life. I offer, to all who will come, cleansing from the old human tendencies, the fleshly inclinations. All who will may experience new life and wholeness, not once but every moment. There is no hopelessness in me, no despair; for nothing is irreversible. I came that you might have life, and have it abundantly.

413

NOVEMBER 23

"No longer do I call you servants...
but I have called you friends..."
– John 15:15

From Fern:

_____ (your name), *come apart from your busy schedule and let us enjoy one another, as Mary came to sit at my feet, just to be in my presence. Martha was concerned for my physical needs, not realizing how soon the physical body would give way to the spiritual. Know that for balance you need sustenance for both your physical and spiritual natures. The loveliest times with your friends are those when you feed one another in both these ways.*

We are friends. We need not always be busy with projects; I need not always be teaching or interpreting or assigning. Remember the times I stole away to spend the night in communion with the Father.

Sometimes it is enough for you and me to be together, to share our love and enjoy our companionship. For we are one in Spirit. We have the same Father, the same home.

We have much to talk about but friends do not always need to talk. There are times when it is enough just to be together, when silence is lovely. Be still and know. Feel the warmth of our love. Sense the peace of the moment. Receive the showers of blessing. Be still...be still...be still.

NOVEMBER 24

"For by grace you have been saved through faith...
not because of works lest anyone should boast."
– Ephesians 2:8-9

From Fern:

_____ (your name), *beware of activity, however holy it may appear; for activity carries within it the seeds of self-importance and competition. Even if denied with the mouth, the temptation to think of stars being added to the crown, another step up the ladder to heaven has been gained. This is an insidious thought, for in that case my suffering was in vain and dying on the cross was for naught. I paid the price for your soul. Worldliness had you and I paid your ransom.*

This is not to say that your participation in bringing in the kingdom is unwanted. It is not to say that you should take to your rocking chair once you have become a Christian. It is to say that your motives must be clear. Why are you busy for me? To impress? To win points? Or is it because your love for me compels you to do, to act, to be, to tell others of that love and of our relationship?

_____, *it must be the latter. My love for and oneness with God was the reason for doing all that I did. My coming to earth in human form was because of my love for you. Let love be the reason for whatever you do.*

NOVEMBER 25

"The opposite of anger is not calmness, it's empathy."
– Mehmet Oz

From Cat:

I truly believe that empathy—identifying with and understanding another person's feelings—should be a required subject taught in every elementary school around the world. It's one of the greatest gifts we can give or receive, the very core of the Golden Rule that's "golden" because it actually works: "Do unto others as you would have them do unto you."

Empathy heals. It transforms. It opens hearts and meaningful dialogue. It unites. It disallows abuse and bullying. When we insist on developing it as a habit rather than a concept, a verb rather than a noun, it causes us to instinctively pause before yelling or criticizing or insulting to ask how we would feel if someone spoke like that to us. Empathy is priceless, but it costs nothing. It's so powerful that there's no aspect of our lives it leaves untouched—it makes us a better partner, a better friend, a better sibling, a better son or daughter, a better employer, a better employee, a better pet owner, a better citizen of the world in general. In fact, come to think of it, I can honestly say that a lack of empathy is the one quality shared by every person I've excused from my life. If you're incapable of empathy, or are capable of it but choose not to use it, you're someone I can't emotionally afford.

Today's the day to start making your empathy skills a priority, and ultimately a habit. Look around at the people closest to you and take the time to really focus on each one of them. As best you can, see through their eyes for a few minutes. Hear through their ears. Live in their body. Process thoughts through their mind. Feel what they feel. As best you can, be them, until a real sense of *them* creates a twinge of empathy in your soul.

And then, expand the exercise to some place full of strangers and choose someone at random to focus on whom you'd ordinarily take for granted—a cashier, for example, or a server or a busboy or a parking valet. Notice them. Let it register with you that they don't just vaporize into thin air when the store or the restaurant or the valet stand closes. They woke up this morning somewhere just like you did, with a probably imperfect life just like yours, with their own set of problems just like yours, and, whether they felt like it or not, showed up to a job that's probably not their dream come true—but they're *working*, God bless them—where they probably hear more complaints than compliments and are probably underpaid in the process. Again, as best you can, see and hear and live and think and feel and imagine being them, and don't shift your focus until you've truly sensed their lives and felt an empathy for them that would make you think twice about being rude or abrupt or complaining or unkind to them, *no matter what their behavior toward you.* You're not in charge of anyone's behavior but your own, and trust me, keeping empathy as a priority and making it a habit is a peaceful place to be and a peaceful place to create.

I'm excited for you to discover how much deeper your life, and the lives of those around you, will be, from simply shining a spotlight on the beautiful art of empathy that's already inside you just waiting for you to start putting it to use every day, every chance you get.

Heavenly Father, You gave me the gift of empathy
and the Golden Rule to tell me how to apply it.
In gratitude, I promise never to withhold it again
and let such a beautiful gift go to waste. Amen.

NOVEMBER 26

"Anyone who is in Christ is a new creation;
the old has passed away, behold, the new has come."
– 2 Corinthians 5:17

From a shepherd out in the hills tending his sheep,
God made Israel's greatest king.
From a tiny, helpless infant
without position or place to be born,
God made the Savior of all the world.

From Fern:

_____ (your name), *you do not know what you can do unless
and until you put your life in my hands. It is not your performance that matters,
but how you allow me to perform through you. I have always chosen the weakest
and/or most unlikely for my great events. My power is made perfect in weakness.
Give me your life that I may accomplish what I wish to do. Salvation for all is my
desire. It is accomplished, but it must be realized. Persons must come to know
that they are my child. Be a Christ to someone today, which is to say, be sensitive
to need, respond, listen with your heart that is not distracted by other duties. Love
not only your children—the "proper," the "acceptable"; but love mine—the
outcast, the alienated, the sinner. They need you most. Be there for them.*

NOVEMBER 27

"Prayer is walking with God
in the cool of the day."
– Genesis 3:8

From Fern:

(Based on Luke 15:11)

Divine parent, You entrusted Your children with life and freedom to employ it as we will. You have allowed us to err, to have free rein to the extent of the tether.

And there You stand in the road, awaiting us to return to You. More than that, You have, in a mysterious way, been all that while beside us.

We have Jesus whispering for us, "Forgive them, for they know not what they do."

We feast on the world's pleasures until they become bitter in our mouths. We defy Your laws until we break ourselves upon them, and we return, dirty and broken, and You say, "Come; come to me, you who are heavy laden, and I will give you rest."

"We love because you *first* loved us," and we never know it as surely as when we return from our journey into a far country.

It hurts out there. Life is cruel out there. Thank You for Your open arms, Your forgiveness, Your never-ceasing love!

NOVEMBER 28

"And I will pray to the Father,
and He will give you another Counselor,
to be with you forever."
– John 14:16

From Fern:

O Lord, so fill me with Your divine self that I do not know how to
distinguish between You and me;

so involve my will that it may be perfectly entwined in Yours, my will
being in total accord;

so lift my spirits that wherever I go, to whomever I meet, will go
optimism, trust, and generosity to be shared all along the way.

Increase my sensitivity not only horizontally but vertically, for I know
that You speak and lead continually. You do not hide or withhold
your hand. It is I who fail to take it.

O Lord of the living and of those who have gone on, tie our lives
together with one another in this realm and across the veil that
separates us. Be with Your children. Bless and keep us, we ask in the
name of Him who invited the little children to come. Amen.

NOVEMBER 29

"Prayer is not conquering God's reluctance,
but taking hold of God's willingness."
– Phillips Brooks

From Fern:

Holy Lord, sustain me through this day; fortify me with Your peace,
for the responsibilities of the day are many and the call is for a steady
step and calmness of mind.

Only as I feel Your presence can I know my way. Only as I sense that
this, too, is a step along the path provided for me, can I walk with
confidence. For each day is a building block toward the total
structure of my life, founded in the Divine Mind of God. Each
experience a stone—some to stumble over, but all to build upon.
And so shall this day be.

It is important, for nothing is wasted. When the structure is
complete—and may it be a beautiful temple to Your glory—then
shall be revealed the light and dark stones, some wet with tears, some
shining with triumph. There it will stand for all to see.

O, may it not crumble into naught, but be a structure in Your
kingdom.

NOVEMBER 30

"Come to me, all who labor
and are heavy laden,
and I will give you rest."
– Matthew 11:28

From Fern:

"Come to me," You have said, dear Jesus. "Come to me," and I see Your hands outstretched, inviting—hands that once were those of youth, then a laborer, and then because of Your suffering for us—for me! "Come to me," You invite, and it begins to dawn that we, Your children, need to "go" nowhere to do that. We "come to ourselves," to our own hearts and souls and minds and find You waiting there!

"Come" in the quiet and find peace, or in the tumult and confusion and find rest for the soul. "Come" in times of need to One who will understand, or in sorrow to find the Comforter. "Come" to talk, to listen, to share. A friend is waiting, a confidant, a support, an encourager. "Come" in joyous times to exhilarate. "Come" to praise the Holy One, and in all this you shall find the supplement and fulfillment for all your other experiences. This is completeness, wholeness, *shalom*.

"I will give you rest" and I will give you all the rest! "Seek first the kingdom and righteousness, and all these things shall be yours as well."

DECEMBER

DECEMBER 1

"You know that old trees just grow stronger,
And old rivers grow wilder every day.
But old people, they just grow lonesome
Waiting for someone to say,
'Hello in there...hello.'"
— John Prine, *Hello in There*

From Cat:

I visited a nursing facility recently to give a talk and share some laughs, some hugs, and some prayers to anyone who might want them.

It was such a privilege to be in the presence of people who were in the twilight of their lives and had so much wisdom to impart, if only someone would ask.

I always ask. I wouldn't miss that opportunity for anything. I'm here to learn, after all, and finding room after room after room of superb, eager teachers was as humbling and joyful as it gets. Two of the women were in their late eighties/early nineties, and I'm not exaggerating when I say that they were sharper and more articulate than a whole lot of younger women I meet!

But who would know that if no one pays attention?

There was an even an adorable seventy-nine-year-old woman named Melba who was wearing Cat Cosmetics lip gloss! It looked as great on her as it does on any eighteen-year-old and took years off her face. It tickled me no end to know that somehow she found and bought my make-up. She may not have been exactly where she wanted to be, but darned if she wasn't going to look good being there!

Of all the things I had to offer, nothing made their eyes light up more than laughter and prayer, a quiet, reassuring connection to their Creator. A laugh and a prayer can get any of us through anything, I always say; and to see those eyes who've seen so much transformed from empty to joyful from something so simple has left my heart full and grateful ever since.

Do I wish every so often that I were Bill Gates, so I could see to it that all of those dear, amazing people will get the care they deserve for however much longer they'll be with us? You bet I do. But I'm not. I'm Catherine Hickland, and I can do what I can.

So can you.

As John Prine put it, "So if you're walking down the street sometime, and you spot some hollow, ancient eyes, don't just pass them by and stare as if you didn't care. Say 'Hello in there...hello.'"

Give love. It's free, and it matters, more than we can ever imagine until we see it in action.

And don't forget to slap on a little lip gloss. If you don't believe me, ask Melba.

Beloved Father, please help me to never get so preoccupied
with the busy-ness that sometimes clutters my life
that I can't find time to be a warrior on Your behalf
for those who are too often forgotten...
and who, by Thy grace, will be me someday. Amen.

DECEMBER 2

"The glory which thou has given me I give to them,
that they may be one, even as we are one."
– John 17:22

From Fern:

_____ (your name), *when you belong to me, you are in a family that far exceeds what the word usually conveys; for you are drawn together into my body and made one. There is a recognizable quality to the relationship so that, in whatever country, however strange your cultures and lifestyles might seem to one another, you* know *that you belong. In the earthly family, all you may have in common is an ancestor. Your thoughts may be totally different. Your attitudes, motivations, and goals may resemble one another not at all. Your one link is the bloodline from which you have come.*

When you are made one in me, you are washed in my blood, made clean in my love. We have the same Father, are filled with the same Spirit, the Spirit of the Father and of the Son. Those who are mine have the same name: Christian; and are in the same bloodline, that which I shed for you on the cross. The more we associate, the more resemblance there will be. Never has there been greater need for persons to know they have a family—you and me.

DECEMBER 3

"I am the light of the world;
he who follows me will not walk in darkness,
but will have the light of life."
– John 8:12

From Fern:

Precious Lord, lead me this day. Let my light, from Your divine presence, lead someone in some way, to You. For You are the truth light to shine upon the path where we shall go. The way is dark ahead but You have promised to be with us and as we go forward, the light moves with us, showing step by step in the narrow way how we may proceed in safety.

O dear God, help me always to depend upon that light and no other. Keep the way clear; for it is easy to be inattentive, to wander off into sideways, and miss the way that leads to ultimate fulfillment—to *life*.

Lord, You would not have it so. You came in Jesus to prevent our missing the true way, the divine light. You gave your very life in order that the narrow path be revealed. I yearn to walk in that way. I yearn to sense my hand in Yours and Your presence beside me, accompanying; before me, leading behind me, protecting.

I need not proceed in fear. In confidence I can go forward this very day.

DECEMBER 4

"I have always been delighted at the prospect
of a new day, a fresh try, one more start, with perhaps a bit of magic
waiting somewhere behind the morning."
– J. B. Priestley

From Cat:

Years ago, on short trips to Los Angeles, I used to stay with
close friends who had a gorgeous little girl named Samantha Rain.
She was a joyful toddler, and I got an up-close-and-personal look at
part of the reason for that: Every single morning when she opened
her eyes, her parents greeted her with huge smiles, a million kisses,
and the words, "It's new day, child!" They made it sound so exciting
and magical, so full of endless possibilities, that it worked on me,
even from the next room. It turned mundane errands and apartment-
hunting into adventures, every phone call and e-mail into potential
surprises, disappointments into opportunities.

Very few of us were given that beautiful reminder when we were
little, but we're grown up now, we get to make our own rules and
choose our own habits, and I want you to join me in this one, starting
today:

When you open your eyes tomorrow, and every day from then
on, I want you to remind yourself, with love and excitement, that it's
a brand new day. Whatever you've been meaning to do, or missed
out on, or chickened out on, or started without finishing, you can do
today! Whatever hurts and frustrations you went to bed with last
night are yesterday's news. They don't matter any more. Today is
about happiness, joy, loving yourself, being the best friend to yourself
you could ever ask for. Don't believe it? That's okay, too. When it
comes to the well-being that no one's responsible for but you, just
fake it 'til you make it and let the rest of your life catch up with you.

Want to get a lot accomplished? Great. Tackle that to-do list.
Feel like cooling your jets? Great. Take a breath, be gentle with
yourself and set aside some time to go out and play. Just live this day
with grace and dignity, NO MATTER WHAT! Don't let anyone
disturb your peace or rattle your cage, even if they're being rude for

428

no reason. Smile back, move along, and be glad you're not having as bad a day as they apparently are.

Today is a gift, from God to you. Enjoy it, love it, LIVE IT, and when you go to bed tonight, don't forget to thank Him and look forward to the fresh today that will be right there waiting for you when you open your eyes again.

Join me. Let's do this together: IT'S A NEW DAY, CHILD!

Precious Lord, I'm so grateful
for every new day You give me,
and You have my word, I'll never again
take this gift for granted.
I'll cherish it and celebrate it
with the joy of a child—*Your* child—
exactly as You'd have me do. Amen.

DECEMBER 5

"No one can serve two masters...
You cannot serve God and mammon."
– Matthew 6:24

From Fern:

_____ (your name), *be cautious in considering financial status. Remember that it is the Lord who has given to some the ability to get wealth. Like the gifts of the Spirit, they were not given to bring honor. To whom much is given, of him much is required. To only one did I say, "Sell all you have and give to the poor." That young man had substituted wealth for the position God should rightly have in his life.*

I accepted support from persons of means. I call persons who will exemplify Christian living and Christian principles whatever their situation. The issue is not what my people have, but their attitude toward what they have.

Be my child. Be sensitive to needs of every kind. Many of those have no answer in the financial realm. In fact, you know that wealth often creates more problems than it solves. Have compassion for the wealthy as well as the poor. Many of them are envied and resented. Many in both situations are blinded by this world and its goods. It is hard for them to establish right priorities.

Tell them how to fill their empty lives. Give money where it will help, but always give love with understanding.

DECEMBER 6

"Seek the Lord while He may be found."
— Isaiah 55:6

From Fern:

Dear God, I stand on the threshold, pausing to come. I feel uncertain. Based upon interpretation of the scriptures by others, I do not know if Your face is stern or approving. I do not know whether it is appropriate to fall forward in awe or run to embrace You.

I know the recommended parts of prayer: ACTS—adoration, confession, thanksgiving, supplication. Do You desire structure and formality, or spontaneity? I know what I want from *my* children. Is it the same as You want from Yours? I look forward to Your words.

God, You once said that no one could look upon Your face and live, and so You sent Jesus that humankind could look upon him and see You. He said, "If You have seen me, You have seen the Father."

He is Your face. In Him we see tenderness and love, inviting and welcoming. He gives me confidence that each of Your children may come in whichever is the most natural way; for You also gave Your own Spirit to indwell in our lives in order that we may relate to You, seek You, and find You waiting for us to turn to You. Thank You for this guidance!

DECEMBER 7

"Peace is not something you wish for; it's something you
make, something you do, something you are,
and something you give away."
– Robert Fulghum

From Cat:

When I started studying the mind through hypnotism, I had no
idea what a profound difference it would make in my life to
understand both aspects of the mind—the conscious and the
subconscious. To my amazement, until then I didn't have the first
clue what the word "relax" really meant, let alone how to achieve it.

Understanding how to quiet my mind has given me keys to
peaceful living, soul-deep prayer through meditation (turns out I
didn't know what that was, either) and ridding my life of negative
energy, from myself and from the world around me.

Among the countless lessons I've learned through my studies is
the fact that the harder we work toward our own inner peace, the less
likely we are to forfeit it in any aspect of our lives. We get to take
control of ourselves and our reactions to external events and other
people's behavior everywhere we go.

There are countless would-be peace-thieves out there. We have
no say in how anyone else chooses to behave, but we most certainly
can decide that we're not handing over our peace and our joy
anymore. We can take a step back and, maybe for the first time,
realize that for the most part, those peace-thieves are flailing and
making noise about nonsense that doesn't even matter. Most of the
time it's about who's "right." And really (big yawn here), *who cares?*

It's time to stop reacting and start demanding peace in your life.
Put an end to peace-thieves, because you can! Walk away from
nonsense without attitude, get quiet, and use your God-given power
to take charge of how you feel.

I had TV on as background noise the other day while I was
doing some mindless housework, and all of a sudden I noticed that
some awful show had come on that was apparently devoted to people,

mostly women, being horribly mean, catty, and vicious to each other at the top of their lungs. I dived on the remote as if it were a live grenade, said out loud, "Not it *my* house!" and turned it off as fast as I could. Why anyone would produce, air, or participate in a show that even implies there's something normal or acceptable about that ugly behavior, I can't begin to guess. (I can hear you out there: "Duh, Catherine! Money and their fifteen minutes of fame, hello-o-o-o!" Sorry. Still not worth it.) But I can do what I've developed a habit of doing about ugly behavior in my life in general: not in *my* house, followed by an immediate, resounding CLICK!

And because we teach people how to treat us, and attract the energy we put out, those around us will figure out, sooner rather than later, that if that's how they choose to behave, they're going to have to take it somewhere else. We're not having it.

Demand inner peace from yourself and nothing less. Put some mind-muscle into it, and don't give one bit of power to the peace-thieves around you by engaging them, even for an instant. Smile to yourself as you walk away when they try to pull you into their silly games. That noise is their problem, not yours, and you outgrew those games when you were in junior high. You've fought hard for the peace you've earned, and you're hanging onto it, promoting it and, above all, *living it* with all your might, starting today.

Dear God, help me to walk today and every day
in the footsteps of Your loving son, who stilled the waters,
and, no matter what the circumstance,
as You asked of us in Your holy book,
"make every effort to do what leads to peace." Amen.

DECEMBER 8

"Avoid the godless chatter and contradictions
of what is falsely called knowledge, for by professing it
some have missed the mark as regards the faith."
– 1 Timothy 6:20-21

From Fern:

_____ (your name), *beware of getting caught up in theological jargon. Remember the simplicity of my parables, how I used the natural to illustrate the spiritual. Begin to see that all life is one. You have a tendency to separate what is visible from the invisible, what is secular from the sacred, what is physical from the spiritual. It is one. It came from my mind and hand.*

You were a baby, fed and cared for by those who loved you. You grew. You were educated as you applied yourself. There came a time for your spiritual birth. The same pattern applies. You are to grow and mature. Then you are to parent those who are babes in the faith. Consider nature. Plants have seed for perpetuating their species. One tree produces many apples, each apple having many seeds. Be like the tree. Produce much fruit. Wherever you are, drop a seed that another may take root and grow.

There are cycles and seasons in nature, a time for planting, for growing, for harvesting. Then comes a time for quiet and rest. Intersperse your activities with time for rest. Then be resurrected each morning for a new day, alert and eager for a new opportunity.

DECEMBER 9

"We are His workmanship, created in Christ Jesus
for good works, which God prepared beforehand,
that we should walk in them."
– Ephesians 2:10

From Fern:

Dear God, You have created this world with a plan in mind. It was
neither by folly nor whim—there was a "beforehand," and in that
beforehand there was You! In love You planned and brought forth.
In trust You gave each a work to do, a responsibility to carry.

I pray, my Lord in heaven, that I may carry mine—that amidst all the
confusion and noise I may hear Your voice; that amongst all the
paths I might walk I may see the clear-shining light that singles out
the one on which You would have me go.

Show me the way, reveal to me my tasks, and then strengthen me to
carry them through. Gift me anew with the power of Your Holy
Spirit. Enable me to represent You wherever I go and to whomever I
meet. And help me always to give You the praise. Keep me aware of
the source of my power, my wisdom, my abilities. Help me never to
attempt to draw people to me, but through me to Christ. Let me
serve in the name and Spirit of Jesus.

DECEMBER 10

"Take pride in how far you have come
and have faith in how far you can go."
– Christian Larson

From Cat:

An exhausted-looking client sat down with me recently. She'd been working very hard as a mom, a wife, and a busy career woman, and she reluctantly admitted that she was feeling all used up. Being Wonder Woman was wearing her out, and her physical exhaustion wasn't bothering her nearly as much as the fact that she'd lost herself in the process.

"I love my children. I love my husband. I love my work. I've got the life I dreamed of when I was growing up; I just never imagined it would leave me feeling so empty."

I asked her to tell me what her dreams are now, besides a good night's sleep. After a long, thoughtful silence, she looked at me with tears in her eyes and said, "I'm not sure I have dreams for myself any more."

It struck a deep chord in me, and I'm sure it does in many of you as well. "Dream?! I barely have time to brush my teeth! And look around—my life is full! What's the point of dreams if I don't even have a place to put them?" Right?

I think one of the unfortunate myths about our dreams is that they're supposed to be "out there somewhere," that they're supposed to involve some visible change in career or lifestyle or relationship status. The fact that very often our greatest dreams are realized "in here," in our hearts and souls, doesn't get as much attention as it deserves, because somehow our internal dreams/transformations are perceived as less important than the "big" ones. That's simply not true. Achieving genuine God-centered peace, joy, and fulfillment is really the essence of every dream ever dreamed.

In fact, believing that the answers to our prayers can only be found "out there" can be a set-up for some real disappointments,

436

because they so often involve buying into illusions rather than realities. I still smile to myself about a couple of very successful soap opera actor friends of mine. One of them talked frequently about his dream of owning and operating a hot dog stand on Catalina Island. The other dreamed of opening a book, candle, and incense store in Big Bear. There's nothing wrong with either of those dreams, except that I've never known two people who would have been more miserable if those dreams had come true for them; after a month at most, they would have been so insanely bored they'd have been tearing their hair out and looking for the nearest exit.

I've known women married to insanely wealthy men, who have a live-in staff and full-time nannies. I've known movie stars, superstar recording artists, best-selling authors, even a billionaire, and you know what? Not one of them has a problem-free life. Not one of them leaps excitedly out of bed every morning, rubbing their hands together in anticipation of yet another thrill-packed day.

The bottom line: There's not a perfect life to be found "out there" that you're missing out on or being deprived of.

So you might as well fall in love with the one you've got, flaws and all, starting with *you*.

Yes, I'm talking about falling in love with yourself. No narcissism, please! I've never known a likeable narcissist, and I'm sure I never will. I'm talking about fulfilling an incredibly worthwhile dream that won't require a new wardrobe or adding a room to your house for your new homemade salad dressing factory: the dream of becoming someone you admire, who approaches every requirement in their day not as a chore to be complained about and slogged through, but as an opportunity to do it and do it well, who gives and receives love freely and with gratitude, who can be counted on, who commits to the life they've chosen and throws their shoulder into it, who goes to bed at night with a proud sense of accomplishment and wakes up every morning eager for the challenges ahead, no matter how trivial they might seem.

Falling in love with yourself and your life won't happen in a day or a week or a month. It's a process, one day at a time, a habit to develop so it won't become just another wistful long-term fantasy like those ten Pilates classes you're going to sign up for one of these days, or that novel you're going to write. When on earth are you

437

supposed to find the time to take ten Pilates classes, or write a whole novel? Never. You only find the time to take *one* Pilates class, you just do it ten times. You only write three pages a day, and then another three tomorrow, and then three more, and what do you know—three months later, you've written 270 pages! If you never get started in the first place with those Pilates classes or that novel, consider the possibility that it wasn't actually doing those things that appealed to you, it was just the *idea* of doing them. That's okay. Move right on along until you find those things you want so much that you're more than willing to tackle the day-to-day work it takes to get there—like a certain woman I can think of who didn't become a stage hypnotist by waving a wand, but wanted it so much she went to school, one day and one class at a time, until she ended up hypnotizing people onstage for a living and loving every second of it.

It's that approach I want you to take to *you*! Become your own dream, right where you are and *who* you are, *today*. Fill yourself up with God's light and guidance through prayer; with the joy of raising happy, confident children with good values and the certainty that they're safe, they're well cared for, and they're adored; with the pride of accomplishment in tackling whatever job is ahead of you with the determination to do it right and do it well; with the certainty that, if you have a partner, you chose wisely and healthily, and that if you don't have a partner, you're whole and satisfied and complete without one.

Get in the habit of falling in love with whoever and wherever you are today, so that whoever and wherever you might find yourself being tomorrow, you'll love that person and that place as well, rather than perpetually gazing off in the distance wishing you were them or there instead.

Be the most incredible *you* you can be, an extraordinary one-day-at-a-time work in progress, and I promise, you'll have fulfilled a dream that even some of those people you think you'd trade places with in a heartbeat are still searching for.

> Dearest God, please help me become the greatest fulfillment
> of the plan You had in mind when You breathed life into me,
> by being patient, ready, and willing to do the work every day,
> and looking inside myself first to find and become my dreams,
> because inside myself is where I'll find You. Amen.

DECEMBER 11

"O my God, in thee I trust."
— Psalms 25:2

From Fern:

_____ (your name), *you have persons whom you raise to my attention each day for healing. Beware lest you think of physical healing as the ultimate. Remember that all such healing is temporary. The body returns to dust as it was, but the spirit to God who made it. Pray instead for wholeness, for this was and is my healing. Beware lest you think of the healer as the source. Instead, remember that God is the Source, and it is by the gift of his Spirit that one is given the power to heal.*

Beware lest you think of death as the worst eventuality. I told my disciples that the proper response to my death was rejoicing that I went to be with the Father. When you properly view death you will see it as the Father does, for from God's point of view, all are living.

When you perceive God's protective love, you will know there are times when he passes someone from this realm to the other, so that they will not see the evil that is coming. How often you have thanked Him that your loved ones did not live to see a situation that developed. All this can be summed up in a word: Trust.

DECEMBER 12

"Train up a child in the way he should go,
and when he is old he will not depart from it."
– Proverbs 22:6

From Fern:

Life rolls along, dear God. Weeks go by so speedily, as do months as well. We enter a new one today, and it is like a whole new beginning except that You have fortified us with the experiences of the past.

Thank You, God, for memory! Sometimes I allow that memory to be negative, but all the while I know that wisdom is a result of memory. Wisdom is one of Your divine attributes, but You inject it as You help us remember past experiences, lessons learned.

My Lord, how interesting that youth, generally, do not have wisdom. Their lives are filled with gaining knowledge, and wisdom comes later, as knowledge is applied. How foolish I was in youth—these are the negative memories I have. And yet You allowed me free rein and now such good results. I cannot be critical of youth because I remember. I cannot be intolerant of youth because I remember what it was like to be there. I remember my stubbornness, my audacity in an attempt to cover up my fears, my need for acceptance at whatever cost. I learned how it hurts to "kick against the goads."

Thank you, God, for allowing me to learn the hard way and thereby to gain wisdom.

DECEMBER 13

"We are taught you must blame your father, your sisters,
your brothers, the school, the teachers—but never blame yourself.
It's never your fault. But it's always your fault,
because if you wanted to change
you're the one who has got to change."
– Katharine Hepburn

From Cat:

When she was twenty-three years old, a friend of mine changed her name.

She wasn't an aspiring actress, or running from the law, or someone trying to separate herself from a bad childhood. In fact, she'd had a wonderful childhood, with great, supportive parents. She was a college graduate with a good job and lots of friends.

She was also, like most of us, dealing with several insecurity issues she was rarely conscious of at all. And the idea of changing her name wasn't even on her radar.

But one day, she "just happened" (no such thing as coincidences, remember?) to be given the gift of a reading from a reputable numerologist. She wasn't especially interested, but she didn't want to seem ungrateful, so she went.

He was amazing—very specific, very insightful, and very positive. During the reading, he commented that she'd never really cared much for her given name, which was true but something she hadn't told him, and that her life would flow more smoothly if she changed it. He suggested she send him a list of first names and last names she'd be comfortable with, and he would work with them numerologically and present her with her new name a week or two later. "Try your new name for a month," he told her, "and if you don't notice any significant differences in yourself and your life, then forget I mentioned it."

She discussed it with her parents, who were open-minded enough to say, "Sure, why not, give it a try. Let us know when you get it so we'll know what to call you."

It was New Year's Eve day, 1971, when the numerologist called. She and a friend happened to be going to a large party that night to ring in 1972, so he suggested she stop by on her way. He'd tell her what name he'd come up with from her lists and she could debut it at that night's party. She did, and he gave her the name, told her how to spell it, and then added, "And by the way, you'll always remember the first person you introduce yourself to with your new name, so pay attention."

It became a running joke between her and her friend at the party that none of the strangers at this huge, overcrowded party seemed remotely interested in knowing who she was. They'd been there for more than an hour before someone finally tapped her on the shoulder and she turned to find a very familiar face smiling at her.

"Hi," he said, extended his hand. "I'm Tony Curtis."

She shook his hand and introduced her "new" self, to which he replied, "What a great name. It's nice meeting you." And he walked away, leaving her to wonder if somehow the numerologist had set this up, but it defied all logic and she finally wrote it off as one of life's magical little surprises.

In the next month she effortlessly lost twenty-five pounds, after years of trying every diet known to man with no success, and she was given a promotion at work she'd been hoping for. Within the next six months, she was dating a movie star and a world-class adventurer, both of whom she met "by accident" (see above comment about coincidences), and both of whom pursued her.

She legally changed her name at the end of 1972 and never went back. She's gone on to become a very successful writer, certainly with her share of problems and disappointments but with a wonderful life in general, much of which she feels she owes to the results of an unexpected hour with a numerologist all those years ago.

As I'm sure you've guessed, this is absolutely *not* me advocating a trip to your friendly neighborhood numerologist ASAP. I wouldn't recommend that any more than she would. She and I have talked about it many times, and she didn't need me to tell her that it's not the story of a name change, it's the story of a self-image change and the incredible power our subconscious has in our lives. In her case, she'd attached a lot of "facts" to her given name, including "overweight," that disappeared when she "became" someone who didn't sound to her as if they had a weight problem. She would never have guessed it was a subconscious self-image makeover she really needed until the proof became undeniable.

That's one of the countless reasons I find such joy in hypnotherapy and the access hypnosis provides to the real heart of what we truly believe about ourselves beneath all the hair, make-up, and conscious armor. If I had an hour with each one of you to help you uncover those beliefs and turn the negative ones around, nothing would please me more. If each one of you could come to one of my seminars on trance, or self-hypnosis, that would thrill me, too.

Realistically, though, it's also one of the countless reasons that I urge you to spend time alone every day with yourself and your Wise One, gently, silently digging deep into your soul to become an expert on *you*—the hidden stumbling blocks, the hidden strengths and treasures, and absolutely everything there is to know about the fascinating, complex, utterly unique person you really are.

Can you think of a more wonderful gift to give yourself today?

Heavenly Father, there's so much more I have to learn
about this child You created beyond what I see
in the mirror. Please guide me toward true insight
and wise teachers, with my promise to You
that they will never have had
a more eager, grateful student. Amen.

DECEMBER 14

"Through Him we both have access
in one Spirit to the Father."
– Ephesians 2:18

From Fern:

Heavenly Father, while thanking You for the miraculous gift of the
Holy Spirit. I am aware that no aspect of the Trinity has been more
controversial, more divisive than this. In the 1700s, when America
was being settled, circuit riders took the Christian message to the
frontier. As converts repented and gave You their lives, the physical
evidence of the Holy Spirit was extreme. In the 1800s, Pentecostalism
was born with emphasis on Holy Spirit activity, as it was in the early
church with all the gifts, including tongues, recurring. In the 1960s,
You brought the charismatic movement to what we call mainline
churches with evidence of the Spirit's touch. But those unfamiliar
with the Holy Spirit have regarded all of this with suspicion. They
have, in fact, fearfully wondered if it might be the work of the devil.
They are more repulsed by than attracted to the experience.

*Child, there are true and false experiences. The test of validity is change in the life.
A person filled with the Spirit of Christ will become Christ-like. You will know
them by their fruits.*

DECEMBER 15

"Put on the whole armor of God, that you may be able
to stand against the wiles of the devil."
– Ephesians 6:11

From Fern:

_____ (your name), *you have been praying for the hostages. Pray
for all who are held hostage in ways more subtle than those usually referred to. It
requires effort to stand firm against all the evil forces that come against you and in
time may possess you. For this reason, Apostle Paul gave specific directions for
equipping against them. For persons to whom the supernatural is hard to accept,
this is a difficult teaching. It deals more with thought than actions, and attitudes
before they are expressed. Thought does not precede and determine actions, and
words reveal the attitude already there. The best avoidance is "just say yes" to
Jesus Christ, who is God's yes to the world. I, Jesus, taught you to love and
showed you how to love. I came as light, and darkness fled. I have left that light
shining in you that you may reflect it wherever you go. My followers, lights
wherever they are, light up the world.*

*As long as you are filled with love and light, as long as you expose all your
thoughts to love and light, bathe your attitudes in love and light, you will be
protected from evil forces. They have no other entry into your life.*

DECEMBER 16

"I am the Lord your God,
the Holy One of Israel, your Savior...
You are precious in my eyes, and honored,
and I love you."
– Isaiah 43:3-4

From Fern:

Your love, dear Lord, surrounds me, upholds me, protects me!

How can it be, my God? How can I be precious in Your sight when I find myself so far from what I want to be? What do I want to be? Brave, courageous, sure of my decisions, loyal to you, winning persons to You for Your kingdom; always truthful, always sincere, always seeking the highest.

My God, You know how far short I fall from these aspirations. I think less of myself for that reason, and You do not? You love me in spite of those failings?

Thank You, gracious God, and forgive. Forgive my failing to understand Your kind of love that does not depend upon performance; that does not require certain behavior or thought patterns in order that the beloved be acceptable. O my God, help me to accept such love, to be fed by such love and to learn to so love.

DECEMBER 17

"...What more are you doing than others?"
– Matthew 5:47

Jesus, there are so many tension points in Christian living.
How much shall I do and how much shall I entrust to You?
I want to accept the responsibility for living out my convictions,
but where is the balance point that will prevent
Christian living from becoming mostly activity?

From Fern:

_____ (your name), *you have committed your life to me. You take seriously that I asked, "What more are you doing than others?" and "Him to whom much has been given of him will much be expected." You have been about what you perceive to be the Father's business. What is the balance point? God.*

Keep God central. Center all activity in the Father. Evaluate all busyness in the light of God-love. Your world has become complex. Why? Because the tendency has been to shift the center, to compromise divine law. It operates only when it is accepted and lived literally. The promised blessings were founded on that interpretation. For many, money and what it can buy, the power and prestige it can assure, has become the center. To so live is to base a life on the formula that two plus two equals five. Nothing will then come to a correct result.

DECEMBER 18

"And such were some of you."
– 1 Corinthians 6:11

From Fern:

Lord Jesus, sinless Master, how can You look upon my life and love me? How can You see goodness when it seems to me that my failures must be more obvious? But if You can, and do, as the Scriptures assure me, how can I do less for others?

You have allowed me to see my own weakness. You have shown me that I succumb to temptation time after time. How can I be critical of others who do the same? Some are tempted in one way and some in another. If I am strong where they are weak, I am also weak where they are strong.

God, You have given me a sense of being called to pray for persons of a particular inclination—not to analyze or understand, but simply to lift up to You in prayer those so inclined. Place Your divine hand in blessing and in healing upon their lives, and upon mine.

We need You, Lord. Every day brings challenges. Every day is an opportunity that I do not want to miss. Help me be alert to these factors, but guide me and those for whom I pray in the way that You would have us go.

DECEMBER 19

"No soldier on service
gets entangled in civilian pursuits."
– 2 Timothy 2:4

From Fern:

Lord Jesus, I am reporting for duty this day. I need to re-enlist every morning; for I do not live in camp, but in the world, in community with persons of divine priorities. They beckon me to become involved in their pursuits. Some of them are enticing. They have the appearance of worthiness.

Captain of my life, help me to discern between Your assignments and theirs. In this time reserved for our appointment, give me my orders for the day. Was I drafted, or did I enlist? It matters not. We have a covenant of partnership, and I want nothing as much as I want to serve You.

Forgive me, Lord, for the mental distractions even as we are together now. The "civilian pursuits" seem so present, so urgent and forceful. I *want* to clear my mind of them. I want this time and this day to be wholly Yours. Help me to so focus my life that what I tell You I want is actually true, that I *am* under Your command. It is my honor to carry out Your orders.

DECEMBER 20

"If he is cursing because the Lord has said to him,
'Curse David,' who then shall say,
'Why have you done so?'"
— 2 Samuel 16:10b

From Fern:

Dear Lord, I come today in confession—not for the things I have done or even those I have left undone, but for what I am and what I fail to be. I find in myself haughtiness and pride. In spite of knowing that Jesus was exalted for his humility, I discover that people putting me down makes my hackles rise. My defenses scream internally, "Who does she think she is?" instead of accepting the experience as a lesson I need to learn.

Ever since that realization, God, You have pointed to verses and readings that would speak to my problem. You have shown me that this quality is the most distasteful of all to You, that it was the downfall of angel Lucifer (Isaiah 14:12f).

O dear Lord, help me! Forgive me! Teach me! This is so inborn that it happens spontaneously. I want to overcome it and I know that I cannot on my own accord. Only Jesus' Spirit, living within me, breathing into my soul the very nature of His divine self, can instill this quality in me. Heavenly Savior, rescue me. I pray in Jesus' name and Spirit.

DECEMBER 21

From Cat:

I've told you about one of my all-time favorite books, *The Four Agreements*, by Don Miguel Ruiz. Its subtitle is "A Practical Guide To Personal Freedom," and that's exactly what it is. It elevated my life, and I believe it would do the same for yours.

One of the Four Agreements is "Be impeccable with your word." Impeccable is such a great word—non-negotiable, no margin for error or interpretation. This agreement shouldn't be hard, so why could most of us count on less than two hands the people in our lives we can rely on to simply do what they say they're going to do, or just plain be honest in every conversation, no matter how important or trivial? One broken promise, one "white lie" and credibility goes right out the window, along with trust, and for what? What an easily attainable luxury to live a transparent life in which, at any given moment, we could pass a lie detector test on any subject without breaking a sweat, and in which we're known as someone whose word has real value.

Whether it's as casual a comment as "I'll call you next week to make a lunch date," or (for us business owners) as professionally important as "Your order will ship tomorrow," it matters. It's a promise that the person on the receiving end just might be counting on. If something comes up that prevents you from keeping your word, speak up. If not, do it, for no other reason than because you said you would. And here's the really simple part: If you have no intention of doing it in the first place, don't say it in the first place. How hard is that? Total clarity, no disappointment on their end, no unwanted obligation on yours. I've heard people use the lame explanation, "I just said that to be polite," which begs the obvious question, "How polite is it to let someone down?" Remember, you don't get points for saying it, you get points for keeping your word.

I've also heard the rationalization that "People do that to me all the time, so why shouldn't I?" As a wise man once said to me, "If you emulate behavior you find offensive, you're no better than the person who's offended you." So true! You're not in charge of anyone's behavior but your own, after all, and starting today, you're impeccable with your word. You're going to do exactly what you say you're going to do, exactly when you say you're going to do it, and as a result you're going to be amazed at how much better you and everyone around you feel about your credibility.

And then, of course, there are those people who lie by omission, or use the word "embellish" as a euphemism as if that makes it less of a lie. "I don't see the problem with embellishing a story," they'll say, or, "Of course I embellish my resume. Who doesn't?" Well, a whole lot of people don't, actually, and in the end, "the problem" is that sooner or later, the truth comes out, no matter how big or small the lie might be.

I've never forgotten the story of an actor acquaintance of mine who went to an audition one day. The casting director asked him what he was working on at the moment, and rather than give the honest answer, "I'm driving a cab to pay my bills," he announced that he was understudying a lead actor in a popular Los Angeles play, figuring it was a harmless, obscure enough "embellishment." Unfortunately for him, the casting director happened to be a friend of the lead actor he'd referred to, called to ask about him when the audition was over, and discovered that the lead actor had never heard of this supposed "understudy." Not only did my acquaintance blow any chance he might have had at that job or any possible future jobs with that casting director, but the casting director and the lead actor spread the story far and wide, and my acquaintance is now a full-time cab driver whose acting career vanished with one careless, unnecessary "embellishment."

Whenever you find yourself even remotely tempted to tell (or try to cover up) any kind of lie, never forget the likelihood that someone you're dealing with very probably knows the truth and can expose you in the blink of an eye. And, as Judge Judy puts it so perfectly, "When you tell the truth, you don't have to have a good memory."

So make it a promise to yourself, starting today, to become one of those special few that you and the people you care about can always, *always* count on to be impeccable with your word. I promise, once you make a habit of it, you'll love everything about it.

> Dear God, while I've never intended to live dishonestly,
> I know there have been times when, without thinking,
> I've let myself and others down
> by not being completely truthful.
> Thank You for Your help as I refuse, ever again,
> to squander my credibility, in my ongoing effort
> to live with all the self-respect You intended for me. Amen.

DECEMBER 22

"Behold, I am doing a new thing..."
– Isaiah 43:19

From Fern:

As Newcomer Caller for the Chamber of Commerce, I called on a family who moved into our block. I was intrigued that her husband, an ordained minister, traveled nationally speaking on the subject of ESP. It was a new subject to me, seeming to verge on the occult. It came to me gradually that spiritual experiences do, indeed, come by ways other than our five senses. They *are* extra-sensory. I was very eager to meet the man and made an appointment. My heart was pounding as I went up the steps to the house. I felt myself leaning forward as he told instance after instance when God intervened in the lives of people in the present day!

What I heard that day was, the Bible is true *now!* Until then I'd read it as history. God did wonders *then*. But now? What a revolutionary change when I came to know I can read it in the present tense! Until then I had not understood why God spoke to others, never to me. They said I didn't wait or listen. That day I learned that God doesn't use the ears but the heart. His answers are more feeling than hearing, more thought than sound, but He *does* respond! He's *here* and He's *now!*

DECEMBER 23

"Then you will...pray to me and I will hear you."
— Jeremiah 29:12

From Fern:

I know God answers prayer in His own way and time, sometimes so subtly that we do not realize. When I was very young, going to a country school, a classmate teased me unmercifully. Whatever I had that he wanted he took from me—a new pencil, scarf, handkerchief, whatever.

I knew of nothing to do about it, but suddenly one day I had a thought. I could write a prayer. I would take it home, hold the folded paper in my hands while I knelt beside my bed. I was confident that angels would come and carry it to God, and maybe I could peek and see them! What logically would happen didn't seem to occur to me. The boy saw me writing and, on the way home, took the paper from me. But he must have read it and been touched by it. I don't remember that he ever bothered me again, yet it was years before I realized that God had answered my prayer in such a natural way that I did not know it was He.

I believe this is His way. He keeps His own laws. Seldom does He break into our lives in a cataclysm. When He took human form, He came as a baby. When He speaks, it is in a still, small voice. His healing is generally a process. Our growth physically or spiritually is slow, but always He is near and knowing. It is His way and His promise.

DECEMBER 24

"So teach us to number our days
that we may get a heart of wisdom."
– Psalms 90:12

From Fern:

Dear God, our days indeed are numbered. In chronicling the reigns of kings, one after another "slept with his fathers" and were replaced. One after another "did what was evil in the sight of the Lord." Rare were those who did good. They passed and their influence with them, and the preacher (Ecclesiastes) declared, it is all in vain.

Yes, Lord, it would all be in vain were it not for You who were "before the mountains were brought forth, or (before You) formed the earth and the world. From everlasting to everlasting, thou art God." You love your creation and its creatures so much that You came in Jesus to tell us how we, too, might have everlasting life.

This reinforces the psalmist's words, for it reminds us of the importance of our days—holy gifts given to us by our holy God, to be respected as holy parcels of our lives.

God, with the psalmist I ask that I may be aware of the significance of this day; that I may walk in the light of Your wisdom, that at its end I may be more the person You meant for me to be, when, along with other wonders of this world, You created me.

DECEMBER 25

"Lord, teach us to pray,
as John taught His disciples. When you pray, say..."
– Luke 11:1

From Fern:

Our Father, which unites us all, making us interrelated, one in Spirit.

Who art in heaven, not remote in the highest heaven, but within our own heavenly spirits.

Hallowed be they name. May I do my part to revere Your name.

Thy kingdom come—that glorious relationship when I accept Your reign, Your kingship in my life.

Thy will be done, for Your will is always for good, **on earth as it is in heaven.** What would life be, if Your will were done on earth—in my own life?

Give us this day our daily bread—spiritual as well as physical.

And forgive us our trespasses (as You have promised when we ask) **as we forgive those who trespass against us.** I note the restriction. Help me, dear Jesus, to love as You love and forgive as You forgave.

And lead us not into temptation. It is so strong, so distracting, so subtle, and my tendency is to justify whatever I want to do.

But deliver us from evil, for evil separates me from You. Hold me close! Help me recognize evil when I see it and ask for and depend on Your deliverance.

For thine is the kingdom, and the power, and the glory, forever!

DECEMBER 26

"The Spirit of God was moving..."
– Genesis 1:2

From Fern:

Divine Teacher, as a child progresses in school, so, as humankind has advanced, You have been able to lead us to deeper and more subtle understanding. In Moses' time You gave visible and audible signs of Your presence—earthquakes and thunder, a pillar of cloud by day, of fire by night. You allowed Moses to see Your back but not Your face. You provided bread in the form of manna and water from the rock. You directed the building of a sanctuary as Your dwelling place.

More than a millennium later, Lord, You sent Jesus who said, "God is spirit." He echoed Your I AM and said, "I am the bread of life...I am living water." Apostle Paul said that when Your Spirit lives within, our bodies are Your temple, and we who call You Lord look not to the things that are seen, but to the things that are unseen.

Now, God, You show us that Jesus' presence lives on in his Holy Spirit, healing, teaching, comforting, being the sustenance we need for life. Help me, I pray, to live more by Spirit, less by flesh. Help me emphasize less the doing than the being and becoming.

DECEMBER 27

"For they drank from the supernatural Rock
which followed them,
and the Rock was Christ."
–1 Corinthians 10:4

From Fern:

My Lord and my God, who was the Lord also of Abraham, Isaac, and Jacob, who is the never-changing God on whom we can depend—not virulent one day and docile the next, nor unavailable one time and present later. Your promises are undated. Your goodness is stable. On You we can depend!

Divine Parent, that You chose to be not only Lord and God, but in great magnanimity of Spirit reached out to us as to Jesus, to say, "My child!"

What love, what loveliness, what forgiveness, and what hope in that relationship! You need not have designed a world in which power resides in the invisible—in love, and truth, and beauty. Thank You that You did!

Thank You that You gave us, Your children, the freedom to explore without You—to discover the emptiness, the hopelessness of life apart from You, and then to find when we have "come to our senses" that You have been waiting for our coming!

DECEMBER 28

"As for the rich...
they are to be liberal and generous..."
– 1 Timothy 6:17-18

From Fern:

Thank You, Father, for showing me these words; for the story of the rich young ruler who was to give away all he had, and Your statement that it is hard for the rich to enter the kingdom, have troubled me.

I want to meet all the qualifications for being what You require of your followers. I know that many of those go beyond my common sense to Your uncommon sense, but I have never been convinced of a good result of giving away all that I have, becoming as poor and dependent as those I would seek to help.

You have now given me, Lord, a clear directive through Your servant, Paul. You have already confirmed for me the validity of Your formula: give it and it will be given to you. You have shown me the joy of giving and how it is blended into the joy of loving. You have aroused in me a desire to respond to needs of certain persons, causes, situations. I am thankful for the ability to do that.

Dear, dear God, know that my life and all that is within it, is Yours, to be used according to Your direction. You gave me the ability to earn *our* money and I will use it accountably and generously. I recognize Jesus' call to me that everyone to whom much has been given, of him much will be required. I have been greatly blessed.

DECEMBER 29

"I am the man."
– John 9:9

From Fern:

Lord Jesus, give me the courage to announce my identity. There are times when I am in error and find it hard to admit. There are times when I do not want to confess that I have neglected a responsibility. There are times when I would like to be one of the crowd rather than announcing my beliefs.

Lord, help me to be accountable. If I am guilty of error or neglect, help me admit it even though I may be diminished in the eyes of those who know. If I have firm beliefs, help me state them boldly, even though persons I admire oppose them.

For some day I shall need to be accountable to You, dear God. Some day all that is hidden will be revealed. My honesty now, the posture of declaration, will equip me for that time.

My neighbors' opinion, which is important to me, is not the judgment I should fear. The standard by which I wish to measure my life is Yours. It is not hidden. I have it before me, in Your written word. Help me increasingly to adopt it as my standard, and help me so to live.

DECEMBER 30

"It is good to rub and polish our brain
against that of others."
– Montaigne

From Cat:

It's a physiological fact that when we experience huge, sudden, life-altering events, our brain chemistry can change and cause deep depression, even in those who've never experienced depression before. This is very different from the temporary state of mind of, for example, feeling better when it's raining, or getting the blues on Sundays—the ups and downs of life are normal and unavoidable for all of us.

I heard a story recently that touched me deeply, about a gifted neurosurgeon who'd gone through a series of life-altering events within just a few short months, including the unexpected end of his marriage and the death of a parent. He sank into such a crippling depression that he found himself unable to work, and he slowly but surely began to feel as if he were drowning in his own dark sadness.

One day when he was at a dangerous low, a close friend stopped by and, rather than pointing out how terrible he looked or making him feel worse by telling him it was time to snap out of it, simply invited him to go for a run. The doctor wasn't a runner, but not even caring enough anymore to say no, he accepted the invitation, wore himself out and, to his amazement, slept that night for the first time in months.

The next day he and his friend went running again, and within a week or two he unintentionally slipped into the zone of getting out of his house in the fresh air and moving his body again. Eventually, thanks to the physical and mental self-programming he'd gone through, he returned to his calling as a neurosurgeon and even participated in triathlons, rescued from his pit of depression and back to loving life again.

If you or a loved one is going through a depression that goes beyond a simple case of the blues, please, *please* don't isolate yourself and wait for it to go away. Be pro-active, and go to war against a condition that's not your fault! Either talk to or be that trusted friend who'll give you the gentle, compassionate, non-judgmental nudge you need to get out the door to a qualified, recommended therapist, and/or a support group, and/or one of the steps toward recovery you can start right away: *getting physical.*

You don't have to take up running, or join a gym if you've learned from past experience that you'll never actually go (like the majority of people who buy gym memberships). Find a friend to go walking with. Park at the far end of the lot from the entrance to every store you go to. Join a group in which physical activity is part of the agenda. My personal favorite, and easy to find in almost every town in America: Sign up for a yoga class, which can make an extraordinary difference in the mind and body without pushing you beyond your limits.

Whatever you do, sooner rather than later, take someone's hand or let them take yours and refuse to give in to depression without putting up the fight of your life. There's help out there, there's expertise and love and genuine understanding out there, and your body's right there with you, wanting to move whether your mind feels like it or not, and able to lead you out of the darkness, even if it's only baby steps at a time.

And never, ever forget that *prayer works,* and the rest of us who've been there will be praying for you while you heal and fall in love with your life again.

In the meantime, and forever, know to the core of your soul that you're not alone, and you are loved, with the greatest Love of all.

Heavenly Father, a special prayer for those
who find themselves consumed by the darkness
of depression and despair.
Please shine Your sacred Light so brightly on them
that even they can find it and, in its glow,
see the path that will lead them back to the blessed life
they feel so distant from today. Amen.

DECEMBER 31

From Cat:

Happy anniversary, my precious friend! A year ago today, we began this exciting journey together, and look how far you've come since we first met! This book offered insights, suggestions, and inspirations, but you're the one who did the work, so give yourself a big hug and a round of applause for all the steps you've taken toward fulfilling the infinite potential of that extraordinary child of God you really are.

Fern and I are so grateful to have spent this year with you. It's been our privilege, believe me. You'll be in our hearts and prayers every single day as your exquisite, one-of-a-kind adventure continues.

For now, Numbers 6:24-26 says it all:

May the Lord bless you and keep you.
May the Lord make His face shine upon you
and be gracious unto you.
May the Lord lift up His countenance upon you
and give you peace. Amen.

ABOUT THE AUTHORS

Catherine Hickland

After spending her entire adult life as an actress, on both soap operas and Broadway, Catherine Hickland channeled her fascination with the mind and how it works into a diligent study of the art of hypnosis. She became certified in several areas of hypnotherapy in 2007 and is now the most successful and well-known female stage hypnotist in the country, performing more than two hundred shows a year. A popular speaker and author of *The 30-Day Heartbreak Cure* (Simon & Schuster), Catherine is also a passionate teacher of the mind/body/spirit connection through her seminars, private hypnotherapy sessions, and volunteer work with women in the Federal Prison System. Her Christian faith and devotion to God lie at the core of her dedication to guiding people to their inner peace and freedom; and thanks to her decades of appearing on soap operas for all three networks, she enjoys an international renown that only broadens her audience and her outreach potential.

In 2001, Catherine created and remains CEO of Cat Cosmetics (www.catcosmetics.com), a very successful line of color cosmetics. She's happily married to producer Todd Fisher, and they divide their time between their home in Las Vegas and their ranch in California, which they share with their twenty-four chickens, three horses, a miniature donkey, two geese, thirteen ducks, a pet rooster, and a new baby owl. (And yes, in case you're wondering, Catherine can hypnotize animals.)

Fern Underwood

Fern Underwood was born in a small town in Iowa on February 7, 1915. From her parents, Raymond and Bertha Shoup, she learned the importance of family, hard work, and a sense of humor. From the Depression that swept away her happy childhood on a thriving farm, she learned the importance of frugality and resilience. She married Clifford Underwood on Labor Day, 1940, and was a homemaker and mother to their two children until Clifford's sudden death in 1973,

465

when she took over his chain of auto parts stores for the next twelve years.

Her retirement in 1985 led to travels to Methodist mission stations on five continents as a member of the World Methodist Council, as well as passionate interests in the Bible, writing, and volunteer work with an emphasis on children—interests in which she remains active to this day, despite recent challenges with surgeries and seizures. The walls of her home in Osceola, Iowa are lined with awards from her local Chamber of Conference, the Methodist Church, and the state of Iowa honoring her ongoing insistence that Christianity is a verb, not a noun.

Lindsay Harrison

Born in Osceola, Iowa in 1948 to Clifford and Fern Underwood, Lindsay moved to Los Angeles in 1970, a week after graduating from Iowa State University, to pursue her interest in being a television and screenwriter. That career began in earnest in 1983 and includes nine TV movies, one feature film, and episodic scripts for more than twenty daytime and primetime series.

Her writing career expanded to the publishing world in 2000 and has grown to twenty books, including ten *New York Times* bestsellers, with such notable collaborators as Sylvia Browne, Catherine Hickland, Jeanne Cooper, and Crystal Chappell.

Lindsay is also the co-founder of the Willie-Coppee Fund (www.williecoppeefund.org), a discretionary fund dedicated to helping animals whose medical care exceeds their owners' and rescue groups' ability to pay. She lives in Studio City, California with her three beloved dogs George, Bette, and Sophie.

Made in the USA
Middletown, DE
04 December 2020

26310423R00263